Bloom's Literary Themes

Alienation
The American Dream
Death and Dying
The Grotesque
The Hero's Journey
Human Sexuality
The Labyrinth
Rebirth and Renewal

Bloom's Literary Themes

HUMAN SEXUALITY

Bloom's Literary Themes

HUMAN SEXUALITY

Edited and with an introduction by
Harold Bloom
Sterling Professor of the Humanities
Yale University

Volume Editor
Blake Hobby

BLOOM'S
LITERARY CRITICISM
An imprint of Infobase Publishing

Bloom's Literary Criticism
An imprint of Infobase Publishing
132 West 31st Street
New York NY 10001

Library of Congress Cataloging-in-Publication Data
Human sexuality/ edited and with an introduction by Harold Bloom ; volume editor, Blake Hobby.
    p. cm. — (Bloom's literary themes)
  Includes bibliographical references and index.
  ISBN 978-0-7910-9800-4 (acid-free paper) 1. Sex (psychology) in literature.
2. Sexual ethics in literature. I. Bloom, Harold. II. Hobby, Blake.
  PN56.S5 H78 2009
  809'.93358—dc22   2008042986

Bloom's Literary Criticism books are available at special discounts when purchased in bulk quantities for businesses, associations, institutions, or sales promotions. Please call our Special Sales Department in New York at (212) 967-8800 or (800) 322-8755.

You can find Bloom's Literary Criticism on the World Wide Web at
http://www.chelseahouse.com

Text design by Kerry Casey
Cover design by Takeshi Takahashi

Printed in the United States of America

IBT EJB 10 9 8 7 6 5 4 3 2 1

This book is printed on acid-free paper.

Contents

Series Introduction by Harold Bloom: Themes and Metaphors

1. TOPOS AND TROPE

What we now call a theme or topic or subject initially was named a *topos*, ancient Greek for "place." Literary *topoi* are commonplaces, but also arguments or assertions. A topos can be regarded as literal when opposed to a trope or turning which is figurative and which can be a metaphor or some related departure from the literal: ironies, synecdoches (part for whole), metonymies (representations by contiguity), or hyperboles (overstatements). Themes and metaphors engender one another in all significant literary compositions.

As a theoretician of the relation between the matter and the rhetoric of high literature, I tend to define metaphor as a figure of desire rather than a figure of knowledge. We welcome literary metaphor because it enables fictions to persuade us of beautiful untrue things, as Oscar Wilde phrased it. Literary *topoi* can be regarded as places where we store information, in order to amplify the themes that interest us.

This series of volumes, *Bloom's Literary Themes*, offers students and general readers helpful essays on such perpetually crucial topics as the Hero's Journey, the Labyrinth, the Sublime, Death and Dying, the Taboo, the Trickster, and many more. These subjects are chosen for their prevalence yet also for their centrality. They express the whole concern of human existence now in the twenty-first century of the Common Era. Some of the topics would have seemed odd at another time, another land: the American Dream, Enslavement and Emancipation, Civil Disobedience.

I suspect though that our current preoccupations would have existed always and everywhere, under other names. Tropes change across the centuries: the irony of one age is rarely the irony of another. But the themes of great literature, though immensely varied, undergo transmemberment and show up barely disguised in different contexts. The power of imaginative literature relies upon three constants: aesthetic splendor, cognitive power, wisdom. These are not bound by societal constraints or resentments, and ultimately are universals, and so not culture-bound. Shakespeare, except for the world's scriptures, is the one universal author, whether he is read and played in Bulgaria or Indonesia or wherever. His supremacy at creating human beings breaks through even the barrier of language and puts everyone on his stage. This means that the matter of his work has migrated every-where, reinforcing the common places we all inhabit in his themes.

2. CONTEST AS BOTH THEME AND TROPE

Great writing or the Sublime rarely emanates directly from themes since all authors are mediated by forerunners and by contemporary rivals. Nietzsche enhanced our awareness of the agonistic foundations of ancient Greek literature and culture, from Hesiod's contest with Homer on to the Hellenistic critic Longinus in his treatise *On the Sublime*. Even Shakespeare had to begin by overcoming Christopher Marlowe, only a few months his senior. William Faulkner stemmed from the Polish-English novelist Joseph Conrad and our best living author of prose fiction, Philip Roth, is inconceivable without his descent from the major Jewish literary phenomenon of the twentieth century, Franz Kafka of Prague, who wrote the most lucid German since Goethe.

The contest with past achievement is the hidden theme of all major canonical literature in Western tradition. Literary influence is both an overwhelming metaphor for literature itself, and a common topic for all criticism, whether or not the critic knows her immersion in the incessant flood.

Every theme in this series touches upon a contest with anteriority, whether with the presence of death, the hero's quest, the overcoming of taboos, or all of the other concerns, volume by volume. From Monteverdi through Bach to Stravinsky, or from the Italian Renais-sance through the agon of Matisse and Picasso, the history of all the arts demonstrates the same patterns as literature's thematic struggle with itself. Our country's great original art, jazz, is illuminated by what the great creators called "cutting contests," from Louis Armstrong and

Duke Ellington on to the emergence of Charlie Parker's Bop or revisionist jazz.

A literary theme, however authentic, would come to nothing without rhetorical eloquence or mastery of metaphor. But to experience the study of the common places of invention is an apt training in the apprehension of aesthetic value in poetry and in prose.

Gender and love are hardly confined to literary themes, yet their permanent expression necessarily depends upon answerable style. This volume considers such major authors as Ibsen, Byron, Aristophanes, Chaucer, Shakespeare, Sophocles, Joyce, Pope, Walt Whitman, D. H. Lawrence, and Thomas Hardy—among others—and rightly invokes also Plato and Freud, the leading Western authorities upon eros.

Freud's sexual psychology and Plato's erotic philosophy are partly in conflict, and yet share a remarkable goal: to free thought from its sexual past. It may be, as Freud suggested, that thinking begins with the child's curiosity as to sexual differentiation. If we are to be emancipated from a perpetual moody brooding, we need the kind of clarified consciousness that is the aim of Freudian analysis.

In Plato, we find the Good by mounting the Ladder of Love, where eventually persons fall away and we are alone with Ideal Forms. The last vestige of Platonism in Freud is "reality-testing", by which you learn to accept your own mortality. Can it be that the price of a total freedom of thought from its sexual past is nothing less than death?

Plato and Freud are rivals so formidable that they crowd out most imaginative authorities upon sexual love, and yet they yield to Shakespeare, who knows more even than they can. From Shakespeare we learn, in *Love's Labour's Lost*, that men are more narcissistic than women, and fall in love through the bodily eye, while women are far subtler, and can love more maturely. No one has taught so urgently as Shakespeare that the sexual becomes the erotic when crossed by the shadow of death. Jealousy in its full range from comedy to tragedy finds its proof-texts in *Troilus and Cressida*, *Othello*, and *The Winter's Tale*.

William Blake, prophet of desire, sought to distinguish between the selfish virtues of the natural heart and an imaginatively redemptive passion, but Blake's mythology has proved too difficult for more than a few handfuls in each era to absorb. I myself treasure three memorable instances in modern fiction, where an ironic humor plays itself out in the realms of eros. Proust, in *Swann's Way*, presents Swann agonizing in jealousy before what he takes to be his mistress Odette's window, where he sees a sexual passage-at-arms taking place. "And to think I went through all this suffering for a woman who did not even please me, a woman not really my style," Swann cries out and then discovers he stands before the wrong window. Robert Penn Warren in *All the King's Men* has Jack Burden end an account of his first marriage by intoning: "Goodbye Lois, and I forgive you for everything I ever did to you." Most outrageously, in one of her early novels Iris Murdoch observes: "Falling out of love is one of the great human experiences; you see the world with newly awakened eyes."

The vagaries of human sexuality are infinite. Shakespeare yet once more represents comprehensively and subtly the labyrinths of the drive. Two Antonios, in *The Merchant of Venice* and *Twelfth Night* (did Shakespeare himself play them both?) are extraordinary portraits of authentic homoerotic love, and Richard III's seduction of Anne powerfully conveys the deathly fascination of sado-masochism. *Measure for Measure* is far more sinuous in Angelo's sadistic desires and Isabella's rather terrifying, self-immolating masochism.

What could be termed the Sublime of an eros that throws the world away is rendered superbly by *Antony and Cleopatra*. Goneril and Regan, sister monsters of the deep, murderously lust after Edmund, who appears to have virtually no affect in clear contrast to Lear, always hungrier for more familial love than any among us can hope to receive.

What Freud called "family romances" constitute the foundation of all eros in Shakespeare, as in our own lives. It may be that Shakespeare's deepest insight into human sexuality is the contingent nature of all desire. His women and men are molded by forces they cannot control, particularly the strength of the past, personal and familial.

If there is authentic freedom anywhere in Shakespeare, it has to be Rosalind's in *As You Like It*. She controls all of the play's perspectives, and knows herself and every other character better than we can, until we receive her aid. Wholly exemplary, her freedom to love is one of Shakespeare's finest gifts to us, as we like it indeed.

ANGELS IN AMERICA
(TONY KUSHNER)

"Queer Politics and the Politics of the Queer in Tony Kushner's *Angels in America*"
by Jennifer Glaser,
University of Cincinnati

Critics hailed Tony Kushner for his aesthetic innovations in *Angels in America*. These include his use of Brechtian theatrical techniques, his nod to magical realism in the form of the Angel who appears near the end of part I of the play, and his willingness to embrace global themes such as the end of the Cold War, illness and its aftermath, and the specter of death. Yet far more striking was his uncompromising treatment of human sexuality and the AIDS epidemic that was sweeping through America during the 1980s and 1990s—a relatively novel subject at the time the work was first performed. Although people living with AIDS were depicted in theatrical and film productions prior to *Angels in America*, most notably in Larry Kramer's play *The Normal Heart* (1985) and in Craig Lucas's film *Longtime Companion* (1990), Kushner's play transcended the conventionally tragic representation of the disease by portraying ailing characters whose future health was directly tied to America's own.

The two parts that comprise Kushner's epic *Angels in America*, *Millennium Approaches* (1991) and *Perestroika* (1992), portray the apocalyptic landscape of America as the millennium approaches. Despite Kushner's eschatological preoccupations and his occasional pessimism about America's political scene in these works, they remain

fundamentally optimistic attempts to develop a politics of queer identity commensurate to the task of commenting on millennial America.
As Prior Walter, arguably the central protagonist of *Angels in America*,
says of himself and his brethren in some of the last lines of the play:
"We won't die secret deaths anymore. The world only spins forward.
We will be citizens" (2:280). Throughout the play, Kushner's characters
meditate on the politics of exclusion in America and the larger question
of how the disenfranchised can "be citizens" in America with a voice
in the wider culture (2:280). In *Angels in America*, Kushner explores
the possibilities for a radical queer consciousness and community to
point the way to a redemptive future for an America that has become
lost in a haze of radical individualism and conservative ennui.

As the subtitle of the play, "A Gay Fantasia on National Themes,"
makes clear, Kushner is deeply concerned with the ways in which gay
culture can be used to reconfigure the nation; when asked about his
prominent use of the terms "gay" and "national" during an interview,
Kushner said that "what was important to [him] was the conjunction
of the two words. . .there are other lesbian and gay writers in the States
who are beginning to address issues that connect personal dynamics
and questions of relationships with the political issues that are of such
tremendous significance to the lives of gay men and women" (*Tony
Kushner in Conversation* 18). Kushner's treatment of sexuality in *Angels
in America* melds the erotic with the political. He posits gay identity
not simply as a sexual orientation but as an orientation to the world,
one informed by the marginal position the gay culture has occupied,
a position that for Kushner provides an outsider's view of mainstream
culture.

Set in mid-1980s Manhattan, the play focuses on Louis Ironson, a
gay Jewish man more comfortable with the abstractions of philosophy
and ethics than the very real illness of his HIV-positive partner, Prior
Walter, who struggles to reconcile his increasingly unrequited love
for Louis with his realization that his disease is progressing. Other
key figures include Belize, a black former drag queen who nurtures
Prior through the worst parts of his illness, and Joe Pitt, a Mormon
and committed Republican who is wrestling with his own sexuality.
Kushner's play also focuses on the trials of Joe's Mormon wife, Harper,
and mother, Hannah, as well as on those of iconic twentieth-century
figures such as Roy Cohn and Ethel Rosenberg. The fact that Kushner

chooses to feature only women and gay men in *Angels in America* is a significant one. And, as David Savran notes, despite the fact that much of the play concerns the relationships between various romantic partners, "none of the interlaced couples survives the onslaught of chaos, disease, and revelation. Prior and Louis, Louis and Joe, Joe and Harper have all parted by the end of the play and the romantic dyad (as primary social unit) is replaced in the final scene of *Perestroika* by a utopian concept of (erotic) affiliation and a new definition of family" (209). Even Hannah Pitt, Joe's mother, finds a place in the group as an unconventional maternal figure for Prior. Kushner's focus on these characters and the ways in which their performances of sexuality and gender can create a new idea of "family" as they alter traditional categories prefigures the preoccupations of queer theory. Queer theory, an academic field that deconstructs reified ideas about gender and sexuality, was coming to prominence precisely at the time Kushner's works were first being performed.

As Natalie Meisner puts it, "If any texts could be termed venerable in a field as fledgling as queer theory *Millennium Approaches* and *Perestroika* would certainly be accorded this status. The plays, temporally and historically marked as they are, often serve as a kind of intimate shorthand for queer, performance, and theatre theorists" (177). Queer theory is the offspring of the feminist and LGBT (Lesbian, Gay, Bisexual, and Transgender) movements. Along with seeking to undermine the idea of sex, gender, and sexuality as "natural" and continuous, queer theorists looked to create "a new corpus of academic theorizing that considered sexuality in relation to the persistent pressures of other normalizing regimes pertaining to race, class, gender, geopolitical spatialization, citizenship, nationalism, and the effects of economic globalization and transnational exchange" (Spurlin 9–10). These aims are similar to those of Kushner in *Angels in America*. In recent critical practice, the term "queer" has metamorphosed from noun to verb, and many scholars argue that it is possible "to queer a reading" of a text, to intentionally look at it askew, from a deviant or queer perspective. In *Angels in America*, Kushner's characters are able to "queer" America, gaining an outsider's awareness that allows them to look at the nation from an appropriate critical distance.

In *Angels in America*, Kushner is fascinated by the power of ideas to constitute reality. When Prior Walter and the Valium-addled Harper meet on "the threshold of revelation" in their hallucinatory dream, Prior tells the young woman that he is a homosexual (1:39). Harper, a devout Mormon, declares, "Oh! In my church, we don't believe in homosexuals" (1:38). Prior jokingly replies, "In my church we don't believe in Mormons" (1:38). Here, Kushner plays with the constitutive nature of belief—the manner in which ideology constructs even our sense of what sorts of people can or cannot exist. The conversation between Harper and Prior is made even more ironic and indicative of the blinding nature of belief in that Harper's husband Joe, also a practicing Mormon, is a closeted homosexual, a fact that does not exist for her at all.

In addition to examining the frequently unquestioned links between sex, gender, and desire, queer theorists are often interested in going beyond the study of homosexuality in their work by focusing on transvestitism. Kushner, too, places great importance on the role of both drag and the possibility of a third sex in his theorization of gender identity. Early in *Millennium Approaches*, Prior Walter has a fever dream in which he sits dressed in female clothing at "a fantastic makeup table," applying the "new fall colors" he has swiped from the "Clinique counter at Macy's" (1:36–7). Looking in the mirror, Prior attempts to paint a healthy face upon his ailing one as he muses, "one wants to move through life with elegance and grace, blossoming infrequently but with exquisite taste, and perfect timing, like a rare bloom, a zebra orchid" (1:36). Prior's attempts to embrace "elegance and grace," to don drag even as he is physically dragging, illustrate Kushner's ideas about gay theater being what he calls a "theater of the fabulous," in which formerly powerless characters "become powerful because [they] believe [themselves] to be" ("Thinking about Fabulousness" 74). In contrast to Louis, who "gets butch" when around his family, Prior Walter attempts to continue to be playful with his gender performance—even though drag has become passé in the gay community. This commitment to gender play is part and parcel of his "fabulousness," the life force that sustains him throughout *Angels in America* and that invests him with the authority to wish a blessing of similar fabulousness on the play's audience in the last act (1:25; 2:280). Similarly, the ultimate agent of change in *Angels in America* is an ideal figure for queerness and indeterminacy: the hermaphroditic Angel him/herself, who is described as possessing "eight vaginas" and "a bouquet of phalli," entities that locate him/her outside known sex categories and outside the limitations of both death and daily life (2:174–5).

In *Angels in America* Kushner explores sexuality and gender difference as well as racial and ethnic identity. The first part, *Millennium Approaches*, begins with an epitaph for the American Jew represented by the funeral of Louis Ironson's archetypical Jewish grandmother, Sarah Ironson, whom her rabbi celebrates for being representative of the many, "not a person, but a whole kind of person, the ones who crossed the ocean, the ones who brought with us to America the villages of Russia and Lithuania" (1:16). Her death signals not simply the end of an individual life, but the end of a way of life. Sarah Ironson's descendants "can never make that crossing she made" (1:16). Their names, like their fortunes, are Americanized; the rabbi marvels at one point that there are now Ironsons named "Eric" and "Luke" (1:16). In contrast to the immutable identity suggested by the name "Ironson," literally son of iron, a metal that cannot be melted, the Ironson grandchildren are being incorporated into American culture. At the same time, however, Louis Ironson and his relatives cannot escape entirely "the clay of some Litvak shtetl. . .the air of the steppes—because [Sarah Ironson] carried the old world on her back across the ocean" (1:16). Increasingly, Kushner melds this idea of an immutable Jewish difference (a difference based in part on the history of Jewish dispersal) with an idea of queer difference.

Jonathan Freedman argues that, "along with many other projects, the play undertakes an extensive mapping of the place where figurations of the Jew meet figurations of the sexual other, the deviant, the queer" (91). As Freedman suggests, Kushner does indeed suture Jewishness to queerness in *Angels in America*. However, Freedman's remarks on Kushner's depiction of Jewish identity in *Angels in America* mainly point out how the playwright participates in a long history of anti-Semitic caricature of the Jew as sexually deviant and obscure a central aspect of the connection Kushner draws between Jewishness and homosexual identity. By melding the two, Kushner's play recovers a lost and politically potent position for both Jewish and gay people in America.

Kushner prominently and most problematically explores Jewishness and queerness through the figure of Roy Cohn, the infamous right-wing lawyer and McCarthy henchman. Cohn, a closeted gay man and an exaggeratedly Jewish figure, appears as a "monstrous" and monstrously carnal Jewish deviant in *Angels in America*. At the same time that Cohn often literally embodies an excessive Jewishness, however, so too does the ghost that haunts him, Ethel Rosenberg, the suspected Communist spy whom Cohn sent to death, now a casualty of the Cold War. Rosenberg and Cohn exist as the antipodes of Jewish identity, one the spectral reminder of the Jewish leftist tradition in America and the other the precursor of precisely the kind of neo-conservatism that Louis Ironson, the Jewish character poised between these two Jewish polarities, rails against throughout *Angels in America*. Through Roy Cohn and Ethel Rosenberg and their marked Jewish-ness, Kushner makes a statement about the political rift in Jewish culture that is threatening to deprive Jews of their outsider conscious-ness, which in many ways mirrors queer consciousness.

In *Angels in America*, this queer consciousness emerges most prominently in Kushner's representation of AIDS. When Kushner wrote his play, AIDS was emerging as a significant topic for discussion in both the fields of medicine and social theory. As George Piggford put it, "'AIDS' came to signify by the mid-1980s a series of competing discourses or referential sites that attempted to generate meaning about the syndrome"(170). At this time AIDS was often rendered as a death sentence. But to some AIDS theorists, the disease was instead "an opportunity to reconceptualize the significations of homosexuality and the homosexual community" and "a horrifying literalization of the disease that homosexuality is already perceived to be in homophobic discourse" (Piggford 171). Kushner plays with these competing ideas in *Angels in America*, posing Prior Walter's public exposure to the medical establishment against his private experience.

When the play begins, Prior Walter's disease is becoming more pronounced. Lesions are beginning to appear on his skin, symptoms of the Kaposi's sarcoma that he christens "the wine-dark kiss of the angel of death" (1:27). Although Prior's tongue-in-cheek nod to Homer's *Odyssey* and the "wine-dark" sea Odysseus crossed during his journey home locate him as the hero of Kushner's play, it also places him within the medical discourse of the disease that was prev-alent during the early years of the illness—a discourse that equated AIDS with certain death. Similarly, his experiences with Emily, the nurse who cares for him during his illness, emphasize Prior Walter's increasing corporeality and the fact that AIDS is stripping him of his individuality in the eyes of the medical community. Yet, in another nod to classical mythology, this very infirmity leaves Prior Walter with the powers of a seer. In Prior's private world, he has become a prophet, an entity anointed by the Angel who visits him with the power to see the future as well as the past. The Angel brings a number of Prior's ancestors—"prior" Walters in a dual sense of the word—to see him. The Angel does so not to emphasize that the dying man will be the end of his genealogical line, but to show the ailing Prior the possibilities for a different form of life, the generation of a queer community gathered in time of crisis. Just as Roy Cohn's illness locates him in a queer community despite his attempts to avoid it, to claim that homosexuality does not exist, Prior's disease places him in a position to imagine a future in which a queer outsider consciousness breeds new forms of citizenship, family, and nation.

For, if *Angels in America* is an apocalyptic work addressing Reagan-era politics and the burgeoning AIDS crisis, its final scene is a puzzling reminder of Kushner's continuing allegiance to far more utopian ideals. The last scene of *Angels in America* finds Prior Walter, his friend Belize, and even the tortured Louis Ironson walking cinematically into the sunset as the statue of the Angel of Bethesda stands guard over them. Kushner's "gay fantasia on national themes" reconfigures the future of the nation as an increasingly inclusive entity. Unlike Kushner's earlier play, *A Bright Room Called Day* (1987), which sought to address the contemporary political scene through the allegory of Weimar Germany's past, *Angels in America* is set in a rich present on the cusp of an imagined future. Anticipating the way in which the AIDS epidemic would politicize queer identity and queer the political landscape in America in the 1990s, Kushner's *Angels in America* offers a vision of hope for its audience.

WORKS CITED

Cunningham, Michael. "Thinking about Fabulousness." Reprinted in *Tony Kushner in Conversation*. Ann Arbor: University of Michigan Press, 1998.

Freedman, Jonathan. "Angels, Monsters, and Jews: Intersections of Queer and Jewish Identity in Kushner's *Angels in America*." *PMLA*, Vol. 113, No. 1, Special Topic: Ethnicity. (Jan. 1998), pp. 90–102.

Jones, Adam Mars. "Tony Kushner at the Royal National Theatre of Great
    Britain." Reprinted in *Tony Kushner in Conversation*. Ann Arbor:
    University of Michigan Press, 1998.

Kushner, Tony. *Angels in America: A Gay Fantasia on National Themes*. New York:
    Theatre Communications Group, 1995.

Meisner, Natalie. "Messing with the Idyllic: The Performance of Femininity
    in Kushner's *Angels in America*." *The Yale Journal of Criticism* 16.1 (2003)
    177–189.

Piggford, George. "In Time of Plague: AIDS and Its Significations in Hervé
    Guibert, Tony Kushner, and Thom Gunn." *Cultural Critique*, No. 44.
    (Winter 2000), pp. 169–196.

Savran, David. "Ambivalence, Utopia, and a Queer Sort of Materialism: How
    Angels in America Reconstructs the Nation." *Theatre Journal*, Vol. 47, No.
    2, Gay and Lesbian Queeries. (May 1995), pp. 207–227.

Spurlin, William J. "Theorizing Queer Pedagogy in English Studies after the
    1990s." *College English*, Vol. 65, No. 1, Special Issue: Lesbian and Gay
    Studies/Queer Pedagogies. (Sep. 2002), pp. 9–16.

A DOLL'S HOUSE
(HENRIK IBSEN)

"Henrik Ibsen's *A Doll's House*"
by Kristin Brunnemer,
Pierce College, California

In his time, Henrik Ibsen was a controversial playwright who wrote plays on taboo subjects. From banishment (*Peer Gynt*), to illegitimate children (*The Wild Duck*), to syphilis and euthanasia (*Ghosts*), to suicide (*Hedda Gabler*), Ibsen's characters occupied identities onstage that few in polite Victorian society would dare to mention. Perhaps surprisingly for modern readers, *A Doll's House*, with its plot centered on a woman named Nora who forges her father's signature, takes a loan without consulting her husband, and leaves him and her children to find herself, was considered equally shocking by its first audiences. The play was deemed so daring that, when performed in many countries, the ending was changed so that Nora returns home, finding she cannot leave Torvald or her three children so great is her love and devotion to them (Templeton 113–114). Nora's quest for her personal identity, while scandalous to some at the time, is exactly what made the play so famous—and why it continues to hold such currency as a drama today.

Critical studies of *A Doll's House* often center on the ongoing debate as to whether or not the play offers a feminist message, and whether or not Ibsen meant it to do so. Those who oppose such a feminist reading of the text often turn to Ibsen's own words on the play to the Norwegian Women's Rights League in 1898: " I thank you for the toast, but must disclaim the honor of having consciously worked for the women's rights movement. I am not even quite clear as to just what this women's rights movement really is. To me it has seemed a problem of humanity in general" (Ibsen, quoted in Ricardson 81). Such critics favor a reading of Nora's transformation as humanist rather than feminist, and Eric Bentley, for example, argues that "the play would be just as valid were Torvald the wife and Nora the husband"(30).

Those who read the play as a feminist piece, such as Gail Finney, however, hold that Ibsen's "sensitivity to feminist issues" is revealed in "his creation of female characters" and "their rejection of a strict division between conventional masculine and feminine behavior" (92–93). Likewise, Joan Templeton contests what she calls "the *Doll's House* backlash" wherein the feminist aspects of the play are attacked on "literary grounds" under the pretext that Nora's character between act one and act three undergoes "an incomprehensible transformation" (114). Instead, Templeton argues that "[t]he power of *A Doll's House* lies not 'beyond' but within its feminism; it is a feminist Bildungspiel *par excellence*, dramatizing the protagonist's realization that she might, perhaps, be someone other than her husband's little woman" (138).

The problem, of course, could be that feminism is often difficult to define, a problem noted by bell hooks and Carmen Vasquez. Vasquez argues that feminism, unfortunately, "has come to mean anything you like [. . .] There are as many definitions of Feminism as there are feminists" (Vasquez qtd. in hooks 17). Thus, one scholar's humanism may be another's feminism.

Despite these debates, critics spend little time discussing Nora's transformative identity on its own terms. This is unfortunate because Nora, throughout the course of the play, illustrates many of the levels of American psychologist Abraham Maslow's hierarchy of needs. Moving through the stages of this hierarchy, from physiological elements such as safety, love and belonging, to the desire for esteem and self-actualization, Nora's character exemplifies Maslow's theory that "most behavior occur[s] in response to some kind of motivation, which [is] made up of the interplay among different needs, or drives" (Krapp 309). In her interactions with Kristine, Krogstad, Dr. Rank and, most especially, Torvald, Nora consistently shows how needs— not unconscious, internal motivations—are the key to her growing personal identity.

Abraham Maslow, discontent with psychotherapy of the 1930s, which focused rather exclusively on either Freud's psychoanalysis or B. F. Skinner's behaviorist methods, developed his theory of the hierarchy of needs as a method for understanding what motivates successful, healthy people in the development of their personalities. At the bottom of the hierarchy's scale are physiological needs, such as the need for food, water, shelter, and air. The next level of Maslow's hierarchy, titled safety, consists of the need for financial resources, health, and security. According to Maslow, only after these two stages of need have been successfully satisfied can one progress to the next levels, which consist of the need for love and belonging, the need for esteem, and the need for self-actualization (Krapp 310). Today, the hierarchy is employed in studies of human behavior and identity and even in professional fields such as advertising, marketing, and office relations.

In the first act of the play, Nora returns to her house from shopping in preparation for Christmas festivities. We learn from her early interactions with Torvald that Nora has been concerned about her family's financial situation for quite some time, in part due to her husband's bout with illness in the past. However, with Torvald's new job at the bank beginning in the New Year, the Helmer household anticipates a more stable and affluent future. As Torvald tells Nora, "Ah, it is so gratifying to know that one's gotten a safe, secure job, and with a comfortable salary" (1578). Though Maslow argued that "safety needs are relatively less important for most healthy adults under normal circumstances," there are "exceptional circumstances" that can "activate safety needs in people whose safety needs had previously been satisfied" (Krapp 310). Such is the case with Nora, whose fear for Torvald's health, and by extension her only means of financial security in late Victorian society, prompted her to forge her father's signature in order to borrow sufficient funds to take the family to Italy for Torvald's recovery.

Nora, as Maslow's theory suggests, has been unable to think of much else besides this need for safety, and to keep her attempts to satisfy it a secret from her husband. "You can imagine, of course, how this thing hangs over me," Nora tells Kristine in Act I (1584). As such, all other needs have been put on hold, and Nora details her preoccupation with safety to Kristine, explaining how she has secretly worked, skimped, and saved to pay back the loan and its attendant interest.

Nora's conversation with Kristine also reveals Nora's new and growing desire for esteem, the third level in the hierarchy of needs, which involves both "the need for self-esteem and the need for esteem from others," according to Maslow (Krapp 311). While Nora initially (and rather thoughtlessly, given Kristine's own dismal circumstances) brags to her friend of Torvald's new job, which will bring in "a huge salary and lots of commissions" (1580), she soon feels patronized by Kristine's insistence that she is "just a child" who "really know[s] so little of life's burdens" (1582). To contest this reading of herself, Nora reveals the actions she took to convey her family to Italy and thus save her husband's life. With her need for safety and security fulfilled by the promise of Torvald's new job, Nora now clearly seeks something greater than security: self-worth. Telling Kristine, of course, isn't prudent, but it furthers the plot along, bringing the play into the classic stage of complication, while revealing Nora's "need to feel that other people respect and recognize [her] as worthwhile" (Knapp 8).

However, a visit by her husband's employee Nils Krogstad soon returns Nora to the second stage in Maslow's hierarchy, reconnecting her with her long-held fears for security. Blackmailing Nora with his knowledge that she has forged her father's signature on the loan she took for the trip to Italy, Krogstad tells Nora that he will reveal her secret, thereby opening her up to legal recourse and social shame, unless she can convince Torvald to keep Krogstad at the bank. Ironically, Krogstad blackmails Nora because, he, too, is fearful about his level of security and esteem; this job, Krogstad reveals, is "the first rung" of the ladder he must climb to achieve social acceptance after tarnishing his reputation in an unnamed scandal. "My boys are growing up," he tells Nora. "For their sakes, I'll have to win back as much respect as possible" (1590). Krogstad, like Nora, has been operating at deprivation levels in Maslow's realm of security, and, as Maslow suggests, a person worried about safety and security will "focus on satisfying this need to the exclusion of all other needs, living 'almost for safety alone'" (Krapp 310).

Just as Nora has set aside thoughts of legal recourse and social shame in her attempts to secure Torvald's health, so, too, has Krogstad sought this same level of security without thought for the impact his blackmail will have on Nora. For these reasons, Errol Durbach argues that "Krogstad is a mirror that throws back at Nora the reflection of a persecuted criminal in an unforgiving society [. . .] Krogstad and Nora are fellow criminals beneath skin" (78–79). Brian Johnston, likewise, recognizes that "Krogstad's determination to secure the future of his sons is no more ignoble a motive than Nora's past wishes to save her husband's life and to spare her dying father" (150). Nevertheless, Krogstad's intimidations do more than threaten Nora's safety; they terrorize her into pondering suicide as a solution (Ibsen 1619).

Significantly, *A Doll's House* also reveals Nora's desire for the third stage in Maslow's hierarchy, love and belonging, which is equally strong in the first and second acts of the play. Maslow makes a distinction between two types of love, Deprivation-Love and Being-Love: Deprivation-Love, the "essentially selfish need to give and receive affection from others," is a lower form than Being-Love, the "unselfish desire for what is best for the loved one" (Krapp 310). Nora does initially focus on Deprivation-Love, manifesting a desire to garner care and concern from her family (Knapp 310). Basking in Torvald's diminutive nicknames for her, such as "lark" and "little squirrel," Nora centers her existence on pleasing Torvald so that she, in turn, can receive the satisfaction of being desired and cherished. Likewise, Nora's interactions with her children, her "dolls," are similarly motivated. This sense of Nora's love being deprivation-based rather than unselfish is also clearly exhibited by Nora's concern that Torvald might love her less in the future, "when he stops enjoying [her] dancing and dressing up and reciting for him" (Ibsen 1583). However, Nora's fear of this lack is so great she quickly stops herself from such thoughts: "How ridiculous! That'll never happen" (1583).

Nora also exhibits Deprivation-Love in her interactions with Dr. Rank, the Helmers' dying family friend whose love for Nora is more romantic in nature than fatherly. Nora is a rather shameless flirt when it comes to acquiring Dr. Rank's affections, and Ibsen's stage direction for Nora and Rank's scene alone together is filled with appropriately coy instructions: the actress is directed to put "both hands on his shoulders" and to hit "him lightly on the ear with [her] stockings" (1603). The dialogue of the scene is equally flirtatious, with Nora telling him to "imagine then that I'm dancing only for you" before remembering to add, "yes, and of course, for Torvald too—that's understood" (Ibsen 1603). Moreover, throughout the scene, Nora desires Rank's affections not just for her own need for friendship and intimacy, but also in hopes that Rank will ultimately be like her fantasy of an "old gentleman" whom, as she tells Kristine, she has long daydreamed will rescue her from her financial predicaments (1584). Nora's flirtations are thus quite purposeful, performed with the hope of securing "an exceptionally big favor" from Rank to help her escape Krogstad's blackmail (1604).

Yet, Nora also shows her facility for Being-Love in this scene as well, offering the first suggestion that she is capable of greater aware-ness and self-actualization than has been previously demonstrated by her actions thus far in the play. When Rank confesses to Nora that his affections for her could rival Torvald's, that his "body and soul are at [her] command," Nora is unable to press him into service: "I don't need any help. You'll see—it's only my fantasies. That's what it is. Of course!" (Ibsen 1604). Likewise, Nora obliquely confesses her own feelings for Rank to him, feelings that are beyond friendship or the mere desire to exchange affections. "There are some people that one loves most and other people that one would almost prefer being with," she tells him (1605). To clarify, Nora explains that Torvald, like her father, must be the one she "loves most," but when she lived in her father's house, she actually preferred the company of the maids "because they never tried to improve me." Similarly, Dr. Rank symbolizes Nora's ability for Being-Love, one of the conditions of such love being the capacity to "love and accept a person's failing and foibles rather than trying to change them" (Krapp 310). With Dr. Rank, Nora exchanges this deeper form of love, indicating for the first time in the play, what Brian Johnston calls "the evolutionary process whereby the 'mini-Nora' of the opening scenes becomes the 'super-Nora' of the close" (137).

Ironically, this "super-Nora" emerges not when the threats to her safety, love, belonging, and esteem are removed, but, rather, when Nora's fears come to pass. When her husband opens Krogstad's letter, thereby revealing her actions, he reacts with great anger; the "miracu-lous event" that Nora yearns for, whereby Torvald would "step forward" to take the blame, never materializes. Instead, he worries only about his reputation and social standing, his own need for society's approval and esteem. Nora, however, in having her worst fears materialize, is freed from them. Realizing that they have only been play-acting the perfect marriage, Nora changes, symbolically, out of her dance/perfor-mance costume and into her departure clothes, and prepares to leave Torvald. She tells him in what is perhaps the play's most well known scene:

> I went from Papa's hands into yours. You arranged everything to your own taste, and so I got the same taste as you—or

pretended to; I can't remember. I guess a little of both, first one, then the other. Now when I look back, it seems as if I'd lived here like a beggar—just from hand to mouth. I've lived by doing tricks for you, Torvald. But that's the way you wanted it. It's a great sin what you and Papa did to me. You're to blame that nothing's become of me [. . .] I've been your doll-wife here, just as at home I was Papa's doll-child" (Ibsen 1623).

This key scene, where Nora confronts Torvald and emancipates herself from their child-like play-marriage, still holds great social currency as a feminist manifesto, leading to the play's resurgence in popularity during the 1960s and early 1970s when the feminist movement in the United States began what scholars call a second wave. Nora, in leaving behind a marriage in which she is not an equal but a "doll-child," rejects her secondary status in society. "I'm a human being, no less than you" (1624), she tells Torvald. The scene, too, also reveals Nora's growing desire to move beyond the initial stages of identity, into Maslow's highest realm: self-actualization.

Self-actualization, as Maslow described it, involves "the need to fulfill one's potential, to be what one *can* be" (Krapp 311). Here, too, Nora demonstrates this yearning for self-actualization, in her desire for education, for time to "think over these things for [her]self" (Ibsen 1624), even at the expense of lower needs such as safety, belonging, and social esteem. Maslow argues that a person moving toward self-actualization would be "often less restricted by cultural norms and social expectations" than others not operating at this level, and this appears to be true for Nora, who rejects Torvald's attempts to keep her through shaming her, cajoling her, even forbidding her departure and declaring her sick with fever (Krapp 311). For Torvald, who is still operating at the level of esteem, social standing is everything. "Abandon your home, your husband, your children! And you're not even thinking what people will say," he tells her (1624). Nora, however, feels a different calling, one less concerned with social norms than with exploring her true identity: "I can't be concerned about that. I only know how essential this is [. . .] I have other duties equally sacred [. . .] duties to myself" (1624). For Nora to achieve self-actualization, she must leave behind Torvald, who desires only her willingness to engage with him at the Deprivation-Love level upon which they have built their marriage. As Sandra Saari contends, "At the end of Act 3, Nora has rationally thought herself into freedom from Torvald's interpretation of reality. She then sets out to define reality for herself" (Saari 1994).

Krogstad, Nora's mirror, also seems to move beyond his initial fears for his security and esteem in rekindling his "Being-Love" with Kristine. In another gesture read as a feminist aspect of the play, Kristine proposes to Krogstad that they unite, if not in marriage, then, at least, in forming a union that allows them, "two shipwrecked people," to "reach across to each other" (Ibsen 1613). Errol Durbach writes that this moment, when "[Kristine] offers Krogstad not sacrifice, but alliance, a life of mutual support, a joining of forces in which individual need is not subordinated to social or sexual expectations, and where strength derives from channeling energy and work into a common enterprise," is "Krogstad's Metamorphosis" (85). It stands in direct contrast to the Helmers' own version of marriage. Like Nora, in the final scene, Krogstad is moved to find an identity beyond financial security and social standing. He is now more concerned with personal happiness and self-fulfillment.

Throughout the play Kristine serves as a foil to Nora and Krogstad, demonstrating a path away from Maslow's lower needs or drives and onward toward a self-created, self-actualized space where one need not compromise one's identity and self. Of all the characters, Kristine has had the greatest difficulty in satisfying her physiological and safety needs, yet she is also, paradoxically, the character least motivated by these drives. Like Nora at the play's conclusion, Kristine is free of their hold on her. Referring to her first marriage, in which she agreed to forfeit her Being-Love for Krogstad and her personal happiness for her deceased husband's ability to provide for her family's physiological and safety needs, Kristine tells Krogstad that "anyone who's sold herself for somebody else once isn't going to do it again" (Ibsen 1614). For these reasons, it is obvious why Nora's first stop in her journey to self-actualization begins by spending the night at Kristine's rather than staying in the doll's house she has built with Torvald.

Neither Krogstad's nor Nora's self-actualization is performed onstage for the audience; instead, we are left at the curtain's closing with Torvald contemplating "the greatest miracle" that can only be possible when characters "transform" themselves (Ibsen 1626). This quest for personal identity takes place beyond the stage, beyond our view, outside the realm of society, for self-actualization is an internal manifestation rather than an externally motivated drive. Like Maslow, who believed that an important characteristic of self-actualization was the ability to experience and to recognize "peak experiences," so, too, do Ibsen's characters throughout his plays find themselves in "growth promoting" situations that allow them "to look at [their] live[s] in new ways and to find new meaning in life" (Krapp 311). The characters in *A Doll's House* are no exception to this, offering viewers what Durbach calls "a myth of transformation" whereby Nora leaves behind her childhood identity in order to embrace an independent, self-actualized, autonomous one (133). Whether labeled humanist or feminist, this transformation is perhaps why Ibsen's play still feels so contemporary, why *A Doll's House* is still so studied and so often performed today.

WORKS CITED

Bentley, Eric. "Ibsen: Pro and Con." *Henrik Ibsen*. Ed. Harold Bloom. Philadelphia: Chelsea House, 1999. 25–36.

Durbach, Errol. *A Doll's House: Ibsen's Myth of Transformation*. Boston: Twayne Publishers, 1991.

hooks, bell. *Feminist Theory: From Margin to Center*. Boston: South End Press, 1984.

Ibsen, Henrik. *A Doll's House*. 1879. Trans. Rolf Fjelde. *Literature and Its Writers*, 2nd edition. Eds. Ann Charters and Samuel Charters. Boston and New York: Bedford/St Martin's, 2001. 1575–1627.

Johnston, Brian. *Text and Supertext in Ibsen's Drama*. University Park: Pennsylvania State University Press, 1989.

Krapp, Kristine, ed. "Maslow, Abraham H." *Psychologists and Their Theories for Students*, Vol. 2. Detroit: Gale, 2005. 303–324.

Richardson, Angelique. *The New Woman in Fiction and in Fact: Fin de Siecle Feminisms*. New York: Palgrave Macmillan, 2001.

Saari, Sandra. "Female Becomes Human: Nora Transformed in *A Doll's House*. *Literature and Its Writers*, 2nd edition. Eds. Ann Charters and Samuel Charters. Boston and New York: Bedford/St Martin's, 2001. 1993–1994.

Templeton, Joan. *Ibsen's Women*. Cambridge: Cambridge University Press, 1997.

Don Juan
(Lord Byron)

"Thieves, Boxers, Sodomites, Poets:
Being Flash to Byron's *Don Juan*"
by Gary Dyer,
in PMLA (2001)

INTRODUCTION

In his essay on *Don Juan*, Gary Dyer "explores Lord Byron's fluency in the techniques of covert communication that marked the cultures of sodomy, boxing, and crime," each of which necessitated "cant" dialects (Dyer calls these "flash"). In Byron's time, certain people had to use "flash" to avoid the risk of criminal prosecution. Thus, Dyer's essay explores the criminality of both Byron's language but also his homosexual acts, acts that technically made him a "sodomite." In the end, Dyer argues that it is important to read a section of dialect in the work in light of its cultural implications.

Dyer, Gary. "Thieves, Boxers, Sodomites, Poets: Being Flash to Byron's *Don Juan*." *PMLA* Vol. 116, No. 3 (May 2001): 562–578.

FLASH, to be *flash to* any matter or meaning, is to understand
or comprehend it, and is synonymous with being *fly, down,* or
awake [...].

> —James Hardy Vaux, "New and Comprehensive
> Vocabulary of the Flash Language," 1812 (173–74)

Verbum sapientibus sat est. ("A word to the knowing ones is
sufficient.")

> —proverb

In canto 11 of *Don Juan*, written in October 1822, Byron's
protagonist is reflecting on his first view of London from Shooter's
Hill when he is ambushed by thieves, one of whom he shoots in
the abdomen. After the others flee, the dying assailant, named Tom,
speaks using dialect: "max" for gin, "I've got my gruel" for "I've been
killed" (11.16.2–3). His dialect is lost on the Spaniard Juan, who "did
not understand a word / Of English" (11.12.1–2). Byron anticipated
Tom's idiom when he recorded that the robber was wounded in his
"pudding" (11.13.4), and after Tom expires, Byron adopts this idiom
himself, writing that the dead man

> was once a kiddy upon town,
> A thorough varmint, and a *real* swell,
> Full flash, all fancy, until fairly diddled,
> His pockets first, and then his body riddled. (11.17.5–8)

Byron goes on to write that Juan felt remorse because

> He from the world had cut off a great man,
> Who in his time had made heroic bustle.
> Who in a row like Tom could lead the van,
> Booze in the ken, or at the spellken hustle?
> Who queer a flat? Who (spite of Bow-street's ban)
> On the high toby-spice so flash the muzzle?
> Who on a lark, with black-eyed Sal (his blowing)
> So prime, so swell, so nutty, and so knowing?
> (11.19.1–8)

These terms are obtrusive because they seem ill-suited to paraphrase the meditations of Juan, who does not know standard English, much less its slang.

This essay explores Lord Byron's fluency in the techniques of covert communication that marked the cultures of sodomy, boxing, and crime, a familiarity that underlies certain prominent characteristics of *Don Juan*. Each of these "cant" dialects or codes was necessitated, at least initially, by the risk of legal prosecution, and although you might use such a code without desiring to conceal anything, you would nevertheless indicate that others had felt some threat that engendered the code. Sodomy could be punished with death; if the accused was privileged or fortunate, he would suffer exile or disgrace.[1] Although boxing was only tangentially illegal, its distinctive slang ("flash") betrayed the sport's ties to the culture of people like Tom: thieves, beggars, and prostitutes—an underclass for whom the gallows was an ever-present threat and secrecy a necessity. For Byron these communities overlapped: he and his Cambridge friends Charles Skinner Matthews and John Cam Hobhouse were not only active or aspiring "sodomites" but also members of "the Fancy," the fans and patrons of boxing. Because of their sexual practices, Byron and his friends were no less criminal in English law than Tom was.

The slang in the Shooter's Hill scene hints at encrypted meanings, and this hinting is complicated by Byron's epithets for Tom, who was "[f]ull flash" and "so knowing." *Flash* was not only a noun that denoted a particular kind of language but also an adjective that meant "in the know" or "clued in." Byron "uses different levels of poetic coding to define his audiences," Jerome J. McGann has noted (193–94). As I aim to show, we gain when we recognize why the word *flash* often is the best term for Byron's means of definition. Keats referred to *Don Juan* as a "flash poem" after reading no more than the first two cantos (192), and he was on to something.

Revealing encrypted meanings in specific passages of *Don Juan* can be worthwhile, but it is more important to contextualize and interpret Byron's indications that such meanings are there. Eve Kosofsky Sedgwick has observed that in the nineteenth century "knowledge meant sexual knowledge, and secrets sexual secrets" (73).[2] In Byron's writings secrecy does not necessarily *mean* sodomy, insofar as sodomy may not be the reality behind a specific code found there (after all,

Byron and his contemporaries had plenty of other secrets, with penalties that were less harsh yet still unsettling). Rather, sodomy's role was a paradox: it was the exemplary secret, infamous, unmentionable, and deadly, except that by the same token it was too dangerous to be chosen as an example. So, instead of sodomy's standing in for secrets in general, other secrets had to stand in for sodomy and other disguises for sodomy's disguises. (The substitutions can be intricate: as I show later, one thing Tom's attempted robbery evokes is blackmail.) In canto 11 Byron uses the cant of thieves and of the Fancy to draw attention to encryption itself, but I am arguing that for this poet encryption could not be detached from the encryption demanded by the most secret among all his secrets.

Nor could polyglot discourse escape entirely the shadow of such inhibitions. One purpose of this essay, as the final section makes clear, is to sound a note of caution about interpreting multivoiced texts as celebratory or transcendent, however tempting it may be. Continually throughout *Don Juan* Byron manipulates diverse languages and dialects, and although critics have usually interpreted this variety as a sign of freedom and exuberance, it is just as much an emblem of constraint. The variety is one more reminder of the perils attending any attempt to describe the politics of a formal feature without tracing its specific history.

I

When eulogizing Tom in flash dialect, Byron supplies a note explaining, "The advance of science and of language has rendered it unnecessary to translate the above good and true English, spoken in its original purity by the select mobility and their patrons." Byron then quotes eight lines from "a song which was very popular, at least in my early days," which uses many of the words found in his tribute to Tom, and he directs baffled readers to "my old friend and corporeal pastor and master, John Jackson, Esq., Professor of Pugilism."[3]

Flash had been adopted and expanded by the Fancy, a community that brought together the "select" members of the "mobility," like the former champion Jackson, with "patrons" like Byron.[4] England saw a mania for boxing from the 1790s through the early nineteenth century. The narrator of Robert Southey's *Letters from England* (1807), "Don Manuel Alvarez Espriella," like Juan a visitor from Spain, records how "the Amateurs of Boxing [. . .] attend the academies of the two great professors Jackson and [Daniel] Mendoza, the Aristotle and Plato of pugilism" (451).[5] Beginning in 1806, Byron was among those studying in Jackson's academy at his rooms in Saint James Street, and Cecil Lang has argued that the "Jack" Johnson who fights alongside Don Juan at the siege of Ismail is a portrait of John Jackson (154–55). Readers of *Don Juan* in 1823, when cantos 6–11 were published, would not have been surprised that one diversion Juan takes up in London is boxing (11.66.2).[6]

As John Ford explains in his history of Regency pugilism, the boxing subculture's language was "a combination of sporting technicalities and cockney and underworld slang" (158). Popular guides like *A Classical Dictionary of the Vulgar Tongue*, compiled by Francis Grose, bore some responsibility for the "advance of science and of language" Byron noted. First published in 1785, Grose's lexicon was revised in 1811 with the addition of considerable "Buckish Slang" and "University Wit" to the original's "Pickpocket Eloquence" (Grose, *Lexicon*), and it would be revised again in 1823 by Pierce Egan. Byron owned the first volume of Egan's widely read compendium *Boxiana* (1812), which would guide the aspirant toward fluency in flash.[7] Even though Byron left England six years before he wrote canto 11, he may have been aware that flash had been disseminated more recently by Egan's popular episodic narrative *Life in London* (1820–21) and its many theatrical adaptations.[8]

In *Life in London* Egan writes that "[h]alf of the world are *up* to [slang]; and it is my intention to make the other half *down* to it" (84n2). But the effort Byron puts into making his readers up or down is half-hearted: whereas Egan provides twenty-two footnotes to gloss the "slang" words in a sixteen-line song (207), Byron makes only a token attempt to help the reader decipher his account of Tom. His note observes that this dialect still is learned best by the privileged few like himself who can join in the male bonding at Jackson's studio (the professor's tutelage was not cheap). Since twenty-first-century readers cannot consult Jackson, we have to go to the dictionaries, and with their aid stanza 19 translates into standard English as follows:

> Juan had removed from the world a great man, who in his
> day had made considerable commotion. Who could lead the

thieves in attack in a fight, drink in the thieves' hideout, or steal
at the theater as Tom could? Who could cheat a fool as well or
rob on horseback despite the threat of constables? Who, when
out with his girlfriend Sal, was so lusty, so well dressed, so
devoted, and so clued in?

However, the resulting translation is less significant than the reader's
need to translate, and the content of the message is less significant
than the encryption.

[...]

In his 1823 *Slang: A Dictionary of the Turf, the Ring, the Chase,
the Pit, of Bon-Ton, and the Varieties of Life*, John Badcock defines
flash broadly as "the language of persons whose transactions demand
concealment, yet require that they should mix with those from whom
it should be concealed" (Bee 79). By writing that "flash lingo" is the
subject of his lexicon, Badcock implicitly equates it with *slang*, and
slang he defines similarly, as the "language, words, phrases, invented by
doctors and boxers, lawyers, thieves, sportsmen and whores, necessarily
or purposely to convey their meaning secretly to each other" (158).
Though he focuses on vulgar flash, Badcock acknowledges that even
doctors and lawyers have their distinctive forms of flash, and he also
gives examples of "court slang," "the slang of periodical literature," and
the slang of political radicalism (159). When Byron wrote canto 11
in Italy, he almost certainly had not read Badcock's dictionary, which
appeared in London the same year, but he knew the different species
of flash and the concept of flash to which Badcock testifies. Flash or
slang is characterized by secrecy, and thieves and prostitutes were not
the only people who needed to encode their secrets. Badcock does not
note the flash of sodomites, but we can.

Before moving on to Byron's fluency in such a flash, we must recognize that there are steps between being flash and being its opposite, a
"flat." Vaux explains that the term "half-flash and half-foolish" refers
to someone with "a smattering of the cant language" who "pretends
to a knowledge of *life* which he really does not possess" (179; see also
Egan, *Life* 143). By describing Tom as "full flash," Byron indicates that
the late thief's socialization into this "knowing" community, dedicated
to the criminal "life," was thorough. He also thereby reminds us that
almost all people, and almost all his readers, are half flash at best;
for them the "advance of science and of language" has been retarded,

not least because they lack an instructor like Jackson. Few of Byron's readers understand Tom's speech, fewer still the flash song, and all are prompted to wonder what else in this poem they are not flash to. Indeed, it is made clear that most readers, then or now, can never be more than half flash to many of Byron's meanings.

II

Recognizing this broader meaning of *flash* refocuses our attention on the similarities and affiliations between flash in the most familiar sense (i.e., the underclass slang adopted and codified by the Fancy) and other forms of flash communication, such as the codes Byron and his friends devised to discuss what they would call "Greek love." Not all the secrets in Byron turn out to be sodomy, but even when a secret is something else, the supreme dangers of sodomy have helped shape the nature of secrecy. Indeed, concealing sodomy obviously taught Byron much of what he knew about concealment.

It is axiomatic, one hopes, that we should expect to find symbolically central to an author's work any acts he or she performed that could have led to the gallows. Byron's same-sex desires and acts bore consequences for him, and hence significance, that had no equivalent in, for example, his potentially seditious satires or his relations with his half sister, neither of which was a capital offense. As Louis Crompton has shown, in the early nineteenth century Britain hanged an average of two men each year for sodomy (16), and if the act was not completed, an "attempt to commit sodomy" warranted confinement to the pillory, which could be deadly because of the public's loathing (21–22). Wealthy men often fled to Europe before trial, and the most prominent among these exiles was the novelist William Beckford.
[...]

III

Don Juan, much like the Greek epistles, demonstrates and thematizes how codes demarcate their audiences (the flash, the half flash, the flats), and this kind of demarcation becomes even more prominent in the English cantos (11–17) than before. Byron invites us to look for hidden meanings, writing that his descriptions of London society contain "much which could not be appreciated / In any manner by the uninitiated" (14.22.7–8). Immediately on Juan's arrival near London, the stanzas on Tom's death indicate that there will be flash meanings, even though no key is provided. But when we get to London, Byron asks us to "recollect the work is only fiction, / And that I sing of neither mine nor me" (11.88.4–5), and he records that he "disdain[s] to write an Atalantis" (11.87.5), meaning a roman à clef like Delarivier Manley's *The New Atalantis* (1709) or, more significant to him, Caroline Lamb's *Glenarvon* (1816). Byron writes merely that Lord Henry Amundeville lived in "Blank-Blank Square" because readers are too fond of "Reaping allusions private and inglorious, / Where none were dreamt of" (13.25.1, 13.25.4–5). He proclaims that "when I speak, I *don't hint*, but *speak out*" (11.88.8). The inconsistency cannot be resolved logically by subsuming one set of claims in the other (and all these passages were written just a few months apart). To complicate matters, neither set can be taken literally with complete assurance. By referring to "the uninitiated," Byron parodies the terminology associated with secret societies, around which a mythology had grown beginning in the 1790s. At the same time, his guarantee that the poem is purely fictional looks like a hollow convention designed to fend off inconvenient speculation.

There are, nonetheless, two ways in which Byron's declaration of hidden meanings overrules his disavowal of them. The first I just mentioned: referring to a place as "Blank-Blank" may be *least* likely to cut off inquiry because it suggests an obligation not to specify, similar to the obligation to leave sodomy nameless. Is this obscurity any less enticing than, say, the dashes or asterisks used in satires in Byron's time? The second reason, paradoxically enough, is the inconsistency itself. Contradiction, whether deliberate or accidental, is one of the most common indications that a writer is not being forthright, and by itself it confirms that something is being concealed from most of us.

Byron's retrospective viewpoint in the English cantos is obvious, epitomized by the "ubi sunt" section (11.76–85). The poet gives the impression that he, on returning via his imagination to the country he fled six years earlier, must reflect on the kinds of flash he knew best there, on the reasons for which he sometimes needed to use flash, and on the ideal audience he once had in Hobhouse and Matthews, companions for whom the flash languages of sodomy and boxing could mesh. When Byron's note refers to boxing flash as a vestige of his "early days," he distinguishes his life in the London boxing subculture during 1806–14 from his life in Italy in 1822, when he writes *Don Juan* and spars on his own. He also implicitly distinguishes the sodomitical Byron of 1806–12 from the Byron of 1822, who is in all appearances monogamous and exclusively heterosexual.

Byron's return to British locales is marked by an attempt at highway robbery by someone who is full flash. Here the poem acknowledges the similarity between criminal or pugilistic flash, on the one hand, and sodomitical flash, on the other, in order to remind us of the risks involved in sodomy, such as blackmail. The distinction between the flash and the flats connoted sodomy more readily than it connoted anything else, and this highwayman's flash community stands in for another flash community, one of sexual outlaws, who could face the same deadly penalties.

One indication that sodomy is being evoked is the danger Tom and company represent to Juan. However affectionately Byron remembers his friend Jackson, the poet's response to flash could only be ambivalent, since a full-flash stranger could be a threat as easily as he could be an ally. Betrayal by an informant was a constant theme in the expressive culture recorded by Vaux, Egan, and their imitators, and the flash song in Byron's notes points out this risk: it warns a thief that his mistress, on hearing that he has been arrested, will "turn snitch for the forty," testifying and dispatching him to the gallows for the forty-pound reward (*Works* 5: 747). Whereas Juan cannot understand Tom's dialect, Byron can, and whereas Juan has nothing to fear from an Englishman's being flash in any sense, the same does not hold true for Byron: those who knew what "toby-spice" meant were no problem, but he had to be wary of someone who was flash to phrases like "pl & opt C." The possibility of exposure or blackmail terrorized many in Byron's Britain, and only a few months before he wrote canto 11, a sodomy accusation drove to suicide the British foreign minister, Lord Castlereagh, Byron's enemy.

The English courts had ensured that a robbery attempt by a flash man was an ideal way to represent an attempt at sexual blackmail. In *R v. Jones* (1776) and *R v. Donnally* (1779), the judges of the King's Bench ruled that blackmailing someone with a sodomy accusation constituted robbery, even if the accusation was accurate (Winder 25–26). Just as performing sodomy could lead to the gallows, so too could threatening to expose someone else's sodomy.[17] No other allegation was as dangerous, since no other kind of blackmail was held to constitute robbery (Winder 26–27). The courts' decisions on this matter were summarized in the edition of Blackstone's *Commentaries* that Byron owned ([1803] 243–44n13),[18] and the poet certainly knew that blackmail for sodomy was not only a capital crime but identical legally to highway robbery at knifepoint.

[. . .]

When we take this context into account, the connotations of sodomy and blackmail in the scene at Shooter's Hill are thrown into relief. One of England's disadvantages, the robbery attempt teaches, is that a "gentleman" may be "[e]xposed to lose his life as well as breeches" (11.11.5, 11.11.8). Losing one's pants, conventionally a metonym for losing one's money, can also refer to engaging in sodomy or to having one's sodomy revealed (popular prints that capitalized on the Jocelyn scandal showed the "Arse Bishop" with his breeches hanging down [*Catalogue*, entry 14377, reproduced in McCalman 207]). If a gentleman's being taken is thus exposed, it may indeed cost him his life—probably not consigning him to the gallows but at least exiling him and costing him the life he has led. When robbers demand that Juan choose between his money and his life (11.10.8), he kills one, much as Jocelyn defended his life by jeopardizing Byrne's.

Identifying a species of flash means identifying the group who use it, and although Byron does not translate his specimens of criminal flash, he makes clear who typically use this language. My contention is that Byron adopts and identifies criminal flash for this reason: in exploring the workings of flash (broadly conceived), he cannot choose as his example any kind of sodomites' flash and identify it as such, even though such a flash was the kind of encryption he had needed most acutely. There was no better way available to evoke sexual blackmail than to describe a robbery by a man who was flash to a flash other than the "mysterious." To refer directly to sodomites' need for codes would be to assume a sodomite's perspective, and that was impossible, but no such prohibition ruled out a criminal's perspective. While the robbery scene does not refer to sodomy, it does refer to the sodomite's predicament, a combination of isolation, fellowship, and apprehension not dissimilar to the situation that would come to be called the closet.

Byron's manipulations of insiders and outsiders, of flash readers and flats, becomes comparably complex whenever *Don Juan* refers directly to sodomy. He is addressing the public at large rather than a small, sympathetic circle of associates, yet while he must hide his history of same-sex interests, he hardly conceals sodomy's existence. More readers would understand his references to sodomy in *Don Juan* than could ever decipher the bulletins he dispatched to his friends. [. . .] When Donna Inez bars her son Juan from literature like Vergil's "horrid" eclogue that begins "Formosum Pastor Corydon" (1.42.7–8), Byron's more educated readers would recognize the second eclogue, which records Corydon's infatuation with Alexis; they would also infer what characteristic in particular makes Anacreon's morals "still worse" than Ovid's (1.42.2) and why Juvenal was misguided in "speaking out so plainly" (1.43.5)—Blackstone would have concurred. [. . .]

[T]he manner in which *Don Juan* slyly alludes to same-sex sexuality leaves open the possibility of reading from a sodomite's perspective. For all that readers in 1823 really knew, the poet may have intended this ambiguity. Although I suspect that most contemporary readers who perceived these allusions understood the poet as "knowing" about sodomy but not as complicit in it, it is natural to ask how knowing a man can be yet still claim innocence convincingly—how and why does he know so much? There were readers who were prepared to allow for a sodomite's perspective, either those who had heard rumors about Byron's sexuality or, more interesting, men who since school had relied on classical literature for a history of others feeling as they felt and who now were ready to interpret *Don Juan* similarly, regardless of whether they knew or cared about the author's sexuality.

The result of all these factors is that with sodomy, as with other topics, *Don Juan* appears at moments to address at least two readerships, one more flash than the other. When Byron or the Byronic narrator writes that he no longer is susceptible to "maid, wife, and still less [. . .] widow" (1.216.2), his note cites Horace's claim of now desiring "nec femina, nec puer," neither woman nor boy (*Odes* 4.1.29).[23] Byron's meaning is bifurcated: does leaving out boys indicate that he desired only women, or are we to infer that he, like his Roman predecessor, once pursued boys—and perhaps still pursues them? Even if we are knowing insofar as we comprehend the Latin, we can easily infer that there is a deeper meaning from which we are barred.

[...]

IV

In *Don Juan* Byron enlists at least six national languages besides English (Greek, Latin, Spanish, French, Arabic, Russian), along with diverse technical terminologies and vernaculars, flash among them. As practically every reader notices, the presence of these varied languages is underscored by Byron's practice of rhyming words from disparate sources, pairing Greek with English, elevated language with vulgar, literary language with colloquial, and so on. He repeatedly described *Don Juan* as a blow against "cant,"[24] yet *cant* has more than one sense. Although in the seventeenth and eighteenth centuries the word came to refer to preaching, salesmanship, or hypocrisy, it retained its original neutral meaning, designating more generally any dialect characteristic of a particular community. Much as there is "[n]othing that speaks to all men and all times" (14.16.2), there is no practical alternative to cants in the plural, and, no matter how much *Don Juan* satirizes cant in the narrower sense, it continually exploits cants in general.

[...]

Undeniably there is affirmation or optimism in the poet's movement among languages: it advertises his learning and his knowledge of "life"; it reflects and endorses cosmopolitanism. The pivotal episode with Tom, however, qualifies any utopian vision by evoking disguise and blackmail. Even when Byron uses Latin, French, or the dialect of the Fancy to refer to innocuous or uncontroversial things, his constant reliance on these languages points to the need to disguise his meanings on other subjects. By drawing our attention to Tom's flash, he draws our attention to the pressures and the coercions that can necessitate polyglossia.

Which is why it is important to restore to Byron's masterpiece some forgotten content of its form: this Babel had causes, among them Sodom. That we are often uncertain what a poem means hardly requires comment. What is significant with *Don Juan* is that we are left wondering how much of our uncertainty is due specifically to our not being flash.

NOTES

I would like to thank Rachel Carnell, Lisa Maria Hogeland, Barbara Riebling, Terence Hoagwood, and David Simpson for their suggestions on this essay.

The proverb in the epigraph is given here as Byron might render it (note "Verbum sat" in *Don Juan* 1.53.4). "The knowing ones," a phrase central to this essay, is a faithful translation. In a form of the line in Plautus's *Persa*, "dictum sapienti sat est," "sapienti" is singular (line 729), yet the standard English version of the proverb, "A word to the wise is sufficient," leaves ambiguous how many wise people there are, and in *Blackwood's* in 1820 John Wilson made "sapienti" plural ("Verbum sapientibus") to refer to those who were in on the secrets behind the first Tom Crib–Tom Molineux fight (Wilson 66).

1. The legal term *sodomy* is used here because the threat of prosecution was the factor that most necessitated disguise. The alternative terms are problematic (Byron might endorse the phrase Louis Crompton chooses, "Greek love"). Crompton argues that the codes in Byron's letters reflect "what would today be called a gay identity" (129; see also 11), though what it means to talk about "homosexuality" or being "gay" before the late nineteenth century is a vexing question. Byron and his friends do not fit neatly into historians' accounts of sexuality. Randolph Trumbach has argued that whereas until the early eighteenth century "differences in age justif[ied] sexual relations with males in the libertine's mind," afterward "adult men with homosexual desires were presumed to be members of an effeminate minority," commonly termed "mollies" (6). Clearly Byron and his friends reflect the earlier mores: there is no evidence they considered themselves mollies or thought they would be perceived as such, and for them same-sex relations required some disparity in age or status. Although Andrew Elfenbein suggests that rumors about Byron's sodomy "were probably made more credible because of his often-noticed effeminacy," he notes that "no contemporary accounts explicitly link suspicions about Byron's sexual relations with other males to his effeminacy" (209). Effeminacy sometimes was associated

with same-sex relations, but it was perhaps associated with different-sex relations as often (luxury and hedonism still were effeminate regardless of sexual object choice—witness Byron's Sardanapalus). What the twentieth century was to call sexual orientation was similarly unstable: some assumed that heterosexual and homosexual activities excluded each other, as Byron's half sister Augusta did (Elwin 130); some assumed they were compatible, which we can infer was Byron's attitude. These questions are peripheral here because my argument depends on just one fact about Byron's sexuality: the penalties and disgrace attached to contact he and his friends desired, practiced, and discussed.

2. By the end of the century, Sedgwick goes so far as to argue, issues "of knowledge and ignorance themselves, of innocence and initiation, of secrecy and disclosure" became "integrally infused" with the subject of homosexuality (74).

3. *Works* 5: 747; see also Byron, *Letters* 6: 20. The fullest analyses of this scene are in Christensen 304–20; Elledge.

4. Byron was present to witness a change in the class connotations of *flash*: as Eric Partridge has noted, the word originally meant "relative to criminals, vagabonds, and prostitutes," but in the nineteenth century it "came to mean the idiom of the man-about-town" (Grose, *Classical Dictionary*, s.v. "cant"). The idiom remained but now was adopted by a higher social class by way of the subculture of sport, particularly boxing. Francis Grose's *Classical Dictionary of the Vulgar Tongue* had to be updated in 1811 because its author had not foreseen in the 1780s that "young men of fashion would [. . .] be as distinguished for the vulgarity of their jargon as the inhabitants of Newgate" (Grose, *Lexicon* v; see also Bee 80).

5. See also Byron, *Hints from Horace* (1811), lines 597–98. On the parallels between *Letters from England* and *Don Juan*, see Graham 44–60.

6. For other boxing references in *Don Juan*, see 2.92.6–8, 8.43.5–6, 8.110.7, 11.55.1–4, 11.66.2, and 13.18.7. On Regency boxing in general, see Ford; on Byron's interest in the sport, see G. Gross. On Jackson, see One of the Fancy (Egan) 281–96 and Ford 132–36 in particular. For bibliography on boxing publications

in the period, see Magriel. Hazlitt's famous essay "The Fight" (1822) commemorates Bill Neate's victory over Tom Hickman. For other contemporary perspectives on boxing and the Fancy, see Southey 414–15, 451–52; Barber 66n; and Luttrell 31–33; for boxing "professors" in fiction, see A Late Resident 195 and Cliffe 98.

7. Byron, *Prose* 238. His library also included a 1795 "Dictionary of Cant and Flash Language" (235), which I have yet to identify. There were other lexicons published in Byron's lifetime: George Andrewes's *A Dictionary of the Slang and Cant Languages: Ancient and Modern* (1809); the "New and Comprehensive Vocabulary of the Flash Language" (dated 1812), included in James Hardy Vaux's *Memoirs* (1819; 147–227); *The Modern Flash Dictionary* (1821?); and John Badcock's *Slang* (1823). Much of the flash in *Don Juan* 11.13–19 was of recent vintage: several terms are absent from the first three editions of Grose (1785, 1788, 1796) but appear in the 1811 revision and in Vaux's 1812 lexicon.

8. It is tempting to suppose that Byron's description of Tom as "so nutty, and so knowing" echoes a song from *Life in London*, in which "ev'ry face" in the metropolis is "[s]o natty and so *knowing*" (118). On Byron and Egan, see Sales.

17. Without the threat of violence, an act could not constitute robbery, yet the court pointed out that such a threat was present here: accused sodomites could be assaulted by the mob, and furthermore many men valued their physical safety less than their reputations (Winder 26).

18. In 1807 Byron recorded that he had read Blackstone (*Prose* 5), and he owned the 1803 edition featuring Edward Christian's annotations (233).

23. Originally Byron left out "nec puer," but Hobhouse evidently thought omission would betray more than inclusion, so the poet reinstated the phrase (*Works* 5: 681; see also Byron, *Letters* 2: 47, 49).

24. See *Don Juan* 1.1.3; *Works* 5: 297; and *Prose* 128. Byron continually blamed "cant" for attempts to bowdlerize *Don Juan* and for objections to its morality (see *Don Juan* 4.98.7; *Letters* 6: 76–77, 91, 95, 104, 105, 232, 234, 256).

WORKS CITED

Andrewes, George. *A Dictionary of the Slang and Cant Languages: Ancient and Modern*. London: George Smeeton, 1809.

Bakhtin, Mikhail. *Problems of Dostoevsky's Poetics*. Ed. and trans. Caryl Emerson. Introd. Wayne Booth. Minneapolis: U of Minnesota P, 1984.

[Barber, John]. *The Times; or, Views of Society*. London: William Fearman, 1819.

Bee, Jon [John Badcock]. *Slang: A Dictionary of the Turf, the Ring, the Chase, the Pit, of Bon-Ton, and the Varieties of Life, Forming the Completest and Most Authentic Lexicon Balatronicum Hitherto Offered to the Notice of the Sporting World*. London: T. Hughes, 1823.

Blackstone, William. *Commentaries on the Laws of England, in Four Books*. Vol. 4. Oxford: Clarendon, 1765–69. 4 vols.

———. *Commentaries on the Laws of England, in Four Books*. Notes and additions by Edward Christian. 14th ed. Vol. 4. London: Cadell and Davies, 1803. 4 vols.

Borowitz, Albert. *The Thurtell-Hunt Murder Case: Dark Mirror to Regency England*. Baton Rouge: Louisiana State UP, 1987.

Byron, George Gordon. *Byron's Letters and Journals*. Ed. Leslie A. Marchand. 13 vols. Cambridge: Harvard UP, 1973–94.

———. *The Complete Miscellaneous Prose*. Ed. Andrew Nicholson. Oxford: Clarendon, 1991.

———. *The Complete Poetical Works*. Ed. Jerome J. McGann. 7 vols. Oxford: Clarendon, 1980–93.

———. *Don Juan*. Byron, *Works* 5: 3–662.

———. *Hints from Horace*. Byron, *Works* 1: 288–318.

A Catalogue of Political and Personal Satires in the British Museum. Ed. Frederic G. Stephens and M. Dorothy George. 11 vols. London: British Museum, 1870–1954.

Christensen, Jerome. *Lord Byron's Strength: Romantic Writing and Commercial Society*. Baltimore: Johns Hopkins UP, 1993.

[Cliffe, Leigh]. *Supreme Bon Ton: and Bon Ton by Profession*. Vol. 1. London: John C. Spence, 1820. 3 vols.

Clubbe, John. "Byron's London." *Approaches to Teaching Byron's Poetry*. Ed. Frederick W. Shilstone. New York: MLA, 1991. 152–57.

Crompton, Louis. *Byron and Greek Love: Homophobia in Nineteenth-Century England*. Berkeley: U of California P, 1985.

Donelan, Charles. *Romanticism and Male Fantasy in Byron's* Don Juan: *A Marketable Vice*. New York: St. Martin's, 2000.

Dowling, Linda C. *Hellenism and Homosexuality in Victorian Oxford.* Ithaca: Cornell UP, 1994.

Egan, Pierce. *Boxiana; or, Sketches of Modern Pugilism, from the Championship of Crib to the Present Time.* London: Sherwood, Neely, and Jones, 1818.

———. *Life in London; or, The Day and Night Scenes of Jerry Hawthorn, Esq. and His Elegant Friend Corinthian Tom, Accompanied by Bob Logic, the Oxonian, in Their Rambles and Sprees through the Metropolis.* London: Sherwood, Neely, and Jones, 1821.

Eisler, Benita. *Byron: Child of Passion, Fool of Fame.* New York: Knopf, 1999.

Elfenbein, Andrew. *Byron and the Victorians.* Cambridge: Cambridge UP, 1995.

Elledge, Paul. "Never Say(ing) Goodbye: Mediated Valediction in Byron's *Don Juan XI*," *Byron Journal* 20 (1992): 17–26.

Elwin, Malcolm. *Lord Byron's Family: Annabella, Ada, and Augusta, 1816–1824.* Ed. Peter Thomson. London: Murray, 1975.

"Flash." Adj. 3, def. 3. *The Oxford English Dictionary.* 2nd ed. 1989.

Ford, John. *Prizefighting: The Age of Regency Boximania.* Newton Abbot: David, 1971.

Graham, Peter W. Don Juan *and Regency England.* Charlottesville: UP of Virginia, 1990.

Grose, Francis. *A Classical Dictionary of the Vulgar Tongue.* 1796. Ed. Eric Partridge. 3rd ed. New York: Barnes, 1963.

[Grose, Francis]. *Lexicon Balatronicum. A Dictionary of Buckish Slang, University Wit, and Pickpocket Eloquence. Compiled Originally by Captain Grose. And Now Considerably Altered and Enlarged, with the Modern Changes and Improvements, by a Member of the Whip Club.* London: C. Chappel, 1811.

Gross, George C. "Lord Byron and the Fancy." *Arete: The Journal of Sport Literature* 2.2 (1985): 143–67.

Gross, Jonathan David. "'One Half What I Should Say': Byron's Gay Narrator in *Don Juan.*" *European Romantic Review* 9 (1998): 323–50.

Hazlitt, William. "The Fight." *The Complete Works of William Hazlitt.* Ed. P. P. Howe. Vol. 17. London: Dent, 1933. 72–86. 21 vols. 1930–34.

Hobhouse, John Cam. *Byron's Bulldog: The Letters of John Cam Hobhouse to Lord Byron.* Columbus: Ohio State UP, 1984.

Irving, Washington. "Buckthorne; or, The Young Man of Great Expectations." Bracebridge Hall, Tales of a Traveller, The Alhambra. New York: Lib. of Amer., 1991. 499–542.

Keats, John. *The Letters of John Keats.* Ed. Hyder Edward Rollins. Vol. 2. Cambridge: Harvard UP, 1958. 2 vols.

Lang, Cecil Y. "Narcissus Jilted: Byron, *Don Juan*, and the Biographical
    Imperative." *Historical Studies and Literary Criticism*. Ed. Jerome J.
    McGann. Madison: U of Wisconsin P, 1985. 143–79.

A Late Resident [William Jerdan and Michael Nugent]. Six *Weeks at Long's*.
    Vol. 3. London, 1817. 3 vols.

Lucan. *The Civil War*. Books 1–9. Cambridge: Harvard UP, 1957.

[Luttrell, Henry]. *Advice to Julia: A Letter in Rhyme*. London: John Murray,
    1820.

Magriel, Paul. "Bibliography of Boxing: A Chronological Check List of Books
    in English Published before 1900." *Bulletin of the New York Public Library*
    52 (1948): 263–88.

Malcolmson, Robert W. *Popular Recreations in English Society, 1700–1850*.
    Cambridge: Cambridge UP, 1973.

Martin, Philip W. "Reading *Don Juan* with Bakhtin." *Don Juan*. By George
    Gordon Byron. Ed. Nigel Wood. Buckingham: Open UP, 1993. 90–121.

Mazeppa *Travestied: A Poem. With an Introductory Address to the Goddess of
    "Milling," and Her Worshippers, "the Fancy."* London: C. Chapple, 1820.

McCalman, Iain. *Radical Underworld: Prophets, Revolutionaries, and
    Pornographers in London, 1795–1840*. Cambridge: Cambridge UP, 1988.

McGann, Jerome J. "Byron and 'the Truth in Masquerade.'" *Romantic
    Revisions*. Ed. Robert Brinkley and Keith Hanley. Cambridge: Cambridge
    UP, 1992. 191–209.

The Modern Flash Dictionary. London: G. Smeeton, [1821?].

Moore, Thomas. *The Journal of Thomas Moore*. Ed. Wilfred S. Dowden. Vol. 1.
    Newark: U of Delaware P, 1983. 6 vols.

Norton, Rictor. *Mother Clap's Molly House: The Gay Subculture in England,
    1700–1830*. London: GMP, 1992.

One of the Fancy [Pierce Egan]. *Boxiana; or, Sketches of Ancient and Modern
    Pugilism; from the Days of the Renowned Broughton and Slack, to the Heroes
    of the Present Milling Æra!* London: G. Smeeton, 1812.

One of the Fancy [Thomas Moore]. *Tom Crib's Memorial to Congress*. London:
    Longman, Hurst, Rees, Orme, and Brown, 1819.

[Oxberry, William]. *Pancratia; or, A History of Pugilism*. London: W. Oxberry,
    1812.

Petronius. *Satyricon*. Trans. Michael Heseltine. Rev. E. H. Warmington.
    Cambridge: Harvard UP, 1969.

Plautus. *Persa*. Trans. Paul Nixon. Cambridge: Harvard UP, 1963.

[Reynolds, John Hamilton]. *The Fancy: A Selection from the Poetical Remains of the Late Peter Corcoran, of Gray's Inn, Student at Law. With a Brief Memoir of His Life*. London: Taylor and Hessey, 1820.

Sales, Roger. "Pierce Egan and the Representation of London." *Reviewing Romanticism*. Ed. Philip W. Martin and Robin Jarvis. London: Macmillan, 1992. 154–69.

Sedgwick, Eve Kosofsky. *Epistemology of the Closet*. Berkeley: U of California P, 1990.

Southey, Robert. *Letters from England*. Ed. Jack Simmons. London: Cresset, 1951.

Trumbach, Randolph. *Heterosexuality and the Third Gender in Enlightenment London*. Chicago: U of Chicago P, 1998. Vol. 1 of *Sex and the Gender Revolution*.

Vaux, James Hardy. *Memoirs of James Hardy Vaux*. Vol. 2. London: W. Clowes, 1819. 2 vols.

[Wilson, John]. "Boxiana, No VIII, the Sable School of Pugilism." *Blackwood's Edinburgh Magazine* Oct. 1820: 60–67.

Winder, W. H. D. "The Development of Blackmail." *Modern Law Review* 4 (1941): 21–50.

"Farewell to Love"
(John Donne)

"Two Problems in Donne's 'Farewell to Love'"
by Katherine T. Emerson,
in *Modern Language Notes* (1957)

Introduction

In this examination of Donne scholarship and manuscripts, Katherine T. Emerson focuses on sexual language and sexual imagery in "Farewell to Love." Ultimately, she finds the language under question is not meant to be taken literally but rather as part of Donne's rich word play.

Lines 28–30 of Donne's "Farewell to Love" have been called by John Hayward "the most unintelligible in the whole canon of Donne's poetry."[1] They have received perhaps more than their share of attention but up to now have defied satisfactory interpretation. Part of the problem lies in the fact that the poem exists in only two manuscripts, which, according to Miss Helen Gardner,[2] are unreliable and too closely related to serve as checks on the accuracy of one another. The first printing of the poem, in 1635, seems to be derived from

Emerson, Katherine T. "Two Problems in Donne's 'Farewell to Love.'" *Modern Language Notes* Vol. 72, No. 2 (February 1957): 93–95.

one of these, the O'Flaherty Manuscript, and therefore offers no additional help.

Donne conjectures that Nature may have attached the curse of subsequent boredom to the sex act in order to restrain man from life-consuming overindulgence,

> Because that other curse of being short,
> And onely for a minute made to be
> Eager, desires to raise posteritie. (1635 text)

The earlier reference, in line 16, to the acute brevity of sexual pleasure ("being had, enjoying it decayes"), seems to indicate fairly clearly that this is the curse referred to, rather than the curse of man's mortality, as Sir Herbert Grierson has suggested in his edition of Donne's poetry (London, 1912).

Miss Gardner suggests that "made" be considered as a finite verb in the past tense, having "curse" as its subject and "desires" as its object. This interpretation renders the passage intelligible virtually as it stands in the manuscripts but makes it seem unduly awkward. Her reading gives the lines the same meaning, except for tense, as Grierson's emendation, which is:

> Because that other curse of being short,
> And onely for a minute made to be,
> (Eagers desire) to raise posterity.

But an unsolved problem remains: how is the phrase "to raise posterity" to be taken? For Grierson it has a literal meaning: by begetting posterity man attempts to circumvent his curse of mortality. Miss Gardner also takes it literally. George Williamson[3] and J. C. Maxwell[4] feel that Donne had no such serious thoughts as man's posterity in mind during the composition of the poem, and argue that it is the posterity of the act itself, with its attendant curse, which is to be raised through repetition. Both of these interpretations leave something to be desired, the first because it is inharmonious with the carefree mood and amatory subject of the poem, the second because it is probably somewhat farther fetched than we can expect from even Donne's poetry and is, as Miss Gardner has noted, inappropriate in a poem in which Donne is concerned with the process by which actual—not figurative—posterity may be raised.

A more straightforward interpretation of the passage seems to be that the brevity of the sex act urges man, in his quest for satisfaction, to repeat the act: it sharpens his desire "to raise posterity"—which phrase can most happily be read as Donne's cynical euphemism for "to engage in sexual intercourse." The phrase derives sardonic humor from the fact that man as discussed in this poem is not at all concerned with raising posterity, but rather with the "sport" (l. 27) by which this is accomplished. Thus the phrase is wholly appropriate to the mood and subject of the poem, which is a cynical discussion of sexual love.

In the concluding stanza, which immediately follows these lines, Donne makes plans for avoiding contact with any ladies whose beauties might move him once again to pursue love. It concludes:

> If all faile,
> 'Tis but applying worme-seed to the Taile. (ll. 39–40)

Hayward's note on these lines is: "Wormseed ... is a powerful anaphrodisiac. The Latin word for tail is *penis*, and tail in this sense is common in Elizabethan literature." On the strength of this note, the lines have been taken to mean that if all else fails, one can always resort to anaphrodisiacs. This interpretation has been accepted without dissent.[5] But the grammar of the sentence does not lend itself readily to this interpretation. In order to have this meaning, surely the lines would require the addition of some phrase such as "a matter of" after "but." Without such a phrase there is, in the interpretation based on Hayward's note, no antecedent for the "it" contracted in "'Tis." *What* is "but applying worme-seed to the Taile"?

An interpretation consistent with the grammar of the sentence is that line 40 is a metaphor, with this sense: "If these expedients fail, what more could one expect? For they are, after all, directed only at avoiding the occasion rather than rooting out the cause of the difficulty. They are as purposeless as it would be to apply wormseed to the tail, since wormseed can be effective [either as an anthelmintic or as an anaphrodisiac—the sense of the metaphor is the same in either case] only when taken orally." In sort, the attempt to avoid beauty is a futile application of one's energies while a disposition to love remains. By this reading, "all" in line 39, representing all the plans which Donne has just proposed, is the antecedent of the "it" that is troublesome in the other interpretation. The present-tense "'Tis" is then normal for the situation. Thus the wormseed seems here to be a metaphor, rather than a possible last resort. However, the erotic connotations of the two key words enrich Donne's use of them in a way especially appropriate to the poem and typical of the poet's intricate imagery.

Notes

1. In the Nonesuch edition of Donne's *Complete Poetry and Selected Prose* (Bloomsbury, 1929), p. 192.
2. *TLS*, June 10, 1949, p. 381.
3. *MP*, xxxvi (1939), 301–303.
4. *TLS*, May 6, 1949, p. 297.
5. Professor George Williamson, in *MP*, xxxvi, 303, recognizes the possibility that the lines may represent either "a metaphor of futility" or a "cynical last resort," though he appears to favor the latter.

GIOVANNI'S ROOM
(JAMES BALDWIN)

"*Giovanni's Room* and Human Sexuality"
by Lorena Russell,
University of North Carolina at Asheville

James Baldwin's *Giovanni's Room* (1956) explores an individual's shame and personal conflict as he comes to grips with his emerging gay sexuality. The story is told from the first-person perspective of David, an American who is living in Paris sometime during the mid-twentieth century. The bulk of the story takes place after David has proposed to his girlfriend Hella. While Hella is away traveling in Spain, mulling over the proposal, David develops a sexual relationship with Giovanni, an Italian bartender. Although Giovanni is not David's first homosexual partner, this is the affair that seemingly cements his gay identity, and prompts him to reconsider his previous path in life. David's rejection of Giovanni will ultimately contribute to the latter's death, and the novel traces David's reckoning with how his internalized homophobia has literally destroyed lives. Through David's struggle towards self-understanding, readers are challenged to consider the costs of prejudice and the kinds of suffering individuals who stand outside the norms of the majority must endure as they grow in their self-acceptance.

Because the novel addresses the potentially deadly costs of growing up gay in a homophobic society, homosexual identity is framed as a problematic site of personal struggle. The novel begins with a quote from the gay American poet, Walt Whitman: "I am the man, I suffered, I was there." This epigraph points to the novel's central theme of suffering and situates that theme within the context of the American gay male sensibility.

Baldwin's novel opens in the present tense, a device that effectively bonds the reader with the narrator, who reveals that he is on the verge of "the most terrible morning of my life" (3). At this moment, his girlfriend Hella is on her way back to America, and his ex-lover, Giovanni, faces execution by guillotine at dawn. We also learn that the protagonist is not, as we might expect of an African-American author, a black man, but rather a white man with blond hair. As David imagines his pending train trip to Paris, he describes the quotidian nature of the journey. Like his features ("a face you have seen many times"), his description of the train ride counters his suffering with the everyday appearance of "normality." This contrast between the tempestuous struggle within and the appearance of normality without becomes just one of the themes that the intimacy of the first-person narrative allows.

David's reflections prioritize his internal struggle and suffering as he comes to grips with his sexual identity. He considers how he first became attached to Hella. He saw her drinking at a bar and imagined that she "would be fun to have fun with" but never felt an erotic attraction to her (Baldwin 4). David reflects further on his impulsive proposal of marriage to Hella, which he understands as an attempt on his part to find some kind of moral mooring in reaction to the sexual freedom he found in France. The security of marriage, the fact that it represents an acceptable social script, makes it an easy, if less than honest choice, for both Hella and David.

For *Giovanni's Room* is a book about self-delusion as much as it is a book about self-discovery, a reflection on David's struggle to accept himself as a gay man. His attempt to run from the reality of his sexuality brought him to France, and now he considers his previous resolve to never sleep with a man after his initial encounter:

> There is something fantastic in the spectacle I know present to myself of having run so far, so hard, across the ocean even, only to find myself brought up short once more before the bulldog in my own backyard—the yard, in the meantime, having grown smaller and the bulldog bigger. (6)

Up until this point, David had spent his life running from his sexuality ("the bulldog"), but here in France, through his affair with Giovanni, he finds himself facing a reality that can no longer be so easily denied. He remembers his first gay sexual encounter when he shared a bed with a fellow teenager named "Joey":

> [...] this time when I touched him something happened in him and in me which made this touch different from any touch either of us had ever known [...] And I realized that my heart was beating in an awful way and that Joey was trembling against me and the light in the room was very bright and hot...we kissed, as it were, by accident. Then, for the first time in my life, I was really aware of another person's body, of another person's smell. We had our arms around each other. It was like holding in my hand some rare, exhausted, nearly doomed bird which I had miraculously happened to find. I was very frightened; I am sure he was frightened too, and we shut our eyes. (8)

This passage offers a good example of how *Giovanni's Room* comments on human sexuality. In recalling this suppressed memory, David recounts his desire in an honest and detailed fashion. But fear is never far from intimacy in *Giovanni's Room*, as his confession reveals the fright accompanying his pleasure. Thus, his memory of Joey also becomes an occasion for David to try to understand the deep sense of shame and despair that coincides with his sexual awakening. Even as he enjoys Joey's body with its "power and the promise and the mystery" he is simultaneously aware that that same body represents "the black opening of a cavern in which I would be tortured till madness came, in which I would lose my manhood" (9). Despite the satisfaction the sexual initiation represents, David also remembers the deep sense of social shame and stigma: "I was afraid. I could have cried, cried for shame and terror, cried for not understanding how this could have happened in me" (9).

Not surprisingly, when David awakes he breaks off the friendship and severs the relationship: "I picked up with a rougher, older crowd and was very nasty to Joey" (10). His response to his homosexual desire was to separate himself from Joey by adopting a homophobic attitude, thereby signaling his status as heterosexual. In doing so,

David refutes his own sexuality and simultaneously forecloses the possibility of experiencing intimacy with another human. Now, as an adult, he recognizes how that moment marked the beginning of a flight "which has brought me to this darkening window" (10). The narrative invites the reader to empathize with David's conflicted feelings of pleasure and of aversion, and to understand the level of psychological struggle and pain that his sexual desire has wrought as it plays out against the negativity of social stigma.

Giovanni's Room does not depend on a plot structure, but functions more as a psychological novel, one that works (as is typical in modernist fiction) through the interior psychology of the characters. Here David's interior perspective is used in part to highlight the disparity between the character's feelings and social mores. The novel reminds us repeatedly that one's internal feelings relate to one's social context. It is noteworthy, for example, that David "comes out" in Paris, away from the more conservative sexual norms of the United States. While Giovanni will tease David about his internalized homophobia, David in turn complains about Giovanni's willingness to accommodate Hella's presence concurrently with their relationship. When Giovanni basically calls David a prude for his unwillingness to maintain the two relationships simultaneously, David retorts "it *is* a crime—in my country and, after all, I didn't grow up here, I grew up *there*" (emphasis in original, 81). A large part of David's issue with accepting himself as a gay man goes back to his nationality and his internalized, puritanical attitudes towards sexuality.

While David's retort suggests a critique of American Puritanism, even in Paris it is clear that as gay men David and Giovanni occupy a different and troubled space, as they unsuccessfully try to reconcile their sexual identities and personal histories with societal expectations. Many of the settings in the novel point to their status outside of mainstream society. They meet at a gay bar, one of the few places where homosexuals can feel free to be themselves. Giovanni's work as a bartender means that they typically move about the city at night, in the twilight spaces of the *demi monde*.

Furthermore, the room they stay in, which is Giovanni's room, comes to represent the safe and erotic space that is also the metaphorical closet for David and Giovanni. The room is encircled by a garden, a space that seems to encroach on the room in a threatening kind of way. As Kathleen Drowne makes clear, the claustrophobic and disorderly spaces in the novel, most clearly felt within Giovanni's room, mirror the disorder and internal chaos of disjunctive identities:

> More than mere sexual impurity or even 'deviance,' this cluttered, disorderly, unsanitary room that Giovanni owns and David shares also suggests the profound psychological disorganization and ambivalence that characterize both men's lives. As such, this place becomes much more than merely a site of the story's action; it takes on the role of a mirror, or a gauge, of the hidden aspects of David and Giovanni that manifest themselves in the condition of the room ... (Drowne 79)

Drowne's reading of the text concludes that David's attempts to reconcile himself to his identity ultimately fail, as the chaos and dirt that was so characteristic of Giovanni's room will follow him to the south of France.

Moreover, this tiny maid's room with its painted windows and claustrophobic dimensions represents the ambiguities of a closet. It is secretive not only because it is precious and therefore coveted, but also because, as the setting for the couple's sexual acts, it becomes a location of feelings of shame and social disapproval. In some ways the contradictory attributes of the room (at once safe and chaotic, erotic and threatening) reveal the social and personal ambivalences of "coming out." As one develops and evolves a sense of synchronicity with one's self and one's desires, one simultaneously risks the very real threat of social and familial alienation. While on one level David achieves a sense of peace through his relationship with Giovanni, on another he is acutely aware that he is risking his relationship with his family and the majority of society.

While this dynamic of the closet is very familiar to gay men and women today, there are other ways that *Giovanni's Room* captures some of the dated attitudes and opinions of the past. For example, Baldwin goes to great lengths to situate David vis-à-vis his family history, thus representing psychological theories popular in his time that sought to explain the supposed "deviance" of homosexuality. We learn, for example, that David lost his mother when he was five and still suffers from that loss. As a child he is plagued by morbid nightmares where she appeared "blind with worms, her hair as dry as metal and brittle as a twig, straining to press me against her body; that body so putrescent, so sickening soft, that it opened, as I clawed and cried, into a breach so enormous as to swallow me alive" (10–11). It is not difficult to read the underlying psychology of this passage, which links his mother's deathly presence with David's own repudiation of female sexuality.

Ultimately, however, it is the secretive affair with Joey that comes to determine David's sexual behavior and identity. The affair and its renunciation engenders feelings of fear, shame and disgust:

> [I]ts effect was to make me secretive and cruel. I could not discuss what had happened to me with anyone, I could not even admit to myself; and, while I never thought about it, it remained, nevertheless, at the bottom of my mind, as still and as awful as a decomposing corpse. (16)

The latter image creates a link between David's homosexuality and his dead mother as objects of disgust and abjection.

After his mother dies, David lives with and grows up with his father and aunt, Ellen, who frequently argue over how David should best be raised. His father, a drinker and a womanizer, makes it known that "all [he] want[s] for David is that he grow up to be a man" (15). David's aunt protests that he sets a bad example, and that a man "is not the same thing as a bull" (15). From the beginning, then, David is surrounded by a fear of femininity and a prescribed masculinity, while secretly tortured by the knowledge of his true sexuality. For David, gendered behavior (the practice or acting out of femininity or masculinity) is irrevocably linked to one's sexuality (who one desires sexually). As he matures into a young man, David becomes a master of self-deception, an inhabitant of the closet, as he "had decided to allow no room in the universe for something which shamed and frightened [him]" (20). Although he does engage in a number of brief homosexual affairs ("all drunken, all sordid") he manages to live his life in denial of his sexual desires (20). When one of his lovers is court marshaled and dismissed from the army, he comes close to facing the truth of his identity, but instead flees to France. As he describes it:

> I think now that if I had had any intimation that the self I was going to find would turn out to be only the same self

from which I had spent so much time in flight, I would have
stayed at home. But again, I think I knew, at the very bottom
of my heart, exactly what I was doing when I took the boat
for France (21).

Because of his sexuality, David's movement towards self-awareness
is marked by a series of tensions and conflicts. He lives in the closet,
in constant negotiation of "elaborate systems of evasion, of illusion"
(20). On one level he is a heterosexual man, "wandering through the
forests of desperate women" (21), but on another level he is alone,
suppressed, and displaced. His flight to Paris thus complicates any
easy understanding of what it might mean to "find one's self," especially when full acceptance of one's self is at odds with societal norms
and prejudices.

Much of society's prejudice against homosexuality is expressed
through David's internalized homophobia. His preoccupation with
disgust and abjection grow out of his feelings of self-loathing. When
he is kicked out of his hotel, he notes, "Parisian hotel-keepers have
a way of smelling poverty . . . they throw whatever stinks outside"
(22). When his father tries to convince him to come home and
"settle down," David thinks of "the sediment at the bottom of a
stagnant pond" (22). His most severe disgust he saves for a description of an effeminate man he meets at Guillaume's bar. He has
nothing but contempt for these effeminate gay men, *les folles*, and
describes his uneasiness in the presence of one as arising out of the
response one might have of "the sight of monkeys eating their own
excrement" (27).

He holds his gay friend Jacques in contempt, but it is Jacques who
can offer David the solid advice to "Come out, come out, wherever
you are!" (57). It is Jacques who advises David to follow his heart and
to love Giovanni: "'Love him and let him love you. Do you think
anything else under heaven really matters?'" (57). Finally, it is Jacques
who reminds David that he ultimately controls his own attitudes
towards homosexuality:

> And if you think of them as dirty, then they *will* be dirty—they
> will be dirty because you will be giving nothing, you will be
> despising your flesh and his. But you can make your time
> together anything but dirty; you can give each other something

which will make both of you better—forever—if you will *not* be
ashamed, if you will only *not* play it safe. (57)

This advice suggests the power to turn homosexual love into something
sacred rather than profane is within David's grasp. But to take control
over one's feelings in the face of one's negative socialization proves to
be a hard lesson for David to learn. Even the bar owner Guillaume, who
will become the victim of Giovanni's misplaced rage, warns Giovanni
against David's conflict. As Giovanni reports to David, Guillaume told
him "you were just an American boy. . .doing things in France which
you would not dare to do at home, and that you would leave me very
soon" (108). In fact, these words succinctly capture David's treatment
of Giovanni. While David ultimately recognizes that his contempt for
Jacques "involved [his] self-contempt," for most of the story the elder
Jacques and Guillaume are held in contempt as "dirty water," capable
of fouling the younger David and Giovanni (23, 45).

David's ambivalence about his own identity leads to his projec-
tion of feelings of disgust onto others. In another scene, a gay man in
the bar who earns a description more deserving of Dracula than any
human approaches him:

> It carried a glass, it walked on its toes, the flat hips moved with
> a dead, horrifying lasciviousness. It seemed to make no sound;
> this was due to the roar of the bar, which was like the roaring
> of the sea, heard at night, from far away. It glittered in the dim
> light; the thin, black hair was violent with oil, combed forward,
> hanging in bangs; the eyelids gleamed with mascara, the mouth
> raged with lipstick. The face was white and thoroughly bloodless
> with some kind of foundation cream; it stank of powder and a
> gardenia-like perfume. The shirt, open coquettishly to the navel,
> revealed a hairless chest and a silver crucifix. . . (39)

Giovanni struggles in many of the same ways as David. He too seeks
escape from the reality of his sexuality: "*Je veux m'evader*—this dirty
world, this dirty body" (24). The novel's conclusion suggests an escape
for Giovanni, but it is an escape through the guillotine, through death.
David imagines Giovanni's approach to the door leading to his execution and realizes "that door is the gateway he has sought so long out
of this dirty world, this dirty body" (168).

At the end of the story, David fixates on his own nakedness as he contemplates his penis in the mirror and its prescriptive implication of heterosexual masculinity. He recognizes that, as an effeminate gay man, he must go forward into a life of shame, where his nakedness "which I must hold sacred, though it be never so vile. . .must be scoured perpetually with the salt of my life" (169). David's body, with its sexual organs, becomes a signifier of masculinity and therefore points to the very essence of his conflict as a gay man.

Accordingly, the novel concludes on an ambivalent note. Even as David considers a tentative acceptance of his body, he tears up the letter from Jacques that informed him of Giovanni's execution, thus symbolically renouncing his (homosexual) past:

> The morning weighs on my shoulders with the dreadful weight of hope and I take the blue envelope which Jacques has sent me and tear it slowly into many pieces, watching them dance in the wind, watching the wind carry them away. Yet, as I turn and begin walking towards the waiting people, the wind blows some of them back on me. (169)

Although David tries to walk away from his sexual past by joining the crowd of "normal" people waiting for the bus, the wind blows the torn pieces of paper back to him, suggesting that he cannot escape the knowledge he has acquired in Paris.

Works Cited

Baldwin, James. *Giovanni's Room*. New York: Dell, 2000.

Drowne, Kathleen N. "'An Irrevocable Condition': Constructions of Home and the Writing of Place in *Giovanni's Room*." *Re-Viewing James Baldwin: Things Not Seen*. Eds. D. Quentin Miller and David Leeming. Philadelphia: Temple UP, 2000.

LOLITA
(VLADIMIR NABOKOV)

"Sexuality in Vladimir Nabokov's *Lolita*"
by Paul Benedict Grant,
Sir Wilfred Grenfell College,
Memorial University, Canada

On its American publication in 1958, critic Lionel Trilling defended Vladimir Nabokov's *Lolita* against charges of pornography, claiming, "*Lolita* is not about sex, but about love" (5). The meaning of Trilling's argument is subtler than such a blunt statement suggests, but it creates false expectations in a reader new to the novel: *Lolita* may or may not be about love, but it is undeniably about sex. In downplaying this fact, one risks playing into the hands of the novel's narrator, middle-aged pedophile Humbert Humbert, who claims that he is "not concerned with so-called 'sex' at all," and that the attraction he feels for prepubescent girls is somehow "beyond" the physical (134). The first sentence of his narrative betrays the fact that the sexual aspects of his infatuation are as important as the spiritual: Lolita, a nickname for the twelve-year-old Dolores Haze, is not only the "light of [his] life," she is also the "fire of [his] loins"—that is, the source of his sexual arousal (9).

Humbert, like almost every other character in *Lolita*—heterosexuals, homosexuals, bisexuals, pedophiles, pornographers, voyeurs, and exhibitionists—is defined by his sexuality: it makes him who he is, colors everything he does, motivates every decision he makes. His conception of love is inevitably seen through the lens of his lust. This begs the following question: can sex and love co-exist when one's sexual desires are so obviously perverse? Moreover, if *Lolita is* a love story, as Trilling contends, is it any less genuine because it is told from the point of view of a pedophile? Can we—*should* we—dismiss it out of hand for that reason? Humbert hopes we won't, because as he sees it, his very soul is at stake (308). It should come as no surprise, then, that throughout his story he challenges the reader's notions of normative sexuality and attempts to redefine key terms like sex and love.

Early in the novel, in an attempt to account for his sexual condition, Humbert provides a detailed explanation of his "shameful vice" (264). What society terms pedophilia he calls "nympholepsy," a word that derives from his concept of "nymphets":

> Between the age limits of nine and fourteen there occur maidens who, to certain bewitched travelers, twice or many times older than they, reveal their true nature which is not human, but nymphic (that is, demoniac); and these chosen creatures I propose to designate as "nymphets" . . . there must be a gap of several years . . . between maiden and man to enable the latter to come under a nymphet's spell. (16–17)

What separates nymphets from ordinary girls and drives men like Humbert insane with desire has nothing to do with conventional good looks; rather, it is their "insidious charm" (17) and "mixture. . .of tender dreamy childishness and . . . eerie vulgarity" (44). Male pedophiles, or nympholepts, as Humbert terms them, are "ready to give years and years of life for one chance to touch a nymphet" (88) because "there is no other bliss on earth comparable to that of fondling a nymphet. It . . . belongs to another class, another plane of sensitivity" (166). Since nymphets are so singular, it takes a special kind of man to detect one: "A normal man given a group photograph of school girls. . .will not necessarily choose the nymphet among them. You have to be an artist and a madman . . . in order to discern at once, by ineffable signs. . .the little deadly demon among the wholesome children" (17). Humbert sees himself as one of these men: an artist who has fallen under the spell of "nymphean evil" (125). He describes Dolores as no ordinary twelve-year-old girl, but "some immortal daemon disguised as a female child" (139). The reverse is the truth: he is a "predator" (42) and Dolores is his "prey" (49).

By lusting after little girls, Humbert violates one of western society's strongest taboos; in order to show "that it [is] all a question of attitude, that there [is] really nothing wrong in being moved to distraction by girl-children" (19), he cites cases that seem to prove these taboos are relative: "Dante fell madly in love with his Beatrice when she was nine ... And when Petrarch fell madly in love with his Laureen, she was a fair-haired nymphet of twelve" (19). Again, Humbert places himself in the company of artists, who are connoisseurs of beauty, not criminals; as he claims, "The gentle and dreamy regions through which I crept were the patrimonies of poets—*not* crime's prowling ground" (131). What he fails to mention is that Dante was only nine years old when he met Beatrice, who was only a year younger, and that Petrarch was twenty-three years old when he met Laura, whose age has never been determined. He further argues that an ancient Roman law that allowed girls to marry at twelve "is still preserved ... in some of the United States," and that "fifteen is lawful everywhere." Again, he is being selective: in the late 1940s and early 1950s, when the story is set, this Roman law was preserved in only ten states, and fifteen was *not* lawful everywhere. Clearly, Humbert is not to be trusted as a narrator.

Psychiatrist John Ray, Jr. calls Humbert "abnormal" (5), but as these passages show, Humbert seeks to redefine the notion of what "normal" means. If he can convince his readers that society has a hypocritical value system and that he is living in a world of sexual double standards, he can escape censure. To that end, he tries to overturn the conventional notion of pedophiles:

> the majority of sex offenders that hanker for some throbbing, sweet-moaning, physical but not necessarily coital, relation with a girl-child, are innocuous, inadequate, passive, timid strangers who merely ask the community to allow them to pursue their practically harmless, so-called aberrant behaviour, their little hot wet private acts of sexual deviation without the police and society cracking down upon them. We are not sex fiends! We do not rape as good soldiers do. We are unhappy, mild, dog-eyed gentlemen ... (87–88)

Convention is turned on its head here: pedophilia is "practically harmless" and only allegedly aberrant; pedophiles are not violators, but victims of society, not "sex fiends," but timid gentlemen; "good soldiers," commonly regarded as guardians of morality, have been known to commit rape, so if they go unpunished why should *he* be considered guilty?

While Humbert seeks to justify his pedophilia by drawing on literary and legal precedents, he also tries to excuse his behavior by blaming it on circumstance. Although he states that his sexual condition could be genetic—an "inherent singularity" (13)—he traces its source to an "incomplete childhood romance" (167) with an "initial girl-child" (9), Annabel Leigh, when he was thirteen. On two occasions, he and Annabel were on the verge of having sex, but were thwarted. Her sudden death shortly thereafter became a "permanent obstacle to any further romance throughout the cold years of [his] youth" (14). His unfulfilled feelings follow him into adulthood until he is able to satisfy them with Dolores: "the ache remained with me … until at last … I broke [Annabel's] spell by incarnating her in another" (15). Insofar as this childhood sexual trauma shapes his character, it is typically Freudian. However, Humbert mocks psychoanalysis throughout his confession. This contradiction enables him to trifle with his readers as he trifles with his psychiatrists, "teasing them with fake 'primal scenes' … and never allowing them the slightest glimpse of [his] real sexual predicament" (34). The story of Annabel could be a complete fabrication, a psychologically credible excuse that serves to rationalize (but not vindicate) his actions as an adult.

Thus far, Humbert's attempts to explain his sexual condition read like a series of excuses by which he tries to escape responsibility for his actions. He paints himself as a passive victim and Dolores as a depraved demon, claims that western society has a warped perception of pedophiles, and portrays the cause of his pedophilia as being either genetic or circumstantial—either way, he is not to blame, and is a prisoner of his desire. Finally, if these arguments fail to convince, he can fall back on the fact that nympholepts are artists, and "sex is but the ancilla of art" (259).

According to Humbert, his childhood experience makes it impossible for him to have normal sexual relations with women: "My adult life … proved monstrously twofold. Overtly, I had so-called normal relationships … I was consumed by a hell furnace of localized lust for every passing nymphet" (18). He finds "the sensations. . .derived from natural fornication" unsatisfying; any pleasure he obtains from women depends on how closely they resemble (or can be made to resemble) little girls. Monique appeals to him because "her young body. . .still retained … a childish something" (21); he is initially attracted to Valeria because of the "the imitation she gave of a little girl" (25); in order to fulfill his conjugal duties with Charlotte, he "evoke[s] the child while caressing the mother" (76); and after Dolores leaves him, he takes up with Rita, who has an "oddly prepubescent" body (259).

As this list suggests, despite the problems he has maintaining relationships with women, Humbert has no shortage of female admirers. He repeatedly refers to himself as "an exceptionally handsome male" and writes of the effect his good looks have "on women of every age and environment" (104). When he first meets Charlotte, he assumes she has sexual designs on her "glamorous lodger" (49). As for Dolores: "I have all the characteristics which, according to writers on the sex interests of children, start the responses stirring in a little girl: clean-cut jaw, muscular hand, deep sonorous voice, broad shoulder" (43). How could she fail to be drawn to such "a great big handsome hunk of movieland manhood"? (39) By casting himself in this role of the admired object, Humbert not only displays one of his defining characteristics—narcissism—but abdicates responsibility for his actions: he is not the hunter, but the hunted.

To reinforce this idea, Humbert depicts Dolores as being sexually precocious. He describes how she plants a passionate kiss on his lips before she leaves for camp (66); how, on being reunited, she refers to them as "lovers" (114) and kisses him as though she were a dominatrix: "I touched her hot, opening lips with the utmost piety, tiny sips, nothing salacious; but she, with an impatient wriggle, pressed her mouth to mine so hard that I felt her big front teeth and shared in the peppermint taste of her saliva" (113). Although he knows this is "an innocent game on her part … in imitation of some simulacrum of fake romance" (113), he stresses her forwardness. This lends weight to Dolores' exaggerated description of herself (or, to be more precise, Humbert's exaggerated description of Dolores) as a "disgusting girl" (123) who is "absolutely filthy in thought, word and deed" (114).

This shifting of responsibility reaches its climax when Humbert and Dolores have sexual intercourse, and he claims that *she* seduced *him* (132). To his chagrin, he learns that he is "not even her first lover": she has already been "debauched" by 13-year-old Charlie Holmes (135). She and her friend, Barbara, had sex with Charlie several times: "At first, Lo had refused 'to try what it was like,' but curiosity and camaraderie prevailed, and soon she and Barbara were doing it by turns with the silent, coarse and surly but indefatigable Charlie, who had as much sex appeal as a raw carrot but sported a fascinating collection of contraceptives" (137). This revelation allows Humbert to relinquish responsibility again: "I am not a criminal sexual psychopath taking indecent liberties with a child. The rapist was Charlie Holmes; I am the therapist—a matter of nice spacing in the way of distinction" (150). It also allows him to paint Dolores as being "utterly and hopelessly depraved":

> She saw the stark act merely as part of a youngster's furtive world, unknown to adults. What adults did for purposes of procreation was no business of hers. My life [penis] was handled by Lo in an energetic, matter-of-fact manner as if it were an insensate gadget unconnected with me. While eager to impress me with the world of tough kids, she was not quite prepared for certain discrepancies between a kid's life and mine. Pride alone prevented her from giving up; for, in my strange predicament, I feigned supreme stupidity and had her have her way—at least while I could still bear it. (133–134)

Humbert knows that Dolores has no conception of the significance of what she is doing, but he pretends to be ignorant so that she is forced to take the role of teacher to his pupil. This role reversal is taken to horribly ironic extremes when he later accuses her, with astonishing hypocrisy, "of having impaired the morals of an adult" (150).

The aftermath of this episode reveals much about both characters. "With the ebb of lust," Humbert feels a sense of shame, but this does not stand in the way of his sexual desire: "mingled with the pangs of guilt was the agonizing thought that her mood might prevent me from making love to her again" (140). This becomes a habitual post-coital experience for him: signs of penitence soon give way to lust (285). Dolores' reaction, by contrast, shifts from "queer dullness" (139) to mild hysteria, betraying her emotional confusion. She accuses him of having "torn something inside her" (141), yells at him when he hints they could have intercourse again, then jokes: "'I was a daisy-fresh girl, and look at what you've done to me. I ought to call the police and tell them you raped me. Oh, you dirty, dirty old man'" (141). This demonstrates that Dolores knows that what Humbert has done is punishable by law, but that she hasn't decided how she feels about the situation. Later, when she realizes how he took advantage of her, she again refers to the incident as rape (202), but with a greater sense of the gravity of the allegation.

Humbert may describe sex offenders like himself as passive, timid and mild, but as a lover he is none of these things. Sex becomes a "duty" (165) Dolores must fulfill, even when she is sick (198, 239). He treats her as nothing more than a sexual object, submitting her body to "fabulous, insane exertions" until he has "had [his] fill of her" (285), and forces himself on her whenever desire strikes: "gently but firmly clasping [my fingers] around the nape of her neck, I would lead my reluctant pet to our small home for a quick connection before dinner" (164). At times, these 'connections' are "particularly violent" (159–160); he seems to have a liking for "strenuous intercourse" (140). There are hints that Dolores fights back—on one occasion, a stranger asks Humbert where he received some scratches (164)—but she has to submit to his demands because she has "nowhere else to go" (142).

Lionel Trilling's contention that "no lover has thought of his beloved with so much tenderness" as Humbert does (9-10) requires qualification. It is true that Humbert describes Dolores' body in loving detail, but he hardly mentions her thoughts, which he finds "disgustingly conventional" (148). His own needs are paramount: "it was always my habit and method to ignore Lolita's states of mind while comforting my own base self" (287). The fact that he is prepared to drug her in order to have sex with her proves he would rather have a "completely anesthetized little nude" (124) than a girl with a will of her own (Dolores' diminutive, 'Dolly,' has this secondary, grotesque meaning). Only by pretending she has "no will, no consciousness—indeed, no life of her own" (62) can he operate. It is only later that he faces the truth and recognizes the damage he has caused.

Needless to say, Dolores derives no pleasure from having sex with Humbert, as he admits: "Never did she vibrate under my touch, and a strident 'what d'you think you are doing?' was all I got for my pains" (166). Initially, he has trouble persuading her to have sex—"it would take hours of blandishments, threats and promises to make her lend me for a few seconds her brown limbs" (147)—but she soon realizes the extent of her power over him and prostitutes herself with him in order to earn pocket money (184). She also uses sex as a threat when arguing with him, saying, "she would sleep with the very first fellow who asked her" (205). Dolores' attitude toward sex becomes increasingly blasé: she sees it as nothing more than a form of currency, an act divorced from feeling. It is not surprising that years later, when Humbert gives her money, she automatically thinks he wants sex in return (278). Her relationship with Humbert has many adverse consequences on her sexual and social development. Humbert refuses to let her go on dates with boys her own age. Ironically, because she seems outwardly uninterested in boys, Headmistress Pratt believes that "the onset of sexual maturing seems to give [Dolores] trouble" (193). Pratt thinks Dolores "remains morbidly uninterested in sexual matters, or to be exact, represses her curiosity in order to save her ignorance and self dignity" (195). The truth is, Dolores' sexual maturation has been irreparably damaged by her "sex play" with Humbert (196).

When not abdicating responsibility, Humbert seeks to justify his behavior by expressing his love for Dolores; however, his sincerity is questionable given that his passion for her is not exclusive. When he is on the brink of possessing her for the first time, he still manages to register the presence of another nymphet (126); after he has sex with her, he presses her for sexual secrets about one of her classmates (139); during their first cross-country trip, he parks outside schools and has her caress him while he ogles other girls (161); and when visiting Beardsley School, he has her fondle him under the desk while he gazes at a girl in her class (198). He enjoys "having a bevy of page girls, consolation prize nymphets, around [his] Lolita" (190) because it lends variety to his lust, and if any "ever surpassed her in desirability" he tells us, "it was so two or three times at the most" (161).

As these examples show, sex, not love, is Humbert's primary concern, and this is confirmed when Dolores escapes his clutches with Clare Quilty. One would expect this event to affect Humbert's sexual habits, but it does not: "I would be a knave to say, and the reader a fool to believe, that the shock of losing Lolita cured me of my pederosis. My accursed nature could not change, no matter how my love for her did. On playgrounds and beaches, my sullen and stealthy eye, against my will, still sought out the flash of a nymphet's limbs" (257). Even when he is en route to his last meeting with Dolores and the man he intends to kill for taking her from him, he cannot suppress his sexual desire: "the ancient beast in me was casting about for some lightly clad child I might hold against me for a minute, after the killing was over and nothing mattered anymore" (268). These are not the words or the actions of someone in love; on the contrary, they signify sexual addiction.

Humbert claims to have "fallen in love with Lolita forever" and says he could not live without her (64-65), but even before they cohabit he is wondering what he will do when "she would cease being a nymphet and turn into a young girl" (65). Such thoughts are never far from his mind when they are together:

> Depending on the condition of my glands and ganglia, I could switch in the course of the same day . . . from the thought that around 1950 I would have to get rid somehow of a difficult adolescent whose magic nymphage had evaporated—to the thought that with patience and luck I might have her produce eventually a nymphet with my blood in her exquisite veins, a Lolita the Second, who would be eight or nine around 1960 . . . (174)

When he sees Dolores for the final time, he finds her nymphage has indeed evaporated. Married and "hugely pregnant" (269), she has lost her sexual allure. Consequently, he feels no jealousy when imagining her having sex with her husband, Dick: "he and his Dolly had had unrestrained intercourse . . . at least a hundred and eighty times, probably much more . . . No grudge" (274). This reaction seems to signal a change in his attitude toward Dolores: with the sexual aspect removed, he finally sees her not as a nymphet, but as a person, and professes his love for her:

> There she was (my Lolita!) hopelessly worn at seventeen . . . and I looked and looked at her, and knew as clearly as I know I am to die, that I loved her more than anything I had ever seen or imagined on earth, or hoped for anywhere else . . . You may jeer at me, and threaten to clear the court, but . . . I insist the world know how much I loved my Lolita, *this* Lolita, pale and polluted, and big with another's child. (277–278)

As Trilling observes, this passage goes some way toward convincing the reader of Humbert's sincerity, as do the pages that follow, where he reflects on what he has done to Dolores. Lolita, the nymphet of his imagination, reveals herself to be what she has been all along: "a North American girl-child named Dolores Haze" who has been "deprived of her childhood by a maniac" (283). Humbert confesses to "depths of calculated carnality" (284), accepts that "nothing could make my Lolita forget the foul lust I had inflicted upon her" (283), and expresses what appear to be genuine feelings of remorse for the "poor, bruised child" (284), declaring his love again in the face of his shame (283). It is a bravura performance—but is it *only* that, a show staged for the benefit of his readers? Those who are unsure suspend judgment; those who take him at his word interpret what follows— Humbert's killing of Quilty—as confirmation of his sincerity and a form of belated absolution.

When Humbert confronts Quilty, the latter casts himself as Dolores' hero: "I saved her from a beastly pervert . . . I'm not responsible for the rapes of others. Absurd!" (298). He is right: Humbert *is* a beastly pervert who has committed statutory rape. But Quilty is not blameless, since he, too, treated her as a sexual object, trying to persuade her to perform in pornographic movies, or "sexcapades" (298) and throwing her out when she refused to perform fellatio on some "beastly boys" (277). Quilty takes Humbert for a kindred spirit and tries to bribe him by offering him "a young lady with three breasts" and a "unique collection of erotica" (302). Under other circumstances, Humbert might have shown interest in such curios, but he is there to revenge his twisted honor and cannot be bought. He murders Quilty and shows no remorse for the killing, which he views as unimportant compared with what he has done to Dolores: "Had I come before myself, I would have given Humbert at least thirty-five years for rape, and dismissed the rest of the charges" (308).

Like Humbert, Quilty is "an amateur of sex lore" (250), "a complete freak in sex matters" (276), and is "very fond of children" (296). The fact that he is "practically impotent" (298) reveals much about his motivations: sex is a voyeuristic sport for Quilty, a sterile exercise with no promise of fulfillment; he is "sterile vice" (278) personified. For these reasons, some critics view him as the physical embodiment of Humbert's degenerate side, and contend that when

Humbert kills Quilty he is, symbolically, destroying his evil self and making possible his "moral apotheosis" (5). This argument might be acceptable but for the fact that Humbert writes his memoirs after the murder, while awaiting trial. His descriptions of his nympholepsy are too vivid to convince us that he is capable of rehabilitation. His own words have already condemned him: "My accursed nature could not change" (257).

Ironically, however, Dolores' love for Quilty may authenticate Humbert's own status as a lover, and prove that perversion does not preclude the possibility of love. She was warned about Quilty's perversion before she took up with him, but could see past it in a way she could not see past Humbert's deviancy, perhaps because Quilty did not attempt to mask it in under the guise of love, as Humbert did. She is deluded, but the experience does not embitter her; indeed, she can still refer to Quilty as "the only man she had ever been crazy about" (272). Despite its doomed quality and the fact that her feelings are not reciprocated—perhaps precisely *because* of these things—Dolores' relationship with Quilty demonstrates that love can accommodate sexual deviancy, and that consequently, *Lolita* is no less genuine a love story for being written by a pedophile.

When Humbert asks Dolores (a little too persistently) what Quilty tried to persuade her to take part in at Duk Duk Ranch, she is vague: "Weird, filthy, fancy things. I mean, he had two girls and two boys, and three or four men, and the idea was for all of us to tangle in the nude while an old woman took movie pictures" (276). Unsatisfied with this explanation, Humbert presses her for a precise answer, but "she refused to go into particulars with that baby inside her" (277). Her reluctance is telling. It is not a case of sex being less about pleasure and more about procreation now that she is an expectant mother, because sex never *was* a source of pleasure for Dolores; rather, her reluctance has more to do with her wish to protect the purity of her unborn child by not invoking sordid acts. Simply to speak of them would be to somehow sully the innocence of her baby. As it transpires, she and her baby die in childbirth. This poignant symbol of how Dolores' own growth was stunted by another's sexual obsession seems to suggest that sex without love, without a sense of morality and responsibility for others, is, as Humbert finally acknowledges, nothing but "sterile and selfish vice" (278).

WORKS CITED

Bloom, Harold. Ed. *Vladimir Nabokov's Lolita*. New York: Chelsea House, 1987.

Nabokov, Vladimir. *Lolita*. New York: Vintage, 2005.

Trilling, Lionel. "The Last Lover: Vladimir Nabokov's *Lolita*." *Vladimir Nabokov's Lolita*. Ed. Harold Bloom. New York: Chelsea House, 1987. 5–11.

LYRICS
(SAPPHO)

"Sappho and Human Sexuality"
by Sophie Mills,
University of North Carolina at Asheville

There is no text of Sappho, really, just reports, distant sightings, rumors, a few words reputed to be hers.

—Page Dubois

A bad woman might love roses, but a bad woman does not love the small and hidden wild flowers of the field ... as Sappho did.

—D. M. Robinson

Few ancient writers have been imagined in more incarnations than Sappho. Today, at her birthplace of Eressos on Lesbos, her name adorns women's bars, hotels and art centers, as the lesbian in the purely geographical sense has now become the iconic lesbian in the modern sense. According to ancient sources on Sappho's life (collected by David Campbell under the term "Testimonia"), she was variously a tragic victim of love who drowned herself when rejected by Phaon the fisherman, a subject of fourth-century BCE Athenian comic drama, or even a courtesan (Testimonia 22, cf. Campbell 4). (Note: all parenthetical references to ancient texts refer to the poem numbers given in Campbell's *Greek Lyric*). The Sappho of the nineteenth century was a schoolmistress—either a chaste bluestocking or a worldlier figure presiding over a boarding school seething with girlish crushes—or a heartless dominatrix. Biographies of the early Greek male poets are often unreliable, but they are not nearly so sensationalized as Sappho's life has been, and the exceptional quantity of Sapphic fantasy generated over the past 2,700 years may be explained through a combination of her unusual status as an outstanding female poet, her portrayal of desire between women, her poems' tendency to depict men in supporting roles, and a portrayal of romantic love that seems remarkably contemporary: love is sweet-bitter, hard to handle (130), makes the lover sweat and tremble (31). For modern readers, a further stimulus to the Sapphic mystique lies in the survival of a mere fraction of her work: of nine books, we have but one complete poem, ten moderately-sized fragments, one hundred short citations, and about fifty scraps of papyrus. The romantic lure of the fragment and corresponding yearning for recovery have had a vast impact on the study and reception of Sappho. Moreover, before the invention of the printing press producing ancient texts was arduous work, so that as texts written in Athenian Greek came to dominate the market, copyists no longer bothered to transcribe Sappho's east Greek dialect, a prosaic fact that has typically been obscured by outrageous and outraged tales of book-burnings and theories about the suppression of love between women. No wonder the figure of Sappho continues to fascinate those who study her.

While in theory it should be possible to consider Sappho's life, social milieu, and a literary evaluation of her poetry independently from one another, critics have typically been unable to do so. The apparently direct, confessional style of Sappho's poetry has rendered her life and poetry particularly inextricable from one another and has led to the creation of myriad Sapphos, all somewhat in the image of their creators. This essay cannot avoid this trap: words on a battered manuscript are our only positive manifestation of Sappho, but to say anything about those words leads inexorably to invention and assumption. Any attempt to discuss Sappho without bias brings us right up against the limits of our knowledge of the ancient world.

Sappho was born ca. 630 BCE. Names, but little else, are attested for her parents, husband, and daughter, while there is slightly more information about her brothers. Herodotus states that her brother Charaxus bought the freedom of the courtesan Rhodopis at a great expense and was ridiculed by his sister (poems 5 and 15 may allude to this; cf. 202). Another brother poured wine for the townsmen of Mytilene. We are also told that Sappho was exiled to Sicily (203; Testimonia 5). Both of these details suggest that the ancient poet belonged to one of the aristocratic families on Lesbos who were in a long-running power struggle with one another at the time. Commentators from some 800 years after she lived (e.g. 214B) claim that she educated the daughters of nobles in Lesbos and mainland Ionia, but whether her poetry actually made this clear or whether, like modern critics, they were simply using inference and guesswork to round out her biography is unknown.

Such is the historical testimony on Sappho. Her poetry, however, with its emphasis on love between women written in the first person perspective, has generated ample negative judgment: Anacreon, a generation later, suggests jokingly that the women of Lesbos were more interested in their own sex than in men (358). By Roman times and beyond, Sappho's love life was no joke, but "shame[ful]," "irregular," and "impure." Yet alongside these judgments remained traditional accounts of her suicide due to her unrequited love of Phaon and of an omnivorous sexuality not confined to women: at certain times Sappho is figured as two women—chaste lyric poet and nymphomaniac (Testimonia 3, 4)—by a historical tradition unable to reconcile supposedly incompatible strains in her poetry. Even the name of her husband—Cercylas of Andros ("dick from the Isle of Man")—may be a joke name invented by one of the purveyors of the myth of the hyper-sexual Sappho. The fragments of poetry do not present nearly so lurid a picture: did later commentators believe that expressions of desire for women could only have originated from a creature so indiscriminate that she must also desire men unrestrainedly? Or were they perversely acknowledging her same-sex passions by sarcastic jokes about heterosexual liaisons? So often, our fragments of information lack any context that would assist in interpretation: for example, in 121 Sappho writes, "But if you are my friend, take a younger woman's bed, for I will not endure being the elder in a partnership." If this is the poet speaking *in propria persona*, it might, as it were, queer the popular picture of Sappho the lesbian, since the addressee is male, but we simply do not know.

In the only extant complete poem (1), Sappho contemplates an unresponsive female object of affection and recalls an earlier request for help in a love affair from the goddess Aphrodite, who came to the poet's plea and promised assistance. Sappho describes the goddess's gradual descent from Olympus as she is borne in a sparrow-driven chariot. Though Sappho's language is laden with color-adjectives and compound epithets typical of Greek lyric poetry, her syntax is simple and avoids rhetorical flourishes, creating the impression that we are directly witnessing her experience. However, a consciousness of textual uncertainty must at once make such assumptions highly questionable: Sappho may address Aphrodite as *poiklithron'* ("of the decorated throne"), *poikilophron'* ("of the complex mind"), or *poikilothron'* (loosely, "embroidered love charms"), the last of which evokes Homer's famous account of the seduction of Zeus by Hera in the *Iliad*. Sappho, like all Classical poets, is in continuous dialogue with Homer, setting her poetic stamp upon his scenes to assert her own poetic identity, both within and outside his shadow. Whether her imagery here is primarily literary, decorative, psychological, or a combination—Sappho as "Hera," in urgent need of special charms to seduce a cold female ("Zeus")—a reading of the poem is more complex than its apparent immediacy first suggests.

The poem continues, and Aphrodite smilingly asks Sappho who her love is this time and why she is invoking her assistance yet again. Sappho's use of repetition of the phrase "this time" indicates that this is not their first encounter: its tone has been variously interpreted as Sappho's own rueful awareness of her inconstant passions, Aphrodite's impatience, or pathos. It is also a common convention of Greek lyric poetry to characterize falling in love as a cyclical, rather than single, occurrence in a person's life. While there must be some direct connection between literary convention and lived experience, varying degrees of connection are possible, and since we have lost the landscape of multiple literary conventions in which Sappho was located, Aphrodite's words may offer less insight into Sappho's own emotions than either ancient or modern readers have often thought.

Aphrodite then promises that though Sappho's beloved presently "flees, soon she will pursue, if now she won't receive gifts, soon she will give and if she doesn't love now, soon she will love, even against her will." (This pronoun use is the only indication that Sappho's love is female, and considerable emendation is needed for the text to make sense at all.) In the last stanza, Sappho begs the goddess to help her again and to be her *symmachos*, or ally.

What did it mean to Sappho to describe a visitation of the goddess of love in such a context? Since Aphrodite is just an abstraction for us, most modern readers probably assume at some level that the poet's epiphany is metaphorical. But while we do not know enough about religious belief on Lesbos to say whether such an event was considered literally possible, we do know that divine epiphany is unquestionably a staple of Homer, for example, when Athena intervenes in Achilles' dispute with Agamemnon in the *Iliad* (cf. Sappho 5 and 17). If Sappho's epiphany has literary and religious dimensions as well as personal ones, then who is Sappho? Religious mystic? Skilled poet, reworking epic conventions to convey personal experience? Heroine of her own poem, whose excellence brings her the attention from her patron goddess, similar to the attention Homeric heroes received from their divine patrons? Indeed, Sappho's final request that Aphrodite be her *symmachos* is a metaphor from male experience, and a number of scholars have shown linguistic and thematic connections between Sappho 1 and *Iliad* 5, in which the hero Diomedes begs help from the goddess Athena, under whose protection he routs and wounds Aphrodite. Sappho thus explores her emotional experience through soldiers' military experience, and in the process, identifies both with Diomedes, the hero who needs divine help, and Aphrodite, the wounded female seeking consolation. Some complex questions lie under what seems like a simple *cri-de-coeur*.

The central paradox of lyric poetry is that it creates the illusion of immediate personal experience through poetic craft, which can recreate only at some distance the experience it portrays. Sappho signals this distance in her description of Aphrodite's descent from afar, her self-conscious portrayal of her own passions, and even perhaps through the filter of Homeric reminiscence. Moreover, given the strongly oral, public focus of early Greek literary culture, it is highly probable that Sappho was composing not for private satisfaction but for an audience. Once we allow for the latter, Sappho as the romantic witness of her own experience begins to lose ground, and questions of the poet's relationship to her society become more central.

These complexities surround poem 31 in particular, quoted admiringly by an ancient critic for its portrayal of the physical effects of passion and the objectivity of its description. Here, the female speaker tells of a "god-like" man and a woman who laughs and talks to him: the sight of him causes her heart to flutter, she cannot speak, she is aflame with emotion and can neither see or hear as she sweats, shakes, turns greener (or, more accurately, moister) than grass and wants to die. While what we have of the poem focuses on an intense physicality, there is a gradual movement in the text from the claustrophobic descriptions of the woman's internal sensual experiences, to an observation of her from outside, as she becomes able to examine herself with greater detachment. The first, corrupt, and only line of the last extant stanza—"But all must be endured since even a poor man"—indicates a similar movement towards analysis and detachment, and our impression of the poem may be rather misleading. Nor do we know anything of its context: it is always assumed that its speaker is Sappho, but the extant text does not say so.

In this poem, as in the full-length one, seemingly original details turn out to have a literary pedigree: most of Sappho's descriptions of the symptoms of love, fresh though they seem, first appeared in Homer, although in his text they are associated with emotions of fear and pain rather than love. John Winkler further suggests that when in poem 31 the speaker commends a young woman by expressing envy of the man to whom she is attached Sappho is rewriting Odysseus's admiring encounter with Nausicaa in *Odyssey* 6. In the *Odyssey* this man is merely a rhetorical construct, a distant reference: "Whoever marries you is lucky." To assume that the same is true in Sappho's poem radically challenges many standard interpretations which make the man the fulcrum of the poem, and often seem deliberately to deflect attention from the female speaker's passionate appreciation of the female addressee, for example, by arguing that the speaker is jealous of the woman who has the attention of the man she loves. Indeed, for the great German scholar Wilamowitz the poem was only palatable as the celebration of the beauty of a bride on her wedding day; of course, its tone is nothing like that of the poems whose context we know to have been marriage. Perhaps more than any other, this poem has made critics uneasy, partly because of its intense evocation of the physical symptoms of passion among women, and partly because its interpretation is so dependent on context, which is unknown at this point: are these words meant to be private or public, Sappho talking to herself, another woman, or a circle of equals for whom she is evoking experiences common to them all? How far is her sentiment personal and how far is it simply a conventional evocation of passion designed specifically for an audience? After all, poem 112, which was certainly sung publicly at a wedding, perhaps by a chorus of young women, contains some strikingly erotic language. Was that audience largely female or male? If Sappho is consciously invoking Homer, is the poem's intensity in some way diminished?

Reading Sappho is like listening to a partly inaudible series of conversations within a circle of friends. Certain names recur, some in apparently romantic contexts, and a notably frequent theme of these poems is separation from the beloved. In the frustratingly fragmentary 94, an unknown speaker exclaims that she wants to die and that she leaves Sappho unwillingly. This is one of the few fragments which is relatively direct about physical relations between women: the Sappho of the poem reminds her that, "on a soft bed. . .you satisfied desire (*pothos*)." Again, poem 96, though similarly fragmentary, seems to imagine a beautiful woman who has left one place (Lesbos?) for Lydia (on the mainland near Lesbos), but still remembers Atthis with longing and perhaps some sadness as she goes about her business there.

We know little about women's lives in seventh-century Lesbos, but scholars have attempted to fill in the gaps through what is known of other places in Greece where same-sex desire was acknowledged and to some degree institutionalized. In fifth-century Athens, especially among the elite, older men took an erotic and educational interest in younger men. These were temporary relationships for the young men, most of which would eventually take wives and become lovers/mentors in their turn. One late writer claims that Sappho, like Socrates, presided intellectually and erotically over a set of pupils, while Plutarch states that aristocratic women in archaic Sparta had erotic relationships with young girls. While it is hard to judge the veracity of the claims of authors writing 800 years after their subject, the poems of Alcman, a seventh-century Spartan poet, do include specific expressions of same-sex desire among women. Although Alcman's poems were clearly written by a man and intended to be sung by a chorus of women, it has traditionally been assumed that the poems of Sappho were performed as solos by the poet herself.

Since she was considered worthy to write cult songs for divinities, Sappho cannot have had the scandalous reputation in Lesbos that she subsequently acquired. Evidently, the expression of desire by one woman for another was acceptable at that time, whether because male sexual dominance over women was not threatened by such expressions, or because they were not personal, but like the poems of Alcman, consciously offered for public consumption. It is thus possible that the erotic relationships between women suggested by Sappho's poetry might fit into a broader institutional framework of the older woman as instructor or mentor. The poems that mention a forced separation between lovers presuppose some kind of formalized setting in which time with Sappho could only be temporary, and thereby support the idea of lessons. There is substantial evidence throughout archaic Greece for the existence of choruses of adolescent women in which members were taught discipline, grace, and aesthetic appreciation through musical performance. Conceivably, young women learned music and other arts from Sappho in such a chorus before marrying into the local aristocracy. Eroticism among its members might perhaps be but an extension of their concern with aesthetic beauty. Occasionally, anger directed at other women (91, 144, 155) emerges from the fragments of Sappho's writings, although most are too scrappy to be very informative. Perhaps these disputes were purely emotional, but they might also have resulted from a more fundamental breach between their target and an organized group, such as a chorus. In poem 71, Sappho complains that someone chose the love of the ladies of the house of Penthilus; the arch-enemy of Sappho's associate Alcaeus had married into this family, so some of these disputes may include a political dimension. That said, it must be admitted that the emotions expressed in poem 31 and the relationship between relative equals in poem 1 do seem qualitatively different in both their intensity and individuality from both Alcman's "maiden-songs" and the poetry of male poets addressed to adolescent youths of the period. Inevitably, some fundamental questions about Sappho's intentions must remain unanswered.

One contextual fact of her life is clear however: at the time it was expected that a Greek woman must marry. An entire book by Sappho was comprised of songs for weddings, and these songs are well represented in surviving fragments. Particularly noteworthy are those focusing on the young bride's experience, which reveal Sappho's recognition of the centrality of marriage to young women, and the loss and fear involved. The irrevocability of the change that marriage brings to women runs through these poems; for instance, in 114, a girl's virginity tells her "Never shall I come again to you." Imagery of vegetation is also common: a simile in 105a compares a girl to an apple on a branch that the harvesters have not forgotten but could not reach. In this fragment the description of the apple's sweetness and redness clearly signifies the girl's virginity and desirability, while the fact that she is currently unattainable draws our attention to a time when she will, and must, fall. The fragment 105c makes the link between a young girl's virginity and the vulnerability of a flower even more explicit with a description of shepherds trampling a hyacinth, its purple bloom falling to the ground.

Sappho is a poet. Sappho is a woman. Is she, therefore, a "woman poet" whose poetry is different from that of her male contemporaries? This must in some sense be so. Male and female experiences in ancient Greece were utterly different and Sappho's environment plainly shaped the subjects of her poetry. That Sappho revised Homeric characters to create her own world, identifying now with males, now with females, indicates an ability to make multiple identifications that was perhaps a characteristic of women in Greek culture, who must have known both the dominant male culture and their own, while men needed only know one. Similarly, Lesbos was famous for the beauty of its women. Alcaeus in exile reminisces about the beauty contests held there (130B, cf. perhaps Sappho 83), and Sappho's emphasis on grace and beauty, and active condemnation of those who lack them (55, 57) is largely absent from the poetry of her male contemporaries.

In poem 16, Sappho contrasts what "some" say are the most beautiful sights on earth—cavalry, infantry or ships—with her own opinion that it is the sight of whatever one loves. Perhaps this is a conscious assertion of a female viewpoint, as she cites Helen's elopement with Paris, which a traditional narrative like the *Iliad* condemns as destructive, with apparent sympathy as the perfect example of her argument. The fragmentary poem appears to link Helen's feelings with those of Sappho for Anactoria, whose walk and bright eyes she would rather see than all the chariots and infantry of Lydia; here the reprise of the opposition between military life and a love object ends the poem elegantly. Helen is, for once, depicted as the subject, not object, of desire and, unlike women like Medea or Ariadne who pay the price for their sexual autonomy by being abandoned by the men they choose, Sappho's ending precludes any possibility that Helen's act will hurt her. The expression of active female desire is certainly unusual in Greek poetry: more commonly women are passive objects of male desire, and 31 is especially unusual in making Sappho object as well as subject of her own gaze. That said, there is no absolute difference between Sappho's gaze and that of her male contemporaries as poem 1 contains conventional ideas of pursuit by the lover and the flight of the beloved, and even an element of coercion in the promise that the beloved will love "against her will." Although Sappho asks that Aphrodite not subdue *her*, she seems content for the beloved to submit to her desires.

Yet Sappho's poetry is shaped not only by her gender, but also by her aristocratic background and her sense of herself as a poet in relationship to Homer. Thus poem 44, which describes Hector's wedding procession to Troy with his bride Andromache, could be read as either a woman's or a lyric poet's expansion of an epic story implied by the *Iliad*. Typical of Sappho is the visual evocation of the grandeur of this famous Iliadic union: she foregrounds small details that are mere incidentals on the larger epic canvas—the golden clothes, expensive cups, lyres, and singing—and adds details from her own eastern Aegean milieu, such as exotic smells and the sounds of castanets. The two strands of poetic pride and aristocratic sensibility come together again in 55, in which she contrasts herself with an uneducated woman and claims that her poetry will give her immortality and remembrance (cf. 193 and perhaps 65), two common obsessions of aristocratic males, especially those in Homer. And ultimately, the statement of a commentator on Virgil (207) claiming Sappho asserted that Prometheus' crime of stealing fire was punished by the arrival of women on earth forcefully reminds us that our categories of male and female sensibilities are far from aligned with those of the ancient world.

Works Cited

Burnett, A. P. *Three Archaic Poets*. Cambridge, MA: Harvard UP, 1983.

Calame, Claude. "Sappho's Group: An Initiation into Womanhood." *Reading Sappho: Contemporary Approaches*. Ed. E. Greene. Berkeley, CA: University of California P, 1996. 113–124.

Campbell, David trans. *Greek Lyric*, vol. 1. Cambridge, MA, 1982.

DuBois, Page. *Sappho is Burning*. Chicago: University of Chicago Press, 1995.

Greene, Ellen. "Subjects, Objects, and Erotic Symmetry in Sappho's Fragments." *Reading Sappho: Contemporary Approaches*. Ed. Ellen Greene. Berkeley, CA: University of California P, 1996. 84–105.

Lardinois, Andre. "Lesbian Sappho and Sappho of Lesbos." *From Sappho to de Sade: Moments in the History of Sexuality*. Ed. Jan Bremmer. London: Routledge, 1989. 15–35.

Lardinois, Andre. "Who Sang Sappho's Songs?" *Reading Sappho: Contemporary Approaches*. Ed. Ellen Greene. Berkeley, CA: University of California Press, 1996. 150–72.

Page, Denys Lionel. *Sappho and Alcaeus*. Oxford: Clarendon Press, 1955.

Parker, Holt. "Sappho Schoolmistress." *Re-Reading Sappho: Reception and Transmission*. Berkeley, CA: University of California P, 1996. 146–83.

Prins, Yopie. *Victorian Sappho*. Princeton, N.J.: Princeton UP, 1999.

Putnam, Michael C. J. "Throna and Sappho 1.1." *Classical Journal* 56.2 (November 1960): 79–83.

Reynolds, Margaret. *The Sappho Companion*. London: Chatto & Windus, 2000.

Snyder, Jane McIntosh. *Lesbian Desire in the Lyrics of Sappho*. New York: Columbia UP, 1997.

Winkler, John J. "Double Consciousness in Sappho's Lyrics." *The Constraints of Desire: the Anthropology of Sex and Gender in Ancient Greece*. Ed. John J. Winkler. New York: Routledge, 1990.

LYSISTRATA (ARISTOPHANES)

AND

SYMPOSIUM (PLATO)

"The Tragic Comedy of Sex in Aristophanes' Lysistrata and Plato's Symposium"
by Brian S. Hook,
University of North Carolina at Asheville

Students of ancient Greece are free to choose between two opposing views of Greek sexuality. Either the Greeks were very much like we are, or they were not. Texts and images seem to support both views. The two texts considered in this essay, Aristophanes' *Lysistrata* and Aristophanes's speech in Plato's *Symposium*, seem strikingly "modern": in both, sex and sexuality are central and definitive elements of human life and identity, much as the contemporary Western world views them. This essay will examine that apparent "modernity" and set it in its dramatic, social, and political context.

In recent decades, scholars have used texts and images to reconstruct an account of the sexual identity of the ancient Greeks that does not operate strictly along lines of gender or sexual orientation. In this reconstruction, the dividing line is not male/female or heterosexual/homosexual as much as penetrator/penetrated. The penetrator was the active partner, the superior, and the sanctioned by society; the penetrated and passive member was inferior and subject to shame. The adult Athenian male of the upper classes could penetrate women or younger males, freeborn or slave. Infidelity on the married man's part seems to have been accepted as a societal norm, though adultery on the woman's part was condemned. Most alien to us is *paiderastia*,

or the relationship between an older man (the "lover" or *erastes*) and
a younger boy between the ages of 12 and 18 who had not yet grown
a beard (the "beloved" or *eromenos* or *paidika*). Several speakers of
Plato's *Symposium*, including Phaedrus and Pausanias, who precede
Aristophanes, celebrate this relationship as the highest form of love.
However, these speakers principally characterize *paiderastia* as a
temporary relationship, lasting only as long as the boy's youth. During
courtship, the boy was expected to resist his suitor, was not supposed
to enjoy the sexual acts, and was not expected to love his older lover.
What the boy gained from the relationship, supposedly, was ethical
and social guidance.

Neither of the works considered in this essay conforms to this
more fluid view of the sexuality of penetration. The *Lysistrata* and
Aristophanes's speech in Plato's *Symposium* present sex in terms of
natural desire, not in terms of the social conventions described above.
The natural desire of the men in the *Lysistrata* is for their wives; it is
heterosexual. In Aristophanes's speech in the *Symposium*, both heterosexual and homosexual desires are recognized and are qualified by
the argument that all forms of desire are natural for the individual,
as they spring from an original and now lost human nature. For this
reason, these works speak to us since we tend to view our sexuality
and our sexual desire as innate parts of ourselves. For Athenians these
texts employed recognizable characters, settings, and circumstances.
The tensions between the recognizable and the different, I will argue,
approach what we can call tragic. Though we apply the words "tragic"
and "tragedy" far more broadly than the Athenians ever did, ancient
tragedy involves distance: distance between the human and divine,
distance between one's self-knowledge and reality, distance between
one's knowledge and one's actions. The realization of that distance is
usually the source of pain and suffering for the "tragic hero." Behind
both the *Lysistrata* and Aristophanes' speech in the *Symposium* there
lies tragic distance: behind the former lurks the Peloponnesian War,
which brought Athens to defeat seven years after the play's production; and behind the latter lies the palpable ache of human separation
and the threat of even worse. However, there are no tragic recognitions
in Aristophanes or Plato. Those realizations belong to the audience.

Aristophanes' works are the sole extant examples of Athenian
Old Comedy, although we know names and have fragments of works
of other comic playwrights. In Athens, comic and tragic drama were

performed at several annual religious festivals. The festivals for comedies were the Lenaia, held in late February, and the greater Dionysia, held in late March. The *Lysistrata* was performed in 411 BCE, probably at the Lenaia. The plot of the comedy is easily summarized: the women of Greece decide to abstain from sex until the men abstain from war, and they occupy the Acropolis to impound the funds for war. The actual political circumstances were quite serious in 411. Athens and Sparta and their respective allies had been at war for twenty years, since 431. A peace, negotiated in 421, ended when the Athenians undertook an expedition to Sicily in 415. There they suffered a major defeat in 413, and the Spartans took possession of the town of Deceleia, on the northern boundary of Athens' territory, less than ten miles from Athens itself, from which they freely raided the agricultural land of Athens. Some of Athens' allies, whose loyalties were maintained with threats, had begun to revolt. The *Lysistrata* was performed in the midst of these grim circumstances and alludes directly to them.

This is not to say that the *Lysistrata* is a "realist" comedy. The Peloponnesian war is the background of the plot, but comic impossibilities abound. Why would the women's abstinence at home affect their husbands at war? Also, despite blockades and invasions, Spartan, Boeotian, and Corinthian women arrive to discuss Lysistrata's plan at the start of the play. Similarly unrealistic is the presumption that wives are the only sexual outlets for the men. This was not the case in actuality. Two pimps are mentioned in the play (only the names Orsilochus and Cynalopex are mentioned at lines 725 and 957, respectively, but ancient commentators tell us who they were). Athenian men might use slaves sexually (see Aristophanes' *Acharnians* 271–276) or boys (see below). Courtesans and flute-girls attended the symposia. Masturbation was always an option. Nevertheless, these possibilities are not admitted into the world of the *Lysistrata*. Sexual violence against women is also mentioned in the comedy (160–165) and promptly swept off-stage.

The question of the comedy's "feminism" is more difficult than that of its realism. In Aristophanes' plays prior to the *Lysistrata* women played only minor roles, but women are the main characters of this comedy and in his *Thesmophoriazusae*, performed in the same year. The eponymous heroine may have been intended to evoke a priestess of Athena in the late fifth century, whose name was Lysimache. Both names are significant in the context: "Lysimache" means "dissolver of battle" and Lysistrata means "dissolver of armies." Unlike other historical figures who appear in Aristophanes' comedies, such as Socrates in the *Clouds* of 423, Lysistrata is not treated with comic exaggeration or scorn; she is presented respectfully as a wise and authoritative woman. The older women of the chorus are ferocious but act heroically in defense of the city. The younger women of the play, however, are subjected to disparagement: mocked as drunkards, unreliable, themselves addicted to sex and autoeroticism, lazy, interested in trivialities, and incapable of resolve. And yet Aristophanes takes a woman's view of the war in noting that they give sons and husbands to the war, and if their husbands die, the older women often cannot remarry (588–597). Aristophanes wants to have it both ways, using the women as objects of mockery and sympathy.

In the comic vision of the *Lysistrata*, we encounter the modern, usually comic concept of men tempted and refused. The essential nature of men is portrayed as sexual, chastity as unendurable. We recognize this plot. In fact, women in the modern world have used sex strikes—in Poland, Turkey, Colombia, Sudan—to protest political decisions and violence. But the differences between Aristophanes' time and the present cannot be overlooked. In modern dramas, on screen or on stage, the temptress is rarely the wife—she is more often a figure reduced to an essential sexuality that lures a man to leave his wife or an unmarried man his senses. In Aristophanes' comedy, the role of the *wife* as temptress and torturer is as strange for the Athenians as it is for us. Athenian women had little if any power to refuse the demands of men, were confined to the home for work and had no ability to meet outside the home, and were barred from political activity; Lysistrata's speech combining these roles when she uses the carding of wool as a political analogy gives testimony to this state of things. However possible such a "sex strike" and occupation of the Acropolis as depicted in the fictional *Lysistrata* may be now, they most certainly were not then. Aristophanes' audience would no more have recognized this plot as possible than they would have that of his earlier play, *Peace* (414 BCE), in which a character flies to heaven on a giant dung-beetle.

What Aristophanes' audience did recognize, of course, was their own current political and social circumstances. Deceleia, the Spartan-held outpost in Attica, and Sicily, the site of Athens' defeat, are not mentioned in the play, but they loom in the background. When Lysistrata mentions the "armed sons" the women bore and sent away, the magistrate implores her to be silent: "Do not mention past evils" (590). The Athenian defeat took the lives of many men, and the number of widows and orphans must have increased dramatically in the years following 413. Some drastic measures were instituted in that year and in those following. Scholars have found evidence of a "bigamy decree" from this period that possibly allowed Athenian men to marry two wives or at least permitted them to produce legitimate children from two "wives." The magistrate who confronts Lysistrata in front of the Acropolis is also a feature of the time. The costs of the Sicilian disaster were economic as well as human, and the constitutional democracy was expensive to maintain, so in 413, the Athenians appointed a board of ten magistrates, or *probouloi*, to make decisions. In 412 and 411, the principal political question was the fate of Alcibiades, the rogue general who defected to Sparta and then to Persia rather than face charges concerning his role in a sacrilegious act that took place just before the Athenian fleet departed for Sicily. A politician named Peisander, whom Lysistrata mentions (490), promoted Alcibiades' return. The desecration in which Alcibiades allegedly took part involved herms, statues placed around Athens with a head of Hermes atop a square pillar and an erect phallus emerging from one side. When, in the play, the priapic Spartans come to Athens to negotiate a peace agreement the chorus urges them to leave their cloaks on "so that none of the mutilators of the Herms sees you" (1094). With these and other subtle references, Aristophanes may have been recommending against Alcibiades' recall. By including them, he is clearly evoking the topical scandals and politics of his day, although he is proposing a fantasy to solve them. This is the tragic distance of the *Lysistrata*. The political and social circumstances of Greece in the early fifth century BCE were devastatingly real; the comic solutions to them were entirely fantastic. The silent majority, the women of Athens, appeared only on the dramatic, not the political stage, as Lysistrata herself notes (507–515). And the sexual nature and desire of husbands for their wives? Similarly, a fantasy. The audience must have enjoyed the happy ending of the comedy, in which representatives from around Greece ogle the choice parts of a nude, mute female character called Reconciliation, but no real political change followed the production of the play. The rest of the year 411 BCE saw political assassinations and the suspension of democracy itself until Athens regained a brief measure of stability in 410.

In Greek, *symposium* means a "drinking together," and these occasions were important social and cultural events for upper-class Athenian men. No doubt in practice they were often raucous and wine-soaked, but their cultural significance is derived from their association with music, song, and conversation. The symposia, along with the wrestling schools and the battlefields, were the great locales for male bonding. Plato's *Symposium*, however, is notable for the failures of bonding that are described. Agathon wishes Socrates to sit by him so that he may become wiser by "touching" him, and Socrates doubts the possibility (175c7–e2), while Alcibiades tells how he once tried unsuccessfully to seduce Socrates (217a2–219d2). Socrates himself relates a speech by a priestess, Diotima, that describes the bonds between humans as, at best, instrumental in reaching a higher plane of knowledge. In the midst of these anecdotes, Aristophanes offers his speech describing human separation and longing in mythical terms as our now natural state.

The narrative setting of Plato's *Symposium* is very precise: it takes place after Agathon's first victory in the tragic competition at the Greater Dionysia in 416 BCE. Plato describes the second, more sober night of celebration, which Socrates attended. Apollodorus, a follower of Socrates, narrates the account when he is asked to do so by unnamed interlocutors. Apollodorus identifies himself as someone who has followed Socrates for only three years, and says that the original symposium happened many years before. Apollodorus himself heard it from Aristodemus, he says, who was present, but Socrates has confirmed some of the details. There are at least three layers of time and narrative involved in Plato's *Symposium*, and since it involves an account of an ascent to Truth through stages of partial truth, it is important to take these layers into account. Agathon's symposium happened in 416; Apollodorus is reporting it "many years" after Agathon's departure from Athens (172C) and before Socrates's death, thus before 399; scholars generally agree that Plato wrote the *Symposium* after 385 and before 378, based on internal references. This distance between Plato and the events of 416 is not necessarily meant to qualify the reliability of the work: at its center, in fact, we find another story told second-hand, as Socrates claims to repeat what he heard from Diotima. Apollodorus also admits that Aristodemus did not remember all the details of that night perfectly, and that he, Apollodorus, could not remember everything that Aristodemus told him (178A). Aristodemus also omitted several speeches that were given (180C).

Those in attendance at the symposium, having gotten drunk the previous night, agree to spend the evening in conversation (176a5–e10). They choose to give speeches (*logoi*) about love (*eros*), and their speeches form the basic plot of the *Symposium*. There are at least nine participants present; a tenth, Alcibiades, arrives late. They move around the room from left to right, as tradition dictates, offering their *logoi*. Socrates gives the final *logos* until Alcibiades enters. Alcibiades then gives a speech in praise of Socrates.

Aristophanes is one of those present at the symposium. Plato's work appears to be fiction, and there are several Aristophanic references in the *Symposium*. Zeus's fear that the gods will lose their sacrifices if he destroys humans (190c3–5) resembles a situation in Aristophanes's *Birds*; Calonice swears in *Lysistrata* that she will "cut herself in two like a flatfish" (115–116) to end the war, an expression that resembles Aristophanes' description of the halved humans (191d4). Although Aristophanes was over twenty years older than Plato, in one case he seems acquainted with Plato's ideas: when the women of his comedy *Ecclesiazusae* (ca. 391) take over the government of Athens they institute a form of communism that resembles what Plato later describes in *Republic*. Perhaps Plato is honoring this relationship with the elder writer when he gives Aristophanes one of the most memorable speeches in the *Symposium*.

The speech of Aristophanes, the comic poet, is introduced comically, with Aristophanes overcome by hiccoughs when his turn to speak comes. He asks Eryximachus, a doctor seated to his right, to prescribe a cure or to speak in his place. Eryximachus offers to do both. He recommends that Aristophanes first hold his breath, then gargle with water, and then tickle his nose and sneeze. While Eryximachus is delivering his speech describing love as a harmony and a cosmic balance of opposites, we should imagine Aristophanes gargling and sneezing. When Eryximachus finishes, Aristophanes praises his medical advice—but not his speech—and Eryximachus warns Aristophanes against saying something "laughable" (*geloion*). Aristophanes replies that the laughable is the province of his Muse, but that he does fear saying something "ridiculous" (*katagelasta*).

From that comic beginning, Aristophanes introduces a myth of human suffering. He counters Eryximachus's scientific account of love with a patently mythological one, explaining the original nature of humans. Human form was originally double. Each being had four arms, four legs, four ears, two faces facing opposing directions, and two sets of genitals. There were three genders: male, female, and androgynous, or mixed. These beings also had great strength and arrogance, and they made an attack on the gods. Zeus and the other gods did not want to kill them, since they would then lack worshippers and sacrifices, but they could not let the humans act so arrogantly. Zeus decided to split them in two; the humans would then be weaker and more useful to the gods, since their number would double. After Zeus split them, he bid Apollo to turn their heads around (the first humans had only backs, not chests) and to heal the wound. Apollo did so, and drew all the skin together and tied it off at our navels, smoothing most of the wrinkles out but leaving a few to remind us of our original suffering.

The point of the myth comes in what follows. The split humans lost not only their strength, but also more importantly, their sense of wholeness. The "half humans" searched for their missing half; and if they found it, they embraced it and did nothing else. They so desired to be one again that they did not eat, and thus began to die. Zeus felt pity for the creatures and had Apollo make another adjustment: the genitals, which had been in the back of the "half humans," were moved to the front, that is, where they are now. This change also initiated reproduction (Aristophanes says that before this, humans begot offspring in the earth, like cicadas). Therefore, men could beget children within women, or men could experience "fulfillment" (*plêsmonê*) with other men and thus people ceased to die for desire of wholeness. The dynamic of this desire to be joined together is what Aristophanes calls *Eros*: "Therefore for so long *Eros* has been innate in each human and the uniter of our former nature; *Eros* tries to make one from two and to heal our human nature" (191c8–d3).

The three speakers prior to Aristophanes treat Eros purely as a god and discuss the benefits and consequences of his nature. Aristophanes initiates the trend of the last three speakers to define Eros's nature. At the start of his speech, Aristophanes describes Eros as the "most philanthropic of the gods" (189c8), but in this passage he locates Eros within humans as an innate (*emphutos*) force, as an agent of unity. Aristophanes also uses this myth to explain sexual orientation. Halves of an original androgynous being seek their other halves in the opposite sex; halves of an original male or female being seek their other halves in those of the same sex. In the social scheme of penetrator/penetrated, female homosexuality may have been hard to place, but in the scheme of natural desire, it is not. Similarly, a male homosexual relationship that lasts beyond the youth of one partner is not the cultural norm, but Aristophanes imagines a homosexuality unlike the *paiderastia* praised by others before and after him. In fact, Aristophanes opposes culture and nature when he says that those who are "slices of the male" take no thought of marriage or reproduction unless they are forced by custom, but are satisfied to live their whole lives together unmarried" (192b1–3).

Aristophanes' speech vividly illustrates the power of sexual desire, but reminds his audience that this desire is the product of divine punishment. Eros is also essentially irrational, although it transcends a purely physical bond. Aristophanes says that the lovers "are struck by friendship and *oikeiotes*" (192c1) as well as by eros. *Oikeiotes* is a state of belonging or of intimacy (*oikos* is "home" in Greek, so *oikeios* is what belongs to one's home or one's kin). Further on in the *Symposium*, the priestess Diotima expressly rejects Aristophanes' arguments. She says that people do not love or desire what is "their own" (*oikeion*) but rather what is good. She offers as proof that people will allow the amputation of diseased limbs, clearly "their own," in pursuit of the "good" of health (205d10–206a1). Aristophanes never has an opportunity to respond, though he is trying to do so when Alcibiades bursts in (212c4–9).

Despite the obvious erotic goal of reunification, which is innate in each of us according to the myth, Aristophanes' lovers only sense what they want. Aristophanes says that the soul "divines" what it wants like an oracle (*manteuei*) and like an oracle, expresses its desires in enigmatic ways (192c7–d2). If the blacksmith god Hephaistos stood over the lovers as they lay together and asked them if they wanted to be welded and fused back together, so that they would never be apart, Aristophanes claims that no one would deny the offer, "everyone would think he had heard exactly what he had long desired" (192e7–8), even if he could not have articulated it. However it conforms to our experience, this is a grim view of sexual desire: distanced from understanding, rooted in despair, and unable to be fulfilled. In fact, humans run the risk of being split in half again, Aristophanes warns, and he therefore urges piety toward the gods.

At the end of the *Symposium*, Socrates tries to convince Agathon the tragedian and Aristophanes that the same man should be able to write both comedy and tragedy. Many scholars believe that Plato did just this in the *Symposium*, though they differ on the details. I suggest that both texts discussed in this essay present human sexuality in a comic foreground with a tragic background. The tragedy exists in the distance between the fantasy and the reality in the *Lysistrata*, and in the many tensions in the *Symposium*, especially those between human desire and our understanding of it.

WORKS CITED

Aristophanes. *Lysistrata*. Ed. with commentary by J. Henderson. Oxford: Clarendon Press, 1987. Greek text with introduction, notes, and commentary.

MacDouwell, Douglas. *Aristophanes and Athens*. Oxford: Clarendon Press, 1995. Excellent introduction to all Aristophanes' comedies.

Lesher, J., D. Nails, and F. Sheffield, Eds. *Plato's Symposium: Issues in Interpretation and Reception*.Cambridge, MA: Center for Hellenic Studies, Trustees for Harvard University 2006. Collection of scholarly essays on the *Symposium*.

Plato. *Plato's Symposium*. Trans. with introduction and notes by A. Nehamas and P. Woodruff. Hackett Publishing Co.: Indianapolis, 1989.

Rosen, Stanley. *Plato's Symposium*. Yale: New Haven, 1968. Discussion and commentary.

MADAME BOVARY
(GUSTAVE FLAUBERT)

"Madame Bovary"
by Charles Baudelaire,
in *Flaubert: A Collection of Critical Essays (1857)*

INTRODUCTION

In this character analysis of Madame Bovary, Charles Baudelaire, the infamous nineteenth-century poet known for his profoundly modern sentiments and at times shocking revelations about human sexuality, extols the greatness of Flaubert's creation. While we, as twenty-first-century readers, may find his comments about gender and sexuality anachronistic, Baudelaire does offer many insights. Ultimately, he concludes that the character Emma Bovary "is truly great."

I

In the realm of criticism, the situation of the writer who comes after everyone else, the writer in arrears, holds some advantages not enjoyed

---

Baudelaire, Charles. "Madame Bovary." *Flaubert: A Collection of Critical Essays.* Ed. and trans. by Raymond Giraud. Englewood Cliffs, NJ: Prentice-Hall, 1964. pp. 88–96. (Originally published in *L'Artiste*, 18 October 1857)

by the prophetic writer, who heralds success and produces it, so to speak, by the authority of his boldness and devotion.

Mr. Gustave Flaubert no longer needs devotion, if indeed he ever did. Many artists, among them some of the most perceptive and most highly accredited, have praised and honored his excellent book. Criticism now need only suggest some forgotten points of view and stress a bit more forcefully than has been done some elements and insights that have not yet in my opinion been sufficiently praised and commented on. Besides, there is a paradoxical charm, as I was trying to hint, in this position of a writer behind others, coming at some distance after. Freer because he is isolated like a laggard, he has the appearance of recapitulating debates, and because he is obliged to avoid the vehemence of accusation and defense, he is under orders to blaze a new path without any other stimulus than that of justice and love for the beautiful.

II

Since I have pronounced that splendid and terrible word, Justice, let me be allowed—also because I find this very agreeable—to thank the French magistracy for the shining example of impartiality and good taste that it has set in this circumstance. Called upon by a blind zeal, too vehement to be called morality, by a spirit which had mistaken its ground, faced with a novel, the work of a writer hitherto unknown—and what a novel! the most impartial, the most honest—a field, banal like all fields, whipped and soaked like nature herself by all winds and all storms—the magistracy, I say, has shown itself to be as honest and impartial as the book that was brought before it in a holocaust. And better yet let us say, if it is permissible to conjecture on considerations that accompanied the judgment, that if the magistrates had discovered something truly reproachable in the book, they would nevertheless have amnestied it in favor and in gratitude for that BEAUTY in which it is clothed. This remarkable concern for Beauty, in men whose faculties are only called upon for the Just and True, is an extremely touching symptom, compared with the burning concupiscence of a society which has definitely abjured all spiritual love and which, neglecting *its ancient entrails*, no longer cares for anything but its viscera. In short, we can say that this decision, through its high poetic tendency, was definitive, and that victory was accorded to the

Muse, and that all writers, at least all those worthy of the name, have been acquitted in the person of Mr. Gustave Flaubert.

Let us therefore not say, as so many others are affirming with some slight and unconscious ill temper, that the book has owed its immense success to the trial and the acquittal. Without having been harassed, the book would have obtained the same curiosity, created the same astonishment and agitation. Besides, it had won the approval of all literate people a good deal earlier. Already in its first form, in the *Revue de Paris*, in which imprudent cuts had destroyed its harmony, it had excited an ardent interest. The situation of Gustave Flaubert, suddenly illustrious, was simultaneously excellent and bad, and I shall give as well as I can the diverse reasons for this equivocal situation over which his true and marvellous talent was able to triumph.

III

Excellent, for ever since the disappearance of Balzac, that prodigious meteor that will cover our country with a cloud of glory like a bizarre and exceptional dawn, like a polar aurora inundating the frozen desert with its fairy lights—all curiosity relative to the novel had abated and had become dormant.

[. . .]

But I have also said that this situation of the newcomer was bad, alas, for a lugubriously simple reason. For several years the share of its interest that the public grants to spiritual things had been singularly diminished; its budget of enthusiasm had been constantly shrinking. The last years of Louis-Philippe had seen the last explosions of a spirit still capable of being excited by the play of the imagination; but the new novelist found himself confronting an absolutely worn-out society—worse than worn out—stupefied and gluttonous, horrified only by fiction and loving only possession.

Under such conditions a highly cultivated mind, full of enthusiasm for the beautiful but brought up in a hard school, judging both the good and the bad of these circumstances, must have thought: "What is the surest means of stirring all these tired souls? They are really unaware of what they might love; they have a positive disgust only for what is great; naïve, ardent passion and poetic abandon make them blush and wound them. Let us therefore be vulgar in our choice of subjects, since the choice of too lofty a subject is an impertinence for the nineteenth-century reader. And also, let us beware of letting ourselves go and speaking our own minds. We shall be icy in relating passions and adventures that warm the blood of the common herd; as the school says, we shall be objective and impersonal.

"And also, since our ears have been buffeted in these recent times by childish school babblings, as we have heard of a certain literary process called *realism*—a disgusting insult hurled in the face of all analysts, a vague and elastic word signifying for the common man not a new method of creation but a minute description of accessories—we shall profit from the public confusion and universal ignorance. We shall apply a sinewy, picturesque, subtle, and exact style upon a banal canvas. We shall put the hottest and most passionate feelings into the most trivial adventure. The most solemn and decisive words will escape from the stupidest mouths.

"What is stupidity's stamping ground, the setting that is stupidest, most productive of absurdities, most abundant in intolerant imbeciles?

"The provinces.

"Who there are the most intolerable actors?

"The humble people, occupied with minor functions, the exercise of which falsifies their thinking.

"What is the most overdone and prostituted theme, the most hackneyed sob story?

"Adultery.

"I do not require," said the poet to himself, "that my *heroine* be a heroine. Provided that she is sufficiently pretty, that she has fortitude, ambition, and an uncheckable aspiration toward a higher world, she will be interesting. The feat, moreover, will be nobler, and our sinful lady will at least have this merit—comparatively very rare—of being distinguished from the ostentatious chatterers of the era preceding our own.

"I need not worry about style, picturesque arrangement, the description of my settings; I possess all of these qualities more than amply. I shall proceed supported by analysis and logic, and I shall thus prove that all subjects are indiscriminately good or bad according to the manner in which they are treated, and that the most vulgar ones can become the best."

From that moment on, *Madame Bovary*—a wager, a true wager, a bet, like all works of art—was created.

It remained only for the author to accomplish this feat all the way, to strip himself (as much as possible) of his sex and to become a

woman. A wondrous thing resulted from this: in spite of all his thes-
pian zeal, he could not keep from infusing virile blood into the veins
of his creature, and because of her energy and ambition and capacity
for revery, Madame Bovary remained a man. Like the armored Pallas
sprung from the forehead of Zeus, this bizarre androgyne has kept
all of the seductive quality of a virile spirit in a charming feminine
body.

Several critics have said: this work, truly lovely in the detail and
lifelikeness of its descriptions, does not contain a single character
representing morality or expressing the conscience of the author.
Where is the proverbial and legendary character charged with
explaining the fable and directing the intelligence of the reader? In
other words, where is the indictment?

Absurdity! Eternal and incorrigible confusion of functions and
genres! A true work of art needs no indictment. The logic of the work
suffices for all postulations of morality, and it is up to the reader to
draw conclusions from the conclusion.

As for the intimate, profound character in the fable, she is incon-
testably the adulterous woman. She alone, the dishonored victim,
possesses all the graces of the hero. I was saying a moment ago
that she was almost masculine and that the author had adorned her
(unconsciously, perhaps) with all the virile qualities.

Let us examine attentively:

(1) Imagination, that supreme and tyrannical faculty, substituted
for the heart, or what is called the heart, from which reasoning is
ordinarily excluded and which generally dominates in woman as in
the animal;

(2) Sudden energy of action, rapidity of decision, mystical fusion
of reasoning and passion, which characterize men created for action;

(3) Immoderate taste for seduction, domination, and even all the
vulgar means of seduction, going down to charlatanism in costume,
perfumes, and pomade—all summed up in two words: dandyism,
exclusive love of domination.

And yet Madame Bovary gives herself; carried away by the soph-
istries of her imagination, she gives herself magnificently, generously,
in a completely masculine way, to wretches who are not her equals,
exactly as poets give themselves to despicable women.

A new proof of the totally virile quality that nourishes her arterial
blood is that in the final analysis this unfortunate woman suffers less
from visible, exterior shortcomings, the blinding provincialisms of her

husband, than from that total absence of genius, that spiritual inferiority demonstrated by the stupid operation on the clubfoot.

And in this connection, reread the pages which contain that episode, so unjustly treated as parasitical, whereas it serves to throw a vivid light on the whole character of the person. A dark rage that had long been building up bursts out of all the wifely pores of Madame Bovary. Doors slam; the stupefied husband, who has been unable to give any spiritual satisfaction to his romantic wife, is relegated to his bedroom. He is in penitence, ignorant culprit! And Madame Bovary, hopeless, cries out like a little Lady Macbeth yoked to some inadequate captain: "Ah! If I were *at least* married to one of those old bald and bent scholars whose eyes, shielded by green glasses, are always focused on the archives of science! I could proudly take my place by his side; I should at least be the consort of a spiritual king; but to have as a partner in fetters this imbecile who cannot straighten a cripple's foot! Oh!"

This woman in reality is sublime, considering her class, her petty background, and her limited horizon.

(4) Even in her convent education, I find proof of the equivocal temperament of Madame Bovary.

The good sisters noticed in this girl an astonishing aptitude for life, for deriving pleasure and satisfaction from life—there is your man of action!

The girl, however, was deliciously intoxicated by the color of the stained-glass windows, by the oriental hues that the long, ornate windows cast upon her schoolgirl's prayer book; she gorged herself on the solemn music of vespers and, in a paradox, the credit for which must all go to her nervous hysteria, she substitutes in her soul for the true God the God of her fantasy, the God of the future and of chance, a picture-book God with spurs and moustache—there is the hysterical poet!

Hysteria! Why would this physiological mystery not make the basis and substance of a literary work, that mystery that the Academy of Medicine has not yet resolved and which, manifesting itself in women by the sensation of a rising and asphyxiating lump in the throat (I am speaking only of the principal symptom), reveals itself in nervous men by all manner of impotence and also by an aptitude for every excess.

In short, this woman is truly great. She is, above all, deserving of pity, and in spite of the systematic hard-heartedness of the author, who has tried his best to be absent from his work and to play the role of a manipulator of marionettes, all *intellectual* women will be grateful to him for having raised the female to so high a power, so far from the pure animal, and so close to the ideal man, and for having caused her to participate in that double character of calculation and reverie that constitutes the perfect being.

It is said that Madame Bovary is ridiculous. Indeed, here she is, at one moment taking for a hero out of Walter Scott a sort of gentleman—shall I even say, a country squire?—wearing hunting vests and unmatched suits! And now we see her in love with a little notary's clerk (incapable even of committing a dangerous act for his mistress), and finally the poor woman, exhausted, a bizarre Pasiphae relegated to the narrow confines of a village, pursues the ideal in the dance halls and bars of Rouen. What does it matter? Let us say it, let us confess it: she is a Caesar at Carpentras, she is pursuing the Ideal!

I shall certainly not say, like Pétrus Borel, the Lycanthrope of insurrectional memory, that abdicated rebel: "Confronted with all the platitudes and stupidities of the present, are we not left with cigarette paper and adultery?" But I shall affirm that, after all, when all is said and done, when all has been weighed on the most precise scales, our world is a harsh one indeed for having been engendered by Christ, and that it is hardly entitled to cast a stone at adultery, and a few grotesque couplings more or less will not accelerate the rotation of the spheres and will not advance by one second the final destruction of the universe. It is time to put an end to increasingly contagious hypocrisy and for us to recognize how ridiculous it is for men and women who are perverted even in their most trivial doings to cry shame upon a poor author who has deigned with his poet's chastity to cast a veil of glory on bedroom adventures, always repugnant and grotesque when Poetry does not caress them with its opaline, lamplike glow.

If I gave in to this analytic bent I should never finish with *Madame Bovary*. This essentially suggestive book could fill a whole volume of observations. For the moment I shall limit myself to observing that several of the most important episodes were at first either neglected or vituperatively attacked by the critics. Some examples: the episode of the unfortunate operation on the clubfoot, and the one so remarkable, so full of desolation, so truly *modern*, in which the future adulteress—for she is still only at the beginning of her descent, poor woman!—goes to seek aid of the Church, of the divine Mother, of her who has no excuse for not being ever ready, of that Pharmacy where no one has the right to slumber! The good priest, Bournisien, concerned only with the little rascals in his catechism class playing games amid the pews and chairs in the church, replies ingenuously: "Since you are ill, Madame, and since Monsieur Bovary is a doctor, *why don't you consult your husband?*"

What woman, confronted with this cure's inadequacy, in the madness produced by such amnesty would not rush to plunge her head into the swirling waters of adultery? And who among us, in a more naïve age and in troubled circumstances, has not inevitably encountered the incompetent priest?

IV

I had originally intended, with two books by the same author at hand (*Madame Bovary* and *La Tentation de Saint Antoine*, the fragments of which have not yet been assembled in a volume), to suggest a sort of parallel between the two. I wished to establish equations and correspondences. It would have been easy for me to discover beneath the minute web of *Madame Bovary* the high qualities of *irony* and *lyricism* that intensely illuminate *La Tentation de Saint Antoine*. Here the poet had not disguised himself, and his *Bovary*, tempted by all the demons of illusion and heresy, by all the carnal temptations of surrounding matter—his *saint Antoine*, in short, harassed by all the kinds of madness that circumvent us, would have made a stronger apologetic than his little bourgeois novel. In this work, of which the author has unfortunately only given us fragments, there are some dazzling passages. I do not speak only of the prodigious feast of Nebuchadnezzar; of the marvelous appearance of that little goose, the Queen of Sheba, a miniature dancing on the retina of an ascetic; of the charlatanic and bombastic staging of the entrance of Apollonius of Tyana, followed by his elephant-driver, or rather by his keeper, the imbecilic millionaire whom he leads through the world. I should like especially to draw the reader's attention to that quality of pain, subterranean and rebellious, which runs through the whole work, that dark vein which illuminates—what the English call the *subcurrent*—and which serves to guide us through this pandemoniacal bedlam of solitude.

It would have been easy for me to show, as I have already said, that Monsieur Gustave Flaubert voluntarily veiled in *Madame Bovary* the lofty lyrical and ironical qualities displayed without reservation in *La Tentation*, and that this latest work, a secret chamber of his spirit, is obviously the more interesting one for poets and philosophers.

Perhaps some day I shall have the pleasure of accomplishing this task.

"The Miller's Tale," *Canterbury Tales* (Geoffrey Chaucer)

"Sex and Punishment in Geoffrey Chaucer's 'The Miller's Tale'"
by Michael G. Cornelius,
Wilson College, Pennsylvania

The first pilgrim along Geoffrey Chaucer's famed voyage to Canterbury to tell a tale is the Knight, a noble and stately, if slightly sinister, figure. The Knight recounts a traditional medieval romance with classical overtures, replete with references to courtly lovers, daring battles, brave men, and a beautiful bride. In the tale, Palamon and Arcite, lifelong friends and prisoners of Prince Theseus, fall headlong in love with Emily, the younger sister of Theseus's queen. Eventually the two wage war, with Emily as reward for the victor. For centuries, readers and critics alike revered "The Knight's Tale" for its high style and princely tale, thinking it worthy of Chaucer's awesome talents. It has long been deemed a laudable opening to Chaucer's magnum opus and a formidable first volley in the pilgrims' tale-telling game by both readers and critics alike.

Harry Bailey, the pilgrimage's host, next turns to the Monk, a worthy tale-teller to follow the noble knight per the ranks of medieval social hierarchy, and urges him to "quite. . .the Knyghtes tale" (3119). Before the monk can speak up, however, Robin the Miller, "that for drunken was al pale," interrupts, and declares that he intends to requite the knight's romantic epic with a tale of his own (3120). Scholars have always viewed this reversal of social hierarchy—moving

95

from the highest-ranking member on the pilgrimage to one of the lowest—as integral to Chaucer's strategy of satirizing the social classes of his day. By placing the Miller after the Knight, Chaucer informs his readers that he is intent on breaking societal rules and that, quite literally, anything can happen in the pages of this book. Indeed, the story the Miller tells only confirms this assumption, as the Knight's staid romantic epic is followed by a comic, coarse, and downright ribald tale involving a comely woman, Alisoun, and the fates of the three men in her life, John, Nicholas, and Absolon. Told in a style as low as "The Knight's Tale" is high, "The Miller's Tale" seems a perfect remedy to the placid poetry of the Knight, a zesty yarn that thumbs its nose at the very conventions the Knight espouses in his own story.

"The Miller's Tale," however, has much more in common with "The Knight's Tale" than would first appear. Both tell stories of a love triangle affected by a sudden reversal of fortune, and both are eminently if covertly concerned with the fate of the female object of desire in the tale. This is especially true in "The Miller's Tale," where Chaucer spins much dark humor from the sexual escapades of and resulting ramifications to the adulterous Alisoun, her husband John, her paramour Nicholas, and her ardent pursuer Absolon. However, and perhaps most significantly, of the four main characters in the tale, Alisoun ostensibly evades repercussions for her actions; despite the severity of her sexual sin, Alisoun, as Alvin W. Bowker puts it, "escapes reproof" (33).

"The Miller's Tale" is a *fabliau*, a genre of French medieval comic narrative that often involved lowbrow humor and myriad sexual offenses. Henry Marshall Leicester dismisses the *fabliau* as a "dirty joke." Thomas J. Farrell more accurately describes the genre when he notes that "sexual triumph and physical battery" are the hallmarks of a *fabliau*; in these stories, "sex occurs outside the social institution of marriage, and quite often as an extramarital attack on the institution; violence almost inevitably privileges individual vindictiveness (or whim) over social order" (480, 773). With these comments in mind, it is no surprise to find that each of the men in "The Miller's Tale" has experienced violence upon his person. Alisoun's husband John breaks his arm and is labeled a fool by his neighbors because of Nicholas's scheme; Nicholas is branded when attempting to debase the persistent wooer Absolon; and Absolon is humiliated by Alisoun when he begs a kiss at her bedroom window. The violence in the tale is often lauded as poetic justice for each of the transgressions these men has committed, yet many critics have questioned why Alisoun herself remains unpunished, when her own sin is perhaps worse than any that the men have perpetrated. Farrell sums it up well when he writes:

> A sense that the fates suffered by Nicholas and Absolon are appropriate and just seems to be nearly universal: Nicholas's hot love is repaid in kind, and the aroma of Abolson's perfumed infatuation decays noticeably. But when the argument has been extended to include old John, and to define the specific vices being punished in each character, there is more room to doubt. And there is little room for discussion for Alisoun, whose allotted fate—a night of obviously well-enjoyed mirth with Nicholas and a devastating triumph over the despised Absolon—can be called punishment only by the most grotesque definitions of the term. (778)

As Farrell notes, in "The Miller's Tale," the wife's triumph disrupts the social and gendered orders of her day. The tale also reminds the reader of the role women have long played in the same social institution. It is this role, replete with its lack of authority and agency, which provides the key to Alisoun's retribution. Alisoun's supposed lack of punishment in "The Miller's Tale"—and her correlation to the character of Emily in "The Knight's Tale"—demonstrates a Chaucerian critique on the institution of marriage itself and ultimately seems to suggest that Alisoun's sexualized transgressions escape obvious castigation because, by being forced to wed John in the first place, she has already been punished.

A *fabliau* makes an ideal genre to comment on the institution of marriage, and Chaucer wastes no time in criticizing the players in his tale. He begins with the carpenter John, the husband in his farce and one of the key players in arranging the marriage at the center of the story (along with, one imagines, Alisoun's own father). Chaucer reminds his reader of how such marriages are arranged when he describes the first marriage of the other character named Alisoun in *The Canterbury Tales*, the Wife of Bath, who was originally married at the age of twelve. A marriage between a much older man and a much younger bride was often arranged between father and groom; the father appreciably valued the economic stability the older groom offered both his daughter and, by extension, his whole family, while

the groom valued the comely looks and youth of his trophy wife.
While the older groom/younger bride union was common enough in
Chaucer's time, and a popular convention in the literature of Chaucer's
day, the author himself wastes no time in decrying such weddings
(3229–3230).

Chaucer describes John as both greatly loving towards his wife and
continually wary of her. At the beginning of the tale, Chaucer labels
John jealous and insecure (3224–3226). Earlier, though, Chaucer
describes John as a loving husband, in fact, one who loves his wife
more than his own life (3222). When John learns from Nicholas about
the impending flood, he cries, "Allas, my wyf! / And shal she drenche?
Allas, myn Alisoun!" (3522–3523). Initially, these two contrasting
images of John confuse the reader. Mark Miller suggests that "the
fact that John loves Alisoun more than he does his own life, that
the end of the world for him means first of all her death, provides the
wedge in his psyche that opens him to Nicholas's plot" (65). Bowker
considers that it is John's "compassion [for Alisoun] and his credulous-
ness" that allow him to be deceived by Nicholas in the first place (32).
Farrell and Leicester have harsher words for the carpenter: Farrell
notes that "at worst [John] is a fool for marrying a young wife," while
Leicester echoes this sentiment when he writes that John "must be
a fool to care for someone the *fabliau* has fated to betray him" (770,
484). Both critics, however, are reluctant to pass stringent judgment on
John, suggesting that his foolish decision—to marry a beautiful young
wife—is not worth the punishment he receives in the text. Leicester
declares "John ... is the merest device, the old jealous husband whose
presence justifies the transgressive adultery and allows us to enjoy it
without worrying, since such husbands conventionally deserve what
they get" (482). Similarly, Miller writes that "John's ... punishment,
unlike those of Nicholas and Absolon, never even provisionally comes
into focus in the terms provided by a normative naturalism" and that
"John is the only character in the poem for whom altruism is even
raised as a possibility" (64, 65). To Miller and Leicester, clearly, the
punishment does not fit the crime.

However, the critic Paul A. Olson disagrees with Miller and
Leicester:

> The sketchy portrait of John tells us that he is a jealous lover
> and a rich old man who makes money from two businesses:

> carpentry and keeping roomers. Both aspects of his character
> display a possessiveness which asserts itself first in the action
> when he tells his fear—that he may lose his precious Alysoun
> *(sic)* in the flood—and again when he demonstrates that he
> can be taken in by the prospect of having the whole world and
> Alysoun after the flood. (229)

Olson argues that John's possessive nature and stance towards his wife
brands him enough of a "rascal" to merit his just reward (228). Olson
labels John's primary sin a form of avarice, and John demonstrates his
greed for both wealth and his young wife when he dreams of having
the entire world all to himself after everyone else has drowned in
the flood. Though some critics have considered the ending of "The
Miller's Tale" to reflect a form of "poetic justice," Miller decrees that
a more appropriate term for what transpires to each man is "moral
punishment," and that for John, his "cuckoldry is thereby supple-
mented with a broken arm and the strikingly public ridicule heaped
upon him" (780). If Chaucer's rancor towards John seems not to be
borne out by his deeds, it is important to remember that John's major
transgression is the act of marriage in the first place. John's desire is
not for Alisoun, but for any woman of her type—young, beautiful, and
ideally, pliant. Chaucer recounts several such marriages in *The Canterbury Tales*, none of them favorably. The best example occurs in "The
Merchant's Tale," which focuses on the marriage between January,
an old knight, and May, his young, virginal bride. May, of course,
chafes at being wed to such an old man, and quickly casts her eye on
the handsome young stable boy, a groom of a different type. Though
January threatens to uncover May's adultery, the young bride and her
lover ultimately escape detection, like Alisoun, unscathed. This does
not suggest that Chaucer excuses May's adulterous behavior; rather,
he implies that such unequal marriages are doomed from the start.
Thus in contemplating John's punishment, it is important to consider
the *Tales* in its entirety; in that light, the retribution John receives
makes more sense.

The transgressions that Nicholas and Absolon engage in are
perhaps to be expected based on the roles they play in the tale, and
thus their punishments generally go unquestioned. Nicholas, of
course, is the ardent and persistent lover; he woos Alisoun, wears
down her resistance (though to be honest, her resistance wears down

quite easily), and beds her, all while staying under her husband's roof. Nicholas then concocts a scheme to ensure he and Alisoun can spend time alone, and when Absolon interrupts their dalliance Nicholas conspires to add to his earlier humiliation.

Nicholas remains the chief villain of the plot: he seduces Alisoun, conspires against his host, and rejoices in Absolon's comeuppance. He counts fraud, adultery, and even heresy as his chief sins. Bowker speaks harshly of Nicholas's "cruelty and callousness," noting that "Nicholas has the very type of mind that discovers easy prey among the gullible and the innocent" (28–29). Nonetheless, like John the carpenter, Chaucer's portrayal of Nicholas is not one-sided: "We are persuaded to like Nicholas, to shake our heads at his disjunctive pursuit of scholarship, but to overlook his intemperate activities as emblematic of a casual, easy-going fellow, well-disposed toward the world and not without some expectation of the homage it gives him" (28). Chaucer's tendency to create characters that are not complex but rather imbued with dichotomous likable and dislikable qualities belies his intentions as to how his audience should react to them. We are not to sift through John or Nicholas's positive or negative aspects. Rather, Chaucer intends for his readers to react viscerally to them. We like Nicholas because he is so likable; this quality easily deceives the husband. John, on the other hand, we dislike, not because of any particular personality flaws but largely, perhaps, because of the circumstances of his marriage in the first place.

Despite Nicholas's amiability he is punished for his actions. Miller considers Nicholas's branding a punishment against "masculinity," that the "humiliation and pain of being stuck 'amydde the ers' (3810) by Absolon's hot borrowed blade" is emasculating in its affect (59). It seems fitting that a "lecher's" naked form is now permanently marked, like a great scarlet letter "A," as if to indicate shame at his own transgression (Olson 229). Yet it must be telling that Nicholas's punishment stems not from anything he did to John, but rather as a result of an action directed towards Absolon. It is his decision to "leet fle a fart / As greet as it had been a thunder-dent" in Abolson's face that guides the brand onto Nicholas's posterior; strictly speaking, Nicholas is not punished for deceiving, cuckolding, or even injuring John, all of which he is guilty of (3806–3807). In fact, save for the branding, Nicholas ends the tale better off than he started it: because the townsfolk believe John to be mad, Nicholas is freer to engage in his relationship with Alisoun, who, because of her husband's newfound physical and mental state, may be able to exercise more control over his considerable fortune. Thus, the denouement of "The Miller's Tale" finds both Alisoun and Nicholas in good stead, and Nicholas might even suggest that the branding was worth it.

Like John, Absolon is a character the reader instinctively dislikes, though also like John, his transgressions seem much less serious than Nicholas's. Olson labels Nicholas a lecher, but Absolon is only a dandy, a "clown whose ineffectual public demonstrations constitute an obbligato to a sadness seen not only in the irony of his self-ignorance but in the reaction other people have in his performance," as Bowker succinctly puts it (31). Absolon is ridiculous, but unlike Nicholas, he is rarely serious; Absolon's wooing of all the parish wives, "And namely ... this carpenteris wyf" is more about show than solemn intention (3343). The manner in which Absolon woos bears this characterization out: he refers to Alisoun childishly as his "honeycomb," his "sweete cynamome" and "sweete leef," and his "faire bryd" (3698, 3699, 3792, 3726). He likens himself to a "lamb after a tete" (3704). If Chaucer's constant use of natural imagery in Absolon's wooing is designed to poke fun at the numerous animalistic double entendres he is creating, there is no sense that Absolon himself understands the joke. For him, wooing is an act, a show, "a combination of religious pomp and ritual" (Bowker 31). He woos because of his own elevated opinion of himself and his skills as a lover, and not out of any genuine desire for Alisoun or any of the women he has (presumably unsuccessfully) wooed in the past.

Absolon's punishment, then, is perfectly suited for him: when "he kiste hir naked ers / Ful savourly," his overdeveloped ego is not only rapidly deflated, but Absolon is now forced to confront the very object of desire he has long sought—a naked woman (3734–3735). His overreaction is telling. Bowker suggests that Absolon is "wounded in the very place that would most embarrass and upset him"—namely, his pride—and that the result of his nighttime encounter with Alisoun may very well be a cure to his foolish wooing ways (31). Like John, though, Absolon ends the tale worse off than when he began: his illusions about himself have been shattered, and he is left only with his rancor and hollow revenge to soothe his crushed ego. Interestingly, the two men whose indiscretions seem the least harmful end up far worse than Nicholas at the conclusion of the tale: John is left with his broken arm, Absolon with his broken self-image, while Nicholas is left with Alisoun, his relationship and everything else (save his backside) relatively intact.

We, too, are left with Alisoun, whose indiscretions are the worst and whose punishment is almost nonexistent. Alisoun, after all, breaks her own marriage vow, and in her own bed; Alisoun takes advantage of her husband's deception; Alisoun does not look out for her husband's best interest; Alisoun devises Absolon's humiliation. Many critics, including Olson and Farrell, have questioned the common wisdom of calling the punishments "justice": after all, how can justice be served when the greatest transgressor, Alisoun, remains unscathed?

Some critics believe that this freedom from punishment is unwarranted. Olson suggests that in the tale, "Action arises from character," and thus each of the males in the story gets what he respectively deserves (228). In order to explain Alisoun's unscathed state at the end of the tale, Olson suggests that she functions not as a character but rather as the manifestation of each man's transgression: ". . . a man may have three 'wives': carnality, avarice, and pomposity. Alysoun *(sic)* serves for all three" (233). Seen in this light, Alisoun is not a character, but a caricature, representing not a dynamic literary personality but an object that reflects some aspect of the three males who desire her. Miller suggests that this attitude reflects the idea of "'woman' as an object of appreciation. . .little more than a place for a man to find his own pleasure, as is suggested most starkly [in the tale] that the 'there' in which a husband finds God's plenty is his wife's 'pryvetee,' that is her genitals, rather than in *her*" (52). This implies that the tale "links an ideology of gender and erotic desire, and specifically an ideology of normative masculinity" (Miller 50). In other words, "The Miller's Tale" is really, in the end, all about *men*; the men are punished because they have transgressed, while Alisoun, it seems, lacks the character development to have transgressed; if "action arises from character," then Alisoun does not act, but only reacts, and thus no transgressions have occurred.

Yet in examining the scene of Absolon's punishment, where Alisoun takes the lead, Miller queries, "What does it mean for Alisoun, who throughout the tale has functioned as a more or less passive object of desire . . . to become at this fateful moment not merely an object but an agent?" (37). In proposing Alisoun has gained some semblance of "agency," of authority and independence, Miller suggests that Alisoun *does* have the ability to decide some things for herself and, by extension, has the ability to transgress. After all, she initially resists Nicholas before deciding, on her own, to give in to her desire; she dispatches Absolon with girlish glee; and she handles her own husband brilliantly, ensuring that she, of all the players in the tale, ends the story in the most improved position. Leicester enthuses that Alisoun has "resistance, rebellion and independence," and that, "Insofar as the other characters are used as responses to her, she is what is behind or beyond them all" (485, 492). Leicester adds that in the tale everyone *is* their gender role, and acts accordingly, though he never explains why this allows Alisoun to escape sans punishment. In the end, critics seem to suggest that if Alisoun is a dynamic character designed to exhibit her own agency, then Chaucer has fashioned her to sidestep the punishment he so handily doles out to the other characters in the tale.

A clue to the reason for Alisoun's escape from retribution may be found in the previous story, "The Knight's Tale," in the fate of Emily. In the tale, Emily prays to the goddess Diana to allow her to remain unmarried and a virgin but Diana is powerless to intervene and informs Emily, "Thou shalt ben wedded" (2351). Emily, sister-in-law to the king, has no choice but to comply. The same is true for May in "The Merchant's Tale," for the narrator in "The Wife of Bath's Prologue," and for Alisoun here. Chaucer often demonstrated his contempt for such an abuse of power, believing that marriages between equals (such as that of Dorigen and Arveragus in "The Franklin's Tale") were superior to a marriage between an older groom and a younger bride. Perhaps, then, Chaucer does not punish Alisoun because he believes a larger societal force, one that is beyond her control, has already punished her. Thus, while Chaucer does not suggest a radical overhaul of the institution of marriage he does offer a critique of an institution that sells a bride to the highest bidder.

Miller comments that in "The Miller's Tale," "to be a woman is little more than to be the thing men desire" (57). "The Miller's Tale" both reminds us of this inevitability and allows us to forget for a moment its gloomy premise. Ultimately, Chaucer punishes not the freewheeling sexuality inherent in the piece, but rather the actions of the men—the husband, the lover, the wooer—who focus too much on themselves and never enough on the "object" of their desire. If the end of the story allows the reader one more moment to revel in the just desserts Chaucer has meted out, it only forestalls the realization that the worst punishment of all—Alisoun's—will certainly last long after John's arm, Nicholas's burn, and Absolon's ego have all healed.

WORKS CITED

Bowker, Alvin. "Comic Illusion and Dark Reality in 'The Miller's Tale.'" *Modern Language Studies* 4.2 (1974): 27–34.

Chaucer, Geoffrey. *The Canterbury Tales*. Ed. Larry D. Benson. Houghton Mifflin Company: Boston, 2000.

Farrell, Thomas J. "Privacy and the boundaries of Fabliau in the *Miller's Tale*." *ELH* 56.4 (1989): 773–795.

Leicester, H. Marshall. "Newer Currents in Psychoanalytic Criticism, and the Difference 'It' Makes: Gender and Desire in the *Miller's Tale*." *ELH* 61.3 (1994): 473–499.

Miller, Mark. *Philosophical Chaucer: Love, Sex, and Agency in the* Canterbury Tales. Cambridge UP: Cambridge, 2004.

Olson, Paul. "Poetic Justice in *The Miller's Tale*." *Modern Language Quarterly* 24(1963): 227–236.

Robinson, F. N., ed. *Poetical Works of Chaucer*. Cambridge: London, 1957.

MOLL FLANDERS
(DANIEL DEFOE)

"Introduction"
by Mark Schorer,
in *The Fortunes and Misfortunes*
of the Famous Moll Flanders &c. (1950)

INTRODUCTION

In his introduction to the 1950 edition of *Moll Flanders,* Mark
Schorer argues that Defoe's novel can best be understood
by interpreting the novel's depiction of sexuality as the indication of the amoral way in which things are bartered and
exchanged in a mercantile society. Moll and many of the other
downtrodden characters in the book are reduced to things
to be bought and sold in the marketplace. While Schorer
argues that Defoe no doubt intended to emphasize the attributes of irony and even humor in the sexualized character of
Moll, he concludes that her depiction is mainly a tragic one,
functioning as a social commentary on a soulless, market-
consumed culture.

Schorer, Mark. "Introduction." *The Fortunes and Misfortunes of the Famous Moll
Flanders &c.* by Daniel Defoe. New York: Random House, 1950. pp. v–xvii.

I

In the preface to his book, *The Living Novel*, V. S. Pritchett proposes that the novel that lives beyond its time somehow embodies as "new material" the intrinsic values and conflicts that are the peculiar condition of its time. Thus the living novelist is always "on the tip of the wave," not reflecting his age but, for the first time, really discovering the age to itself. Yet "new material" is hardly ever a new "subject." "New material is added only by new seeing, not by new sights. *Moll Flanders* is a book of new material because it is old material—the conventional rogue's tale—seen in a new way." However we may wish to qualify this statement, its essential point must stand; for *Moll Flanders* is the first work of fiction to bring us at a thrust into the very heart of the middle class, even as the middle class was coming into dominant existence. "Seeing" the middle class and "seeing" with its eyes, perhaps without quite knowing, was Defoe's "new way." *Moll Flanders* is all the more entertaining and perhaps all the more true in that here a middle-class intelligence has been located—has been *seen*—in a criminal life.

To say that we are in the heart of the middle class is to say at the same time that we are in the heart of Daniel Defoe. His life is a nearly incredible account of bourgeois activity in the late seventeenth and early eighteenth century, fantastically crowded and always precarious, edging now up toward aristocracy and secret vice, now trembling on the ledge from which it would plunge down into the world of open vice and crime. At the very end, an aged man of seventy, Defoe was forced for reasons still obscure to us to flee his home and live out his last months in hiding. Secret flight was an old and familiar pattern for him, often exciting, often even exhilarating, but the final hiding, which ended with his death in "a lethargy," as his age called it, is pathetic, and if he troubled then to look back over his packed and various years, he might well have found them a spectacle of waste. He seems to us to have been a man so deeply involved in the multiple, immediate activities of daily life that he was never able to pause to observe how remarkable, on various occasions and in a thousand fleeting moments, he actually was, and, in later history, would appear to have been.

He was born merely Daniel Foe in 1660, and remained D. Foe for forty years, when, by an alteration not hard to make, he became the more aristocratic Daniel Defoe. Of aristocracy there was nothing in his blood, nothing in his nature. His father was a dissenting tallow-chandler, and Daniel Defoe received the plain but solid education of a typical Dissenters' academy. The tradition of religious dissent, implicated in the ambitions of the rising lower orders, encouraged a kind of depraved Puritanism that expressed itself in a moralistic piety and a utilitarian morality; and these strains were always to be evident in at least the superficial character of Daniel Defoe. He married pros-perously, considerably improving his economic situation through the match; yet had, as a young man in 1685, enough of indiscretion and imprudence to join Monmouth's rebellion, an unsuccessful Protestant attempt to forestall the succession of James II. At about the same time he had entered the world of trade as a merchant in hosiery (a term that indicates approximately those items we associate today with "haberdashery"), but, never content with merely one activity, he engaged at the same time in the merchandising of various other goods including at least wine and tobacco. His enterprises became more ambitious and more involved, and in 1692, with an already tarnished name, he declared himself bankrupt, indebted to the amount of 17,000 pounds. Between the years 1688 and 1694, he was the subject of at least eight lawsuits for fraud in dealings ranging from ships to civet cats, and he was never again to live quite outside the shadow of the debtors' prison.

In the midst of all this, he had in an amateur way already evinced an interest in authorship by composing at least two sets of clumsy verses of a satirical bias, and when he was faced with the necessity of beginning his economic life again at the age of thirty-three, he turned to journalism. Yet even as he moved into the political activities that contemporary journalism inevitably involved (he was at first a tool of the Whig ministry of William III), he began a new mercantile opera-tion, a tile and brick factory at Tilbury, that survived successfully until his next great disaster.

Once launched on his literary career, his pace was reckless, relent-less. His published works number over four hundred titles. What drove him? It is the great question in Defoe's life, and there has never been an answer. His first important book, the *Essay on Projects* of 1698, shows us a mind not, certainly, noble, but vastly curious, wide ranging, and genuinely concerned with the public good. It is a mind possessed even of a certain humdrum visionary quality, as in that proposal for

the education of women that sprang from his sympathetic recognition
of their hideously depressed condition:

> I have often thought of it as one of the most barbarous
> customs in the world, considering us as a civilized and a Christian
> country, that we deny the advantages of learning to women. We
> reproach the sex every day with folly and impertinence, while I
> am confident, had they the advantages of education equal to us,
> they would be guilty of less than ourselves.

It is a mind that offers everywhere the unpretentious kernels from
which two hundred years of "progress" were to spring; it is the mind
of the middle class, with all its humble folly and its often foolish good.
Thus it is also a rather self-righteously pious mind, a moralizing rather
than a meditative mind, a mind that, even as it is ever alert to the main
chance, is imbued with a somewhat uncritical but not unattractive
tolerance. This last we see in Defoe's only interesting poem, the *True-
Born Englishman* of 1701, which, as a satirical attack on the enemies
of the Dutch King William, is at the same time a plea for sympathy
between varying national strains. And yet, for all this, one cannot feel
that Defoe's motive was ever really altruistic or even disinterested.

His poem brought him money and the friendly eye of the king,
and when the king died in 1701, Defoe was already so deeply implicated in the political intrigue of his time that he had no inclination
to extricate himself. Until now, he had with most Dissenters been a
defender of the Whig position, and it was the Tory attempt to legis-
late against the device of "occasional conformity," whereby a Dissenter
could make himself eligible for public office, that impelled Defoe to
write his most brilliant but personally most disastrous satire. For *The
Shortest Way With Dissenters* he stood three days in the pillory and
thereafter was allowed to languish in Newgate until, his life again and
the brickworks too in ruins, he was inconspicuously rescued by a Tory
politician, Robert Harley, soon to be the new queen's minister and
whose tool Defoe thereafter became. Defoe's newspaper, *The Review*,
influential as it may be in the history of journalism, was founded for
no better reason than Harley's cause. Long before *The Review* died
in 1713, Defoe had come to be regarded as one of the most valuable
men that a faction could employ, and one of the most reprehensible.
Of him, Swift (who likewise served Harley) wrote in 1708, "One of
these authors (the fellow that was pilloried, I have forgot his name)

is indeed so grave, sententious, dogmatical a rogue, that there is no enduring him," and Addison, in 1713, "a false, shuffling, prevaricating rascal—unqualified to give his testimony in a Court of Justice."

By 1713, to be sure, Harley had fallen, Defoe had transferred his services to the Whig minister, Godolphin; and, upon his decline, returned them to the once more ascendant Harley. These are twists and turns of conscience that call up no wonder in us over the fact that, in 1712, in a moment of oblique self-scrutiny, Defoe could have written, "I have seen the bottom of all parties." He had seen, besides, the bottom of his own narrow soul. For Harley he had founded a secret intelligence service, himself the agent, and when he went over to Godolphin, he spied with equal ingeniousness for him. A spy is perhaps the nearest political equivalent to the kind of reporter, in the literary world, that Defoe revealed himself to be in his famous short narrative, *A True Relation of the Apparition of one Mrs. Veal*, which he published in 1706. The prying gift of observation, the sense of fact, the feel for mystery, the delight in sensation and danger—all these would seem to relate these diverse occupations in the single man. The constant risk of exposure and jail (Defoe was jailed again in 1713), the willingness to drop one project (*The Review* died in the same year) and get on to a new one (the *Mercator*, an organ of apology for the current policy of free trade), and, finally, the love of masquerade, to which we will presently come—all these seem, too, to be qualities as necessary to the political as to the journalistic spy. The two, in Defoe, at any rate, were one.

Robert Harley, Earl of Oxford, fell finally (and fell into a Tower cell) in 1714. Queen Anne died in the same week. Defoe, once more, fell temporarily. His immediate major effort at rehabilitation was an enormous work of domestic piety called *The Family Instructor*, a moralistic handbook, written in dialogues, to the conduct of marital and parental affairs in the Christian home. This monument to vulgarized righteousness was a stopgap in a bad moment; it was also, conceivably, a hasty payment to conscience. Defoe was as much at home here as anywhere, and it is borne in on us that his easiest gift was the ability to slide into almost any role and believe it real. Observe the next step: although George I seemed at first to feel no kindliness toward even the gifted hangers-on, like Defoe, of even moderate Tories, like Harley, Defoe was nevertheless in the secret employ of the new party by 1718. And now the two occupations of political and literary espionage come together in fact, for he was employed by the new Whigs to write like a Tory for a Tory periodical, that "the sting of that mischievous paper should be entirely taken out." Nor did he emasculate only one Tory journal, but several at once, and, further, by the time that, in the most notable example, he was working in this artful fashion on Mist's *Weekly Journal*, he wrote at the same time for a Whig paper, *The Whitehall Evening Post*. The deviousness is almost dazzling, and it brought Defoe's relation with Mist to a momentary end.

> What strange adventures could untwist
> Such true-born knaves as Foe and Mist? . . .
> As rats do run from falling houses,
> So Dan another cause espouses;
> Leaves poor Nat sinking in the mire,
> Writes *Whitehall Evening Post* for hire.

The labyrinthine character of political journalism in the eighteenth century is perhaps nowhere more clearly displayed than in the fact that, after this break, Mist sought out Defoe again and rehired him on his own terms.

Defoe was nearly sixty years old, and we should expect to find him now an exhausted literary hack; but it is precisely now that the miracle occurs. In 1719 he published the first of the several works by which his literary fame was to be established. *Robinson Crusoe* is a work of fiction based on fact—the case of Alexander Selkirk. *Moll Flanders*, which followed three years later (almost unbelievably, together with *Due Preparations for the Plague*, *A Journal of the Plague Year*, *Colonel Jack*, and another four-hundred-page book of homiletic dialogues, *Religious Courtship*) was a work of fiction that pretended to be fact. The literary energy that brought these works into being is not to be explained, but the literary evolution is clear enough. They are, indeed, a kind of culmination of all Defoe's history and quality. In *Moll Flanders*, Defoe the bankrupt tradesman and Puritan moralist, Defoe the journalist and popular historian, above all, perhaps, Defoe the pilloried prisoner and Defoe the spy, come together. His imagination is the composite gift of all these characters.

II

Everything about *Moll Flanders*—its kind and Defoe's extension of that kind, its literary method, its paradoxical morality—everything about it has a naïvely direct relation to his own world of experience and interests. The kind is the biography of a rogue, a conventional if low form of literary expression since Elizabethan times. Rogue biographies were usually the lives of real criminals fictionally foreshortened and sensationalized. Their ostensible purpose was to expose the operations of criminals and thereby to warn; their actual purpose was rather to thrill an undiscriminating audience with melodrama. The convention offered Defoe solid elements to which he would almost at once have responded. The world of crime he had experienced and observed with sufficient directness and even fascination to recognize as a subject matter that he was in a superb position to handle, and it is no accident that Moll's paralyzing fear of Newgate is her most forcibly urged emotion. At the same time, the journalist in Defoe would have responded to a subject that lent itself to exposure, and the Puritan, to the elements that allowed the expression of a ready impulse to admonish and exhort. Add to these the convention of the "secret history," which would be as attractive to the intriguing familiar of party ministers as it would be to the journalistic spy, and the several elements that the rogue biography offered to the special talents of Daniel Defoe should be evident.

The method that Defoe developed to animate the *genre* is perfectly calculated to his talents. The Puritan and the journalist together, the first out of genuine suspicions of the idle and the second out of his conviction that nothing is more persuasive than fact, lead Defoe to deny that he is writing fiction at all. On the contrary, he tells us, he is merely editing the diary of a real and notorious character who must, for reputation's sake, present herself under a pseudonym. Thus at once Defoe saves his conscience and puts himself into his favorite position, the assumed role. He is not telling us about Moll Flanders, he is Moll Flanders. The device comes easy to one whose own life had consisted of a series of conflicting roles, and he had had long practice not only in life but in his previous writings. He had written in the past as though he were a Turk, a Scotch soldier, a visionary Scotchman, a Quaker, a lonely but enterprising castaway. Why not now as a sexually abandoned thief? Once the role was assumed, it was easy, too, for the journalist to support the role, or, at any rate, for a journalist with Defoe's special feeling for the telling physical facts in any situation. Out of this gift grows his special kind of verisimilitude, that kind of realism best described as "circumstantial." It is a method that depends not on sensibility but on fact, not on description but on proof, as if a man, wishing to tell us of an excellent dinner, did not bother to say how his food tasted, but merely listed the courses that made up the meal, or, more likely, produced a cancelled check to prove that he had paid a good deal for it. On such evidence, we would hardly doubt that he had eaten it. Thus the centrality in Defoe's method (and the resulting texture) of the bolts of goods, the inventories, the itemized accounts, the landlady's bills, the lists, the ledgers.

Defoe's tone is hardly less important to this method than his persuasive details. How matter-of-fact all this is, for such an extraordinary life! Five marriages, a score of recorded lovers, and, if we can count, a score of children, twelve dead and eight alive when Moll's childbearing ceased at last. *We* exclaim (we may even protest), but Defoe does not. In this story, the birth of a child or the acquisition of a new lover seems hardly as important as the hiring of a coach or the packing of a trunk. Defoe's prevailingly matter-of-fact tone levels all incidents out on a straight narrative plane, and we are lulled into supposing that any account of a life that is so guilelessly without emphasis is necessarily true. Defoe's deepest guile, indeed, always lay in his appearance of being without guile. A narrator with an air of uncomprehending innocence or a narrator so innocent that he comprehends precisely the wrong things in a situation, had been among Defoe's great propagandistic devices throughout his career as a journalist, and over and over again, this device had been the basis of his satire. In *Moll Flanders*, the heroine, like Defoe's earlier narrators, is peculiarly innocent; the meaning of her experience seems to run off her moral skin like quicksilver; nothing touches her; at the end, a woman of seventy, she is almost exactly as bland as she was in the opening scenes, a small girl who wished to be a lady. And this quality again, this very imperceptiveness, lends itself to Defoe's purposes of persuasion. Isn't this, we ask ourselves, exactly what a woman like Moll would be, so wonderfully imperceptive that this is really a book about a remarkable self-deception?

But then the other question comes, and with it, the question whether this is a method adequate to the production of a novel. Whose deception is it—Moll's? or Defoe's? And this question takes us into the third consideration, the paradoxical morality of the book. *Moll Flanders* comes to us professing that its purpose is to warn us not only against a life of crime but against the cost of crime. We cannot for very many pages take that profession seriously, for it is apparent all too soon that nothing in the conduct of the narrative indicates that virtue is either more necessary or more enjoyable than vice. At the end we discover that Moll turns virtuous only after a life of vice has enabled her to do so with security. The actualities of the book, then, enforce the moral assumption of any commercial culture, the belief that virtue and worldly goods form an equation. This is a morality somewhat less than skin deep, with no relation to motives arising from more than a legalistic sense of good and evil; having its relation, rather, to motives arising from the presence or absence of food, drink, linen, damask, silver, and timepieces. It is the morality of measurement, and without in the least intending it, *Moll Flanders* is our classic revelation of the mercantile mind: the morality of measurement which Defoe has apparently neglected to measure.

Defoe's announced purpose is probably a pious humbug, and he probably meant us to read the book as a series of scandalous events. His inexhaustible pleasure in excess (twenty children, not five; twenty lovers, not fifteen; five husbands, including a brother, not three)—this element in the book continues to amuse us. The book becomes indeed a vast joke, a wonderful kind of myth of female endurance, and, like all tall tales, an absurdity. Yet it is not nearly as absurd as that other absurdity that Defoe did not intend at all, the notion that Moll could live a rich and full life of crime, and by mere repentance, emerge spotless in the end, a perfect matron. The point is, of course, that she has no moral being, and that the book has no real moral life. Everything is external. Everything can be weighed, measured, handled, paid for in gold, or expiated by a prison term. To this the whole method of the novel testifies: this is a morality of social circumstance, a morality in which only externals count since only externals show. Thus we may conclude that the real meaning of the book is to be discovered in spite of Defoe, whose point of view is, finally, indistinguishable from the point of view of Moll Flanders; and we may therefore conclude, further, that the book is not the true chronicle of a disreputable female, but the true allegory of an impoverished soul—the author's; not, indeed, an anatomy of the criminal class, but of the middle class striving for security.

Security and morality are almost identical in *Moll Flanders*, and we today are hardly in a position to scorn Defoe's observation that it is easier to be pious with a bank account than without one. Like *Robinson Crusoe*, this is a desperate story of survival, a story that tries to demonstrate the possibility of success through unremitting native wit. Security, clearly, is the end of life:

> This was evidently my case, for I was now a loose, unguided
> creature, and had no help, no assistance, no guide for my

conduct; I knew what I aimed at and what I wanted, but knew nothing how to pursue the end by direct means. I wanted to be placed in a settled state of living, and had I happened to meet with a sober, good husband, I should have been as faithful and true a wife to him as virtue itself could have formed. If I had been otherwise, the vice came in always at the door of necessity, not at the door of inclination; and I understood too well, by the want of it, what the value of a settled life was, to do anything to forfeit the felicity of it.

But if security is the end of life, ingenuity, clever personal enterprise, is its most admirable quality, and, certainly, the only way to security:

I have observed that the account of his life would have made a much more pleasing history than this of mine; and, indeed, nothing in it was more strange than this part, viz. that he had carried on that desperate trade full five-and-twenty years and had never been taken, the success he had met with had been so very uncommon, and such that sometimes he had lived handsomely, and retired in one place for a year or two at a time, keeping himself and a manservant to wait on him, and had often sat in the coffee-houses and heard the very people whom he had robbed give accounts of their being robbed, and of the places and circumstances, so that he could easily remember that it was the same.

Strip *Moll Flanders* of its bland loquacity, its comic excess, its excitement, and we have the revelation of a savage life, a life that is motivated solely by economic need, and a life that is measured at last by those creature comforts that, if we gain them, allow us one final breath in which to praise the Lord. Yet this essence is not the book as we have it, as Defoe wrote it, any more than the acquisitive impulse is the whole of middle-class value. For there is also the secondary interest of the book, which is to reveal to us the condition of women, the small choice (there was only her needle; to be sure, there *was* her needle had she preferred it; but who would ask that she should have?)—the small choice that Moll could have made between disreputable and reputable employment. The infant Moll, born in Newgate, becomes a public charge; education is an impossibility; independent work is likewise an impossibility; and as young men are by nature wolves, so the world at large is wolfish. Women, like men, are forced into the realm of trade, they offer such goods as they have for such prices as they can command.

This secondary interest suggests the softer side of Daniel Defoe, his will to create a less savage world than the world he knew. The paradox of the middle class has always been its hope to create, through its values of mere measurement, values that did not have to measure in its way. And the social pathos of *our* lives is largely to be traced to our illusion that we have done so. This is also the final pathos of Moll Flanders' life, whether Defoe was aware of it or not.

Sympathy exceeds awareness, and throughout *Moll Flanders* (this is probably the main reason that we continue to read it) we are charged by the author's sympathy. It shows as much in the gusto with which he enters Moll's life and participates in her adventures as it does in his tolerance of her errors and her deceits and self-deceits. It shows, furthermore, in a few moments of this vastly episodic narrative when genuinely novelistic values emerge, when, that is, the individual character somehow shines through the social automaton. One such moment occurs when Moll is reunited with her Lancashire husband:

> As soon as he was gone, and I had shut the door, I threw off my hood, and bursting out into tears, "My dear," says I, "do you not know me?" He turned pale, and stood speechless, like one thunderstruck, and, not able to conquer the surprise, said no more but this, "Let me sit down"; and sitting down by a table, he laid his elbow upon the table, and leaning his head on his hand, fixed his eyes on the ground as one stupid. I cried so vehemently, on the other hand, that it was a good while ere I could speak any more; but after I had given some vent to my passion by tears, I repeated the same words, "My dear, do you not know me?" At which he answered, Yes, and said no more a good while.

Such genuinely moving scenes must be observed, of course, against the long stretches of the book where the relentless narrative sense points up the totally deficient sense of plot, where the carelessness of

time and causality destroys the illusion of actuality after all the pains
to achieve it, where the monotonously summarizing method gives
even the fine feeling for separate incident a pallor. These deficiencies
all remind us that this is not, after all, the first English novel.

Yet it is very nearly the first English novel. It is the whole ground-
work. Given twenty more years of literary convention and just a
slightly different set of interests, Defoe would have freed himself from
the tyranny of fact and the morality of circumstance and sprung into
the liberties of formal fiction, where another morality must prevail.
His prose has been called "the prose of democracy," and this has been
the characteristic prose of the novel as we know it in English. The
prose of democracy is a prose without rhetorical refinement even when
it employs rhetorical display; it emerges in sentences as sinewy and
emphatically plain as this: "In short, they robbed together, lay together,
were taken together, and at last were hanged together." It is also a
prose capable of fine, colloquial surprise:

> I made him one present, and it was all I had of value, and that
> was one of the gold watches, of which I mentioned above, that I
> had two in my chest, and this I happened to have with me, and
> I gave it him at his third visit. I told him I had nothing of any
> value to bestow but that, and I desired he would now and then
> kiss it for my sake. I did not indeed tell him that I had stole
> it from a gentlewoman's side, at a meeting-house in London.
> That's by the way.

Such prose projects us into the future of the novel: Jane Austen,
George Eliot, Mark Twain, D. H. Lawrence, Ernest Hemingway.

Yet not entirely. "That's by the way," says Moll; and then comes the
voice of Defoe, saying, too, "Yes, that's by the way." He does not, finally,
judge his material, as a novelist must. He makes us sort out his multiple
materials for him and pass our judgment. Our judgment must therefore fall on him, not on his creature, Moll. In her bland, self-deluded
way, she asks us not to be harsh; and that again is the voice of Defoe,
taking a breath at the end to beg posterity to be kind. As it has been.

MUCH ADO ABOUT NOTHING
(WILLIAM SHAKESPEARE)

"Much Ado About Nothing"
by Charles Cowden Clarke,
in *Shakespeare Characters:*
Chiefly Those Subordinate (1863)

INTRODUCTION

In his extensive 1863 study of Shakespeare's plays, Charles
Cowden Clarke praises the wit, charm, and moral temperament of Beatrice in *Much Ado About Nothing*. As for the
"merry war" between Beatrice and Benedick, however,
Clarke argues that their relationship lacks passion, being
another example "of the ninety-nine hundredths of the
marriages that take place in society, and which are the
result of friendly concoction." Finally, Clarke asserts that by
portraying Beatrice and his other female heroines as intellectually equal to men, Shakespeare had a positive "intellectual influence" on the gender prejudices of his time.

Clarke, Charles Cowden. "Much Ado About Nothing." *Shakespeare Characters;*
Chiefly Those Subordinate. London: Smith, Elder, & Co., 1863. pp. 295–316.

I never knew any one object to the nature and conduct of Beatrice in "Much Ado About Nothing," who was not either dull in faculty, ill-tempered, or an overweening assertor of the exclusive privileges of the male sex.

The late Thomas Campbell, in an edition of the poet, denounces her as "an odious woman." I never saw Mr Campbell, and knew nothing of him personally; I can say nothing, therefore, of his temper, or of his jealousy as regards the privileges claimed by the stronger party in the human world; and most certain am I that he was not a man of "*dull* faculty," for I do know his intellectual character. But I should be inclined to draw a conclusion from the epithet used by that elegant poet and cultivated scholar, that he was a man subject to strong impulses, and to a high degree of nervous irritability; and that he had risen from his task of editing this enchanting play, annoyed and excited by the sparring between Beatrice and Benedick, in which word-encounters she certainly is no "light weight" to him; but to call her "odious" was an injudicious comment, and only true as regards his own individual temperament and feelings. In the general estimation of the world, Beatrice is one of those who wear their characters inside out. They have no reserves with society, for they require none. They may, perhaps, presume upon, or rather forget that they possess a mercurial temperament, which, when unreined, is apt to start from its course and inconvenience their fellow-travellers; but such a propensity is not an "odious" one—it is not hateful; and this is the only feature in the character of Beatrice that Mr Campbell could object to. She is warm-hearted, generous; has a noble contempt of baseness of every kind; is wholly untinctured with jealousy; is the first to break out into invective when her cousin Hero is treated in that scoundrel manner by her affianced husband at the very altar, and even makes it a *sine quâ non* with Benedick to prove his love for herself by challenging the traducer of her cousin.

This last fact, by the way, leads to a natural digression when speaking of the career of Beatrice; and that is, that the very circumstance of her embroiling her lover in a duel for another person is of itself a proof that the *sensual* passion of love had no predominant share in her choice of Benedick for a husband; and in this insignificant— apparently insignificant—but momentous point of conduct, we again, and for the thousandth time, recognise Shakespeare's unsleeping sense of propriety in character. A woman, personally and passionately in love, has been known to involve her lover where her own self-love has been compromised; and even then I should question the quality of the passion; that, however strong it might be, it was weaker than her own self-worship; for the sterling passion of love, by the law of nature, is all-absorbing, all-engrossing, and admits no equal near the throne. But no woman, so enamoured, would place her lover's life in jeopardy for a third party; and this leads me to retrace my position and observe, that the union of Beatrice and Benedick was only a "counterfeit presentment" of ninety-nine hundredths of the marriages that take place in society, and which are the result of friendly concoction. There was no "love," no sexual love, between Benedick and Beatrice; but the self-love of each being fanned into a flame from hearing, through the plot of their friends, that they were mutually, though unknowingly, an object of attachment to each other,—this "self-love," with an emotion of gratitude, exalted their reciprocal respect into the conventional love of every-day society; but there was not a spark of passion in the whole affair. The very discovery that each is an object of supposed interest with the other produces not one word in avowal of passion; and here again Shakespeare is on his guard; and in how masterly a manner has he sustained the several characteristic peculiarities of the two individuals upon that discovery. Beatrice, with her lively demonstrativeness of nature, rushes from the arbour after hearing the conversation of Hero and Ursula respecting her being the object of Benedick's affection. She has fallen into the trap they have laid for her, and she exclaims:—

> "What fire is in mine ears? Can this be true?
> Stand I condemn'd for pride and scorn so much?
> Contempt, farewell; and maiden pride, adieu!
> No glory lives behind the back of such.
> And, Benedick, love on: I will requite thee;
> Taming my wild heart to thy loving hand.
> If thou dost love, my kindness shall incite thee
> To bind our loves up in a holy band."

There is no avowal of passion, methinks, in that speech. It is merely an acquiescent one,—"If thou *dost* love, my *kindness* shall incite thee" to tie the knot. On the other hand, Benedick, being a man of the world, a soldier, too, and not wholly a child to stratagems, comes forward sedately questioning the dialogue respecting himself and Beatrice, between Don Pedro, Claudio, and old Leonato. To give full force to the doubt and caution of Benedick, and at the same time to enrich the plausibility of the plot against him, he would have suspected his young companions, but old Leonato being of the party staggers him. He says to himself, "I should think this a gull, but that the white-bearded fellow speaks it; knavery cannot sure hide himself in such reverence." And never was soliloquy more naturally penned than his communing with himself upon the dialogue he had just heard:—

> "This can be no trick; the conference was sadly borne. [That is, sedately, seriously borne.] They have the truth of this from Hero. They seem to pity the lady. It seems her affections have the full bent. Love me! why, it must be requited. I hear how I am censured; they say I will bear myself proudly if I perceive the love come from her. They say, too, that she will rather die than give any sign of affection. *I did never think to marry.* I mustn't seem proud. Happy are they that can hear their detractions and put them to mending. They say the lady is fair: 'tis a truth, I can bear them witness;—and virtuous; 'tis so, I cannot reprove it: and wise, but for loving me! by my troth, 'tis no addition to her wit; nor no great argument of her folly; for I will be horribly in love with her. I may chance to have some odd quirks and remnants of wit broken on me, because I have railed so long against marriage; but doth not the appetite alter? A man loves the meat in his youth that he cannot endure in his age. Shall quips and sentences, and these paper bullets of the brain, awe a man from the career of his humour? No! The world must be peopled. When I said I would die a bachelor, I did not think I should live till I were married."

Will any one say that there is any expression of love in its exclusiveness in that speech?

I would devote a few more words upon the two characters of Benedick and Beatrice, and principally upon the latter, who is one of our favourites among the heroines in Shakespeare.

Beatrice is not without consciousness of her power of wit; but it is rather the delight that she takes in something that is an effluence of her own glad nature, than for any pride of display. She enjoys its exercise, too, as a means of playful despotism over one whom she secretly admires, while openly tormenting. Her first inquiries after Benedick show the sort of interest she takes in him; and it is none the less for its being veiled by a scoffing style; while what she says of their mutual wit-encounters proves the glory she has in out-taunting him. When her uncle observes to the Messenger, in reply to one of her sarcasms, "There is a kind of merry war betwixt Signior Benedick and her; they never meet, but there is a skirmish of wit between them;" she replies—

> "Alas! he gets nothing by that. In our last conflict four of his five wits went halting off, and now the whole man is governed by one; so that if he have wit enough to keep himself warm, let him bear it for a difference between himself and his horse; for it is all the wealth he hath left to be known for a reasonable creature."

She is suspiciously anxious to point her disdain of him; for when the Messenger remarks,—"I see, lady, the gentleman is not in your books;" she retorts, "No; an he were, I would burn my study." Her native hilarity of heart is evidenced constantly, and in the most attractive manner; for it serves to make the blaze of her intellect show itself as originating in a secret blitheness of temperament. The prince, Don Pedro, says,—"In faith, lady, you have a merry heart;" to which she replies,—"Yea, my lord, I thank it, poor fool, it keeps on the windy side of care." And when, following this up by some smart banter, she gracefully checks herself,—"But I beseech your grace, pardon me; I was born to speak all mirth and no matter:" he rejoins—"Your silence most offends me; and to be merry best becomes you; for out of question you were born in a merry hour." Whereto she answers, "No, sure, my lord, my mother cried; but then there was a star danced, and under that was I born." Well may the prince remark after she has gone out, "By my troth, a pleasant-spirited lady!" To which her uncle, Leonato, replies:—

> "There's little of the melancholy element in her, my lord; she is never sad but when she sleeps; and not ever sad then;

for I have heard my daughter say she hath often dreamed of
unhappiness, and waked herself with laughing."

The fact, is, like many high-spirited women, Beatrice possesses a
fund of hidden tenderness beneath her exterior gaiety and sarcasm,—
none the less profound from being withheld from casual view, and very
seldom allowed to bewray itself. As proofs of this, witness her affection
for her uncle, Leonato, and his strong esteem and love for her,—her
passionate attachment to her cousin Hero, and the occasional, but
extremely significant, betrayals of her partiality for Benedick; her very
seeking out opportunities to torment him being one proof (especially in
a woman of her disposition and breeding) of her preference; for women
do not banter a man they dislike,—they mentally send him to Coventry,
and do not lift him into importance, by offering an objection, still less a
repartee, or a sarcasm. The only time we see Beatrice alone, and giving
utterance to the thoughts of her heart,—that is, in soliloquy, which
is the dramatic medium of representing self-communion—(already
quoted)—her words are full of warm and feminine tenderness,—words
that probably would not seem so pregnant of love-import, coming from
another woman, more prone to express such feeling; but, from Beatrice,
meaning much. It is the very transcript of an honest and candid heart.
Then the poet has given her so potent an antagonist in her wit-fencing,
that her skill is saved from being thought unbefitting. Benedick's wit is
so polished, so manly, so competent, that her womanhood is spared the
disgrace of bearing away the palm in their keen encounters. He always
remains victor; for we feel that he voluntarily refrains from claiming
the conquest he achieves; and he is ever master of the field, though his
chivalrous gallantry chooses to leave her in possession of the ground—
that "ground" so dear to female heart, "the last word." Benedick is a
perfect gentleman, and his wit partakes of his nature; it is forbearing in
proportion to its excellence. One of the causes which render Benedick's
wit more delightful than that of Beatrice, is, that it *knows when to cease*.
Like a true woman, (don't "condemn me to everlasting redemption,"
ladies!) Beatrice is apt to pursue her advantage, when she feels she has
one, to the very utmost. She does not give her antagonist a chance;
and if she could upset him, she would pink him when he was down:
now, Benedick, with the generosity of superior strength, gives way first.
His mode at the last of checking her mettlesome wit, when he finds it
again about to curvet unseasonably against him, is worthy of Benedick's

manly spirit. It is a gallant rebuke; at once gentle and conclusive, it is the most effectual, as it is the most fit, close that he could put to the lady's arch pertinacity. At the close of the drama, when they all come in masked, and the scene of Claudio's second betrothal takes place, Benedick comes forward, saying—

"Soft and fair, Friar.—Which is Beatrice?
"*Beat.* [*Unmasking.*] I answer to that name. What is your will?
"*Bene.* Do not you love me?
"*Beat.* No; no more than reason.
"*Bene.* Why, then, your uncle, and the prince, and Claudio, have been deceived; for they swore you did.
"*Beat.* Do not you love me?
"*Bene.* No; no more than reason.
"*Beat.* Why, then, my cousin, Margaret, and Ursula, are much deceived; for they did swear you did.
"*Bene.* They swore that you were almost sick for me.
"*Beat.* They swore that you were well-nigh dead for me.
"*Bene.* 'Tis no such matter. Then you do not love me?
"*Beat.* No, truly; but in friendly recompence.
"*Leonato.* Come, cousin; I am sure you love the gentleman.
"*Claud.* And I'll be sworn upon it he loves her; for here's a paper written in his hand,—a halting sonnet of his own pure brain, fashioned to Beatrice.
"*Hero.* And here's another, writ in my cousin's hand, stolen from her pocket, containing her affection unto Benedick.
"*Bene.* A miracle! here's our own hands against our hearts! Come, I will have thee; but, by this light, I take thee for pity.
"*Beat.* I would not marry you; but, by this good day, I yield upon great persuasion, and partly to save your life; for I was told you were in a consumption.
"*Bene.* Peace! I will stop your mouth."—[Which he does, with a kiss.]

One of Beatrice's best pieces of wit is her reply to her uncle's wish:—

"Well, niece; I hope to see you one day fitted with a husband.

"*Beat.* Not till God make men of some other metal than earth. Would it not grieve a woman to be over-mastered with a piece of valiant dust? To make an account of her life to a clod of wayward marle? No, uncle, I'll none: Adam's sons are my brethren; and truly I hold it a sin to match in my kindred."

One of Benedick's pleasantest as well as wittiest speeches is that wherein he complains of Beatrice's maltreatment at the masquerade. It is the only time when he seems to be earnestly irritated with her; and no wonder. He says of her behaviour—

"Oh! she misused me past the endurance of a block; an oak, with but one green leaf upon it, would have answered her. My very vizor began to assure life, and scold with her. She told me (not thinking I had been myself) that I was the prince's jester, that I was duller than a great thaw, huddling jest upon jest, with such impossible conveyance upon me, that I stood like a man at a mark, with a whole army shooting at me.".... "I would not marry her though she were endowed with all that Adam had left before he transgressed."

Benedick, being a man of acknowledged wit, as well as of a blithe temperament, has no fancy to be considered a jester,—a professed "jester." His brilliant faculties render him a favourite associate of the prince; but his various higher qualities, as a gentleman and a scholar, give him better claims to liking than those of a gay companion only. It is this that makes Beatrice's calling him the "prince's jester" so intolerable a gibe. She knew it, the hussy! with her woman's shrewdness in finding out precisely what will most gall the man she prefers; and he shows that it touches him to the quick, by reverting to it in soliloquy, and repeating it again to his friends when they come in. A man of lively humour who is excited by his native gaiety of heart to entertain his friends by his pleasantry, at the same time feeling within himself that he possesses yet stronger and worthier grounds for their partiality, has a peculiarly sensitive dread of being taken for a mere jester or buffoon. Benedick's buoyancy of spirit is no effect of levity or frivolity. His humour has depth of feeling as well as mirth in it. His wit has force and geniality, no less than intellectual vivacity. That little sentence, with all its sportive ease, is instinct with moral sound sense—"Happy are they that hear their detractions and can put them to mending." Benedick's wit has penetration and discernment in it. With all his mercurial temperament, too, yet in a grave question this fine character can deliver himself with gravity and a noble sedateness; as where he says, "In a false quarrel there is no true valour." And throughout the challenge-scene he expresses himself with gentlemanly dignity and manly feeling; while we find, from the remarks of the prince upon his change of colour, that he is as deeply hurt as he has temperately spoken. He characterises his own wit, in its gentleness and gallantry towards women, when he says to Beatrice's attendant, "A most manly wit, Margaret; it will not hurt a woman." There is heart in Benedick's playfulness. His love-making, when he is love-taken, is as earnest as it is animated. That is a fine and fervent bit of his wooing-scene with Beatrice, where she asks him if he will go with her to her uncle Leonato's to hear the news, he answers, "I will live in thy heart, die in thy lap, and be buried in thine eyes; and moreover, I will go with thee to thy uncle's." Shakespeare has, with lustrous perfection, vindicated the sound sense and sweet heart that may accompany wit, in the character of Benedick. And after having discussed the mental sparrings and fit-fayings of the two creatures, turn to their first wooing, and see them each displayed to the best advantage—Beatrice, certainly; who in the course of it shows one of those genuine touches of womanly feeling that have been alluded to as redeeming her character from the unfounded as well as ungracious charge of unfeminine hardness. Here is the pith of the scene. When she and Benedick are left alone in the chapel,—the rest of the company having quitted it, after the public shame and scandal heaped upon poor Hero by the mean-spirited Claudio,—Benedick approaches his lady, saying:—

"Lady Beatrice, have you wept all this while?

"*Beat.* Yea, and shall weep a while longer.

"*Bene.* I will not desire that.

"*Beat.* You have no reason; I do it freely.

"*Bene.* Surely, I do believe your fair cousin is wronged.

"*Beat.* Ah, how much that man might deserve of me that would right her!

"*Bene.* Is there any way to show such friendship?

"*Beat.* A very even way, but no such friend.

"*Bene.* May a man do it?

"*Beat.* It is a man's office; *but not yours.*

"*Bene.* I do love nothing in the world so well as you; is not that strange?

"*Beat.* As strange as the thing I know not. It were as possible for me to say, I loved nothing so well as you; but believe me not,—and yet I lie not; I confess nothing, nor I deny nothing. *I am sorry for my cousin.*

"*Bene.* By my sword, Beatrice, thou lovest me.

"*Beat.* Do not swear by it, and eat it.

"*Bene.* I will swear by it that you love me; and I will make him eat it that says I love not you.

"*Beat.* Will you not eat your word?

"*Bene.* With no sauce that can be devised to it. I protest I love thee.

"*Beat.* Why, then,—God forgive me!

"*Bene.* What offence, sweet Beatrice?

"*Beat.* You have staid me in a happy hour; I was about to protest I loved you.

"*Bene.* And do it with all thy heart.

"*Beat.* I love you with so much of my heart, that none is left to protest."

I am mistaken in my taste of true wit and of true feeling if there be not a charming display of both in this very natural, very easy, and very graceful little scene. I wished to urge some extenuation in behalf of Beatrice, because it is not unusual to designate her (as well as Portia) as a "masculine woman." I can only say that every man who expresses this opinion commits a piece of egoism, for both women are endowed with qualities, moral and intellectual, that any man might be proud to inherit. And here again, it is impossible to forego a passing remark upon the generous, indeed, the chivalrous conduct of Shakespeare in portraying his heroines. Of all the writers that ever existed, no one ought to stand so high in the love and gratitude of women as he. He has indeed been their champion, their laureate, their brother, their friend. He has been the man to lift them from a state of vassalage and degradation, wherein they were the mere toys, when not the she-serfs, of a sensual tyranny; and he has asserted their prerogative, as

intellectual creatures, to be the companions (in the best sense), the
advisers, the friends, the equals of men. He has endowed them with
the true spirit of Christianity and brotherly love, "enduring all things,
forgiving all things, hoping all things;" and it is no less remarkable,
that with a prodigality of generosity, he has not unfrequently placed
the heroes in his stories at a disadvantage with them. Observe, for
instance, the two characters of Hero and Claudio in this very play.
She is the absolute perfection of sweetness and generosity, quenching
in forgiveness all the injuries she has received, and bestowing her
heart and confidence where she had every reason to be mistrustful.
Claudio, on the other hand, is a selfish manœuvrer. He tells the prince
that he is in love with Hero, but he opens the conversation about her
by inquiring of him whether Signor Leonato *has a son*; he had an
eye to the cash first, and then the girl, and the circumstance of her
being an only child confirms him in his suit. Claudio is a fellow of
no nobleness of character, for instead of being the last, he is the first
to believe his mistress guilty of infidelity towards him, and he then
adopts the basest and the most brutal mode of punishment by casting
her off at the very altar. Genuine love is incapable of revenge of any
sort, that I assume to be a truism, still less of a concocted and refined
revenge. Claudio is a scoundrel in grain. This question is too ample to
be discussed upon this occasion; but I would merely quote in confirmation of my remark, the characters of Bertram in "All's Well that
Ends Well," of Posthumus Leonatus in "Cymbeline," of Leontes in
"The Winter's Tale," of Othello, (who, indeed, advances much claim
upon our extenuation, and even commiseration, for he was of a noble
nature,) and, lastly, of Proteus in "The Two Gentlemen of Verona."
All these characters appear not only at a disadvantage by, but they are
unworthy of the women with whom they are consorted. Shakespeare
has himself put into the mouth of a man this honest confession. The
Duke in "Twelfth Night" says—

> "However we do praise ourselves,
> Our fancies are more giddy and infirm,
> More longing, wav'ring, sooner lost and worn
> Than women's are."

Again, therefore, Shakespeare is the writer of all others whom
the women should most take to their hearts; for I believe it to be

mainly through his intellectual influence that their claims in the scale of society were acknowledged in England, when, throughout what is denominated the civilised world, their position was not greatly elevated above that of the drudges in modern low life. And have not both parties been gainers by the reformation?—not but that much yet remains to be modified—nevertheless, the moral philosophy of Shakespeare, anticipated by another code, which I am perfectly sure he would have been the first to recognise and avow, has exalted our social system beyond that of the rest of the world.

OEDIPUS REX
(SOPHOCLES)

"The Material and Sources of Dreams"
by Sigmund Freud,
in *The Interpretation of Dreams* (1913)

INTRODUCTION

In this famous passage from *The Interpretation of Dreams*, Sigmund Freud develops his idea of one of the early stages of development in young children, a stage now commonly known (especially among Freudian psychoanalysts and literary scholars) as the "Oedipus complex." According to Freud, adolescents often experience sexual desire for the parent of the opposite sex while also wishing for the death of the parent of the same sex as part of their development from child to adult. Here Freud argues that the Oedipus complex is demonstrated in Sophocles's play *Oedipus Tyrannus*, in which the protagonist, Oedipus, both kills his father and marries his mother.

According to my experience, which is now large, parents play a leading part in the infantile psychology of all later neurotics, and

---

Freud, Sigmund. "The Material and Sources of Dreams." *The Interpretation of Dreams*. Trans. A.A. Brill. New York: Macmillan, 1913. pp. 138–259.

falling in love with one member of the parental couple and hatred of the other help to make up that fateful sum of material furnished by the psychic impulses, which has been formed during the infantile period, and which is of such great importance for the symptoms appearing in the later neurosis. But I do not think that psychoneurotics are here sharply distinguished from normal human beings, in that they are capable of creating something absolutely new and peculiar to themselves. It is far more probable, as is shown also by occasional observation upon normal children, that in their loving or hostile wishes towards their parents psychoneurotics only show in exaggerated form feelings which are present less distinctly and less intensely in the minds of most children. Antiquity has furnished us with legendary material to confirm this fact, and the deep and universal effectiveness of these legends can only be explained by granting a similar universal applicability to the above-mentioned assumption in infantile psychology.

I refer to the legend of King Oedipus and the drama of the same name by Sophocles. Oedipus, the son of Laius, king of Thebes, and of Jocasta, is exposed while a suckling, because an oracle has informed the father that his son, who is still unborn, will be his murderer. He is rescued, and grows up as the king's son at a foreign court, until, being uncertain about his origin, he also consults the oracle, and is advised to avoid his native place, for he is destined to become the murderer of his father and the husband of his mother. On the road leading away from his supposed home he meets King Laius and strikes him dead in a sudden quarrel. Then he comes to the gates of Thebes, where he solves the riddle of the Sphinx who is barring the way, and he is elected king by the Thebans in gratitude, and is presented with the hand of Jocasta. He reigns in peace and honour for a long time, and begets two sons and two daughters upon his unknown mother, until at last a plague breaks out which causes the Thebans to consult the oracle anew. Here Sophocles' tragedy begins. The messengers bring the advice that the plague will stop as soon as the murderer of Laius is driven from the country. But where is he hidden?

"Where are they to be found? How shall we trace the perpetrators of so old a crime where no conjecture leads to discovery?"[1]

The action of the play now consists merely in a revelation, which is gradually completed and artfully delayed—resembling the work of a psychoanalysis—of the fact that Oedipus himself is the murderer of Laius, and the son of the dead man and of Jocasta. Oedipus, profoundly shocked at the monstrosities which he has unknowingly committed, blinds himself and leaves his native place. The oracle has been fulfilled.

The *Oedipus Tyrannus* is a so-called tragedy of fate; its tragic effect is said to be found in the opposition between the powerful will of the gods and the vain resistance of the human beings who are threatened with destruction; resignation to the will of God and confession of one's own helplessness is the lesson which the deeply-moved spectator is to learn from the tragedy. Consequently modern authors have tried to obtain a similar tragic effect by embodying the same opposition in a story of their own invention. But spectators have sat unmoved while a curse or an oracular sentence has been fulfilled on blameless human beings in spite of all their struggles; later tragedies of fate have all remained without effect.

If the *Oedipus Tyrannus* is capable of moving modern men no less than it moved the contemporary Greeks, the explanation of this fact cannot lie merely in the assumption that the effect of the Greek tragedy is based upon the opposition between fate and human will, but is to be sought in the peculiar nature of the material by which the opposition is shown. There must be a voice within us which is prepared to recognise the compelling power of fate in *Oedipus*, while we justly condemn the situations occurring in *Die Ahnfrau* or in other tragedies of later date as arbitrary inventions. And there must be a factor corresponding to this inner voice in the story of King Oedipus. His fate moves us only for the reason that it might have been ours, for the oracle has put the same curse upon us before our birth as upon him. Perhaps we are all destined to direct our first sexual impulses towards our mothers, and our first hatred and violent wishes towards our fathers; our dreams convince us of it. King Oedipus, who has struck his father Laius dead and has married his mother Jocasta, is nothing but the realised wish of our childhood. But more fortunate than he, we have since succeeded, unless we have become psychoneurotics, in withdrawing our sexual impulses from our mothers and in forgetting our jealousy of our fathers. We recoil from the person for whom this primitive wish has been fulfilled with all the force of the repression which these wishes have suffered within us. By his analysis, showing us the guilt of Oedipus, the poet urges us to recognise our own inner self, in which these impulses, even if suppressed, are still present. The comparison with which the chorus leaves us—

> "... Behold! this Oedipus, who unravelled the famous riddle and who was a man of eminent virtue; a man who trusted neither to popularity nor to the fortune of his citizens; see how great a storm of adversity hath at last overtaken him" (Act v. sc. 4).

This warning applies to ourselves and to our pride, to us, who have grown so wise and so powerful in our own estimation since the years of our childhood. Like Oedipus, we live in ignorance of the wishes that offend morality, wishes which nature has forced upon us, and after the revelation of which we want to avert every glance from the scenes of our childhood.

In the very text of Sophocles' tragedy there is an unmistakable reference to the fact that the Oedipus legend originates in an extremely old dream material, which consists of the painful disturbance of the relation towards one's parents by means of the first impulses of sexuality. Jocasta comforts Oedipus—who is not yet enlightened, but who has become worried on account of the oracle—by mentioning to him the dream which is dreamt by so many people, though she attaches no significance to it—

> "For it hath already been the lot of many men in dreams to think themselves partners of their mother's bed. But he passes most easily through life to whom these circumstances are trifles" (Act iv. sc. 3).

The dream of having sexual intercourse with one's mother occurred at that time, as it does to-day, to many people, who tell it with indignation and astonishment. As may be understood, it is the key to the tragedy and the complement to the dream of the death of the father. The story of Oedipus is the reaction of the imagination to these two typical dreams, and just as the dream when occurring to an adult is experienced with feelings of resistance, so the legend must contain terror and self-chastisement. The appearance which it further assumes is the result of an uncomprehending secondary elaboration which tries to make it serve theological purposes. The attempt to reconcile divine omnipotence with human responsibility must, of course, fail with this material as with every other.

NOTE

1. Act i. sc. 2. Translated by George Somers Clark.

A PORTRAIT OF THE ARTIST AS A YOUNG MAN
(JAMES JOYCE)

"Joyce's Epiphanic Mode:
Material Language and the Representation
of Sexuality in *Stephen Hero* and *Portrait*"
by Joshua Jacobs,
in *Twentieth Century Literature* (2000)

INTRODUCTION

Joshua Jacobs examines the sexual language surrounding Stephen Dedalus's "epiphanies" in *A Portrait of the Artist as a Young Man*. By comparing passages from *Portrait* with their prior incarnations in Joyce's manuscript fragments and the unpublished novel *Stephen Hero* (in which Stephen Dedalus is also the protagonist), Jacobs argues that Joyce deliberately and insightfully employs highly sexual language and imagery. Far from simply showing Joyce to be a misogynist, according to Jacobs, the sexual elements of the book actually reveal a complex understanding of language and human sexuality. Stephen's use of language in his erotically charged dreams, fantasies, and epiphanies form both the novel's greatness and its ironical nature. The language in the novel is spoken

---

Jacobs, Joshua. "Joyce's Epiphanic Mode: Material Language and the Representation of Sexuality in *Stephen Hero* and *Portrait*." *Twentieth Century Literature*, Vol. 46, No. 1 (Spring 2000): 20–33.

from the perspective not of a misogynist but of an aspiring
aesthete who attempts to overcome the typical proclivities
we associate with juvenilia: lust, desire, and the ever-present
preoccupation with human sexuality.

⁓

James Joyce's transformations of themes, language, and characters
from one of his own works to another have long been among the
signal preoccupations of Joyce's readers. The manuscript fragments
known as epiphanies, written in the years 1900 to 1903, are the
earliest sources of specific scenes and more general interests which
we can see Joyce draw upon in all his longer works of fiction.[1]
While Joyce's theorization and use of epiphany from *Stephen Hero*
onward have been central to many readers' understandings of his
work as a whole, the connection of this general aspect of Joyce's
work to the specific records of scenes and interactions represented
in the epiphany manuscripts has been of secondary interest. Perhaps
remembering (with some embarrassment) along with Stephen in
Ulysses his "epiphanies written on green oval leaves, deeply deep,
copies to be sent if [he] died to all the great libraries of the world,
including Alexandria" (3.141–42), Joyce's readers have not often
given serious attention to the ways in which his mature works use
the material first developed in these fragments.

The most common critical approach to the epiphany fragments
has been to examine their themes and Dublin locations and to
suggest specific places in Joyce's later fiction in which these epiphanic
elements are deployed. But this focus on the epiphanies as sources
for the later works can obscure the particular workings of language
in the epiphanies and in Joyce's earliest integrations of epiphanic
material into his fiction. The linguistic contexts of these early uses of
the epiphanies—from the passage in *Stephen Hero* in which Stephen
first defines epiphanies, through scenes of Stephen's intense sexual or
artistic feeling in *Portrait*—have a significance beyond their possible
prefiguration of Joyce's later fiction. These moments where Stephen
theorizes epiphanies or experiences overpowering feelings are not, for
the most part, straightforward recyclings of Joyce's original epiphanies;
however, in these passages Joyce's language echoes Stephen's initial

encounter with an epiphanic scene in order to focus the tensions between Stephen's attempts at rigid self-definition and Joyce's more ambiguous constructions of selfhood.

What is chiefly at stake in these climactic passages is Stephen's alternating mastery and helplessness before his nascent sexuality and the extent to which he can define his intellectual and physical self as discrete from his context. Though Stephen tries to assert an intellectual source for his own language, the language Joyce uses to convey Stephen's assertions is insistently grounded in the corporeal and in several characteristic tropes such as murmuring, which stress the material nature of language itself. This dispersion of the source and nature of language beyond the confines of a discrete, fully cognizant agent undermines Stephen's attempts to assert such an agency for himself. By staging the materiality of language and the diffusion of the self within the context of Stephen's sexual crises, Joyce also links Stephen with the corporeality and diffusion of sexuality more firmly than can Stephen's hyperbolic denials or embracings of his sexuality.

I shall argue that, more than merely constituting a progression in theme between the epiphanies and climactic passages in *Portrait*, these moments and the defining passage in *Stephen Hero* are linked by their framing in language this tension between Joyce's and Stephen's constructions of self and sexuality. Because of this continuity of evocative language across distinct climactic moments, we can address this mode of language as a particular force and isolate its specificity and power. I use the term "epiphanic mode" in this essay to refer to this general practice of representing Stephen's nascent selfhood and sexuality, which Joyce develops first in the *Stephen Hero* passage—with its particular tension between the epiphanic text and Stephen's theorization of epiphanies—and then expands in his rendering of Stephen's emotional climaxes in *Portrait*, which have varying connections to the epiphany fragments.

The first explicitly noted example of an epiphany that appears in Joyce's fiction—the "Ballast Office clock" passage of *Stephen Hero*—is a revealing demonstration of Joyce's development from fairly straightforward use of material from the manuscript epiphanies toward the more general practice, or "epiphanic mode," seen in *Portrait*. In the central moment of the relevant sequence in *Stephen Hero*, Stephen overhears a conversation, and is struck by a subsequent artistic imperative:

> The Young Lady—(drawling discreetly) ... O, yes ... I was ... at the ... cha ... pel ...
> The Young Gentleman—(inaudibly) ... I ... (again inaudibly) ... I ...
> The Young Lady—(softly) ... O ... but you're ... ve ... ry ... wick ... ed ...
>
> This triviality made him think of collecting many such moments together in a book of epiphanies. By an epiphany he meant a sudden spiritual manifestation, whether in the vulgarity of speech or of gesture or in a memorable phrase of the mind itself. He believed that it was for the man of letters to record these epiphanies with extreme care, seeing that they themselves are the most delicate and evanescent of moments (211).

Stephen goes on to describe to his friend Cranly his theory of epiphanies, in an early version of his statements on aesthetics in *Portrait* (204–15). Given that in *Portrait* the event of the epiphany itself is removed from the theorization that had been linked to it in *Stephen Hero*, it is not so surprising that much of the critical dialogue has focused on the implications of Stephen's aesthetic critique and how it changes from the earlier work to the later. But the initial framing of this theory in uneasy juxtaposition with a scene of "triviality," and Stephen's description of the "collecting" process as something separate from these scenes as such, suggests that we should avoid mimicking Stephen's attempts to distance the office of the "man of letters" from the events and language of these moments. A closer look at the exemplary epiphany shows that Stephen's self-assured argument for clarity is in fact a reaction against an unsettling multiplicity of language and sexuality.

The epiphany section of *Stephen Hero* begins with Stephen infuriated by his mother's religiosity, an anger that is quickly refocused on Emma Clery. Stephen is frustrated by his inability to fully criticize or ignore her: "In every stray image on the streets he saw her soul manifest itself and every such manifestation renewed the intensity of his disapproval" (210). The narration, explicit in criticizing Stephen in a way the *Portrait* narration is not, then somewhat mockingly relates

Stephen's proposed "theory of dualism which would symbolize the twin eternities of spirit and nature in the twin eternities of male and female." Thus Stephen's nascent desire to stabilize identity provides the background for the epiphanic encounter itself, which defines a correspondence between fragmented, stylized speech and the sexuality that pervades its utterance.

With these structuring factors in mind, Stephen's theoretical attention to the fixed relation of parts to the whole object (or *claritas*; see *Stephen Hero* 213) seems much more a practical attempt at control than an abstract paradigm. The free play and agency of "parts"—parts of the body and the soul within the body—will pervade the representation of Stephen's artistic and personal development in *Portrait*; here we can see this diffusion of discrete identity in the manifestation of Emma's soul in "every stray image of the streets." Given its unbidden repetition, this consuming encounter has as much power to define Stephen as he has power to fix it within his categorizing scrutiny. The particular rephrasing of this line in the paragraph that follows the epiphanic scene—as a "sudden [and thus singular] spiritual manifestation"—suggests Stephen's attempt to make both himself and the ambiguous inspirations of epiphanic scenes stable in time and in language. Equally important is the epiphanic exchange itself, which despite being surrounded by qualifiers such as "triviality" and "vulgarity of speech" is clearly more central to Stephen's imaginative process than the Ballast Office clock (which becomes the official exemplum). The repeated "stage direction," "(again inaudibly)," shows how Stephen's codifying impulse is frustrated by his incomplete observation; also, the separation of syllables by ellipses conveys a materiality of language that I feel corresponds to its sexualized context, particularly in contrast to the graphically unremarkable language that surrounds the epiphany text.

The tension in this passage between the epiphany and Stephen's grapplings with its implications establishes several key tropes of material language and dispersal of the unified self, which Joyce will use in *Portrait* to frame Stephen's drive toward greater rigidity. Joyce's central positioning here of female characters (and their characteristic use of language) as factors that weigh against Stephen's ideals of control and of discrete selfhood suggests how Joyce plans to oppose a female-gendered freedom to the stability Stephen desires. I do not believe that Joyce's use of female characters such as Emma Clery, as well as the prostitute and others in *Portrait*, implies that the feminine and the sexual are interchangeable and that both of these are equally stable and debased characteristics. Rather, Joyce consistently uses female figures to support the internalization of the ambiguities of selfhood in language and sexuality. Jones suggests that this aspect of what I have called the epiphanic mode demonstrates Joyce's general "disrupti[on] through his language of the received symbolic order," which asserts "the limitation of the specular construct of the self as one, the coherence and mastery of 'I,' and [forces one] to acknowledge the scene on which that self is produced: the body of the woman" (182, 190). Joyce's emphasis on the corporeality of female characters, as the scene of the self that Stephen cannot acknowledge, makes them inextricably connected to the production of the epiphanic mode in the climactic scenes discussed here.

While *Portrait*, like *Stephen Hero*, contains materials from the manuscript epiphanies, the novel's salient characteristic for my purposes is not its direct reworkings of Joyce's earlier materials but rather Joyce's extension of the representational strategies of language first seen in the *Stephen Hero* epiphany sequence to climactic moments that are not necessarily prefigured by the manuscripts. Regardless of how closely such climaxes are tied to earlier material, they have in common with the *Stephen Hero* epiphany sequence an ambiguous, sexualized language, which frustrates Stephen's attempts to maintain binaries of intellect and sensuality in himself. The materiality, both in theme and in form, of this "epiphanic mode" of representation is quite pronounced in Stephen's encounter with a prostitute at the end of section 2; and in this passage Joyce establishes several principal figurations of language and the body that continue in these climactic moments throughout the novel.

In this passage Stephen acts to gratify his sexual desire for the first time, and for the first time names this desire as sinful: as he prowls Nighttown, his desire to sin is repeated hypnotically, and with a powerfully physicalized language:

> He felt some dark presence moving irresistibly upon him from the darkness, a presence subtle and murmurous as a flood filling him wholly with itself. Its murmur besieged his ears like the murmur of some multitude in sleep; its subtle streams penetrated his being (*Portrait* 100).

Within the Nighttown milieu, Stephen feels himself overpowered by a "dark presence" rendered as both language and a material invasion. The central figuration of this blurring of speech and matter is the act and effect of murmuring. Among the representational successors to the tropes of the epiphanic exchange in *Stephen Hero*, murmuring in *Portrait* connotes a crucial speech just out of hearing, and is indeed an onomatopoeic rendering of such speech. Because of its materiality—seen here in its "flooding" of Stephen—murmuring continually challenges the idea that speech agency belongs to a discrete self, as murmuring seems to claim not only agency but also issuing substance.

This free play of physicalized language becomes all the more marked in the section's final paragraphs, as Joyce repeatedly cedes the act of speech and other acts to organs acting independently: "He tried to bid his tongue speak" (100), "Her round arms held him firmly to her," "His lips would not bend to kiss her" (101). By distributing agency from a central self, Joyce effects a kind of "organic liberation" and allows a release of sexual power through what Derek Attridge has called a "traffic between vocal and sexual organs" (62). The final paragraph of this section is a paradigm of this trafficking:

> With a sudden movement she bowed his head and joined her lips to his and he read the meaning of her movements in her frank uplifted eyes. It was too much for him. He closed his eyes, surrendering himself to her, body and mind, conscious of nothing in the world but the dark pressure of her softly parting lips. They pressed upon his brain as upon his lips as though they were the vehicle of a vague speech; and between them he felt an unknown and timid pressure, darker than the swoon of sin, softer than sound or odour. (101)

Much has been made of Stephen's surrender to phallic penetration in this sequence, but I would argue that any "surrender" in the context of the epiphanic mode is not within a binary—in which one can either be male/dominant or female/submissive, or (in this case it seems) reverse these pairs—but is a relinquishing of unifying authority in favor of multiplicity. By his deployment of "swooning" in these final pages, Joyce leads Stephen to join in a hitherto-female act of falling from a unitary conception of the body into a potentially liberating field of autonomous organs and senses.

That this valorized falling had been designated as female is made clear by the immediate precedent for the "swoon of sin," the swoon of the "frail swooning form" (100) (nominally that of Emma) that Stephen pursues in Nighttown. This earlier swoon appears as a hyperbolic rendering of idealized female frailty and impalpability, which by its very excess makes swooning a conscious act of playful, powerful escape from being "[held] fast" by a self-aggrandizing vision. Stephen swoons into a state of total palpability that corresponds to a speech that communicates in many registers. The simultaneous rendering of speech and of the speaking body in this final sequence is language at its most incarnate: this "vague speech" (101) (or murmuring) literally presses upon the cognitive centers of hearing and upon the organs of speech, and the lips and tongue that convey this speech become speech themselves. But the most significant coherence of this sexualized, incarnate communication is as a readable text of some sort, as Stephen retains the faculty of reading even in his swooning extremis. This extension of the epiphanic mode into written expression will become central to later climactic sequences as they build toward Stephen's self-definition as an artist.

Stephen's nightmarish vision of goat-beings, the nadir of his self-hatred in section 3 following the sermon, allows us to trace precisely one instance of how Joyce's original conception of the epiphanies themselves developed into the more general epiphanic mode seen in *Portrait*. As the epiphany marked #6,[2] Joyce's first rendering of nightmarish goat-beings is virtually identical to the sequence found in *Portrait* (137–38), with three significant alterations: the repeated ascription of sin to the beings in the epiphany is deleted in *Portrait*, and two phrases are added—the beings are for the first time given the properties of moving "hither and thither," and of issuing "soft language" as they enclose Stephen:

> They moved in slow circles, circling closer and closer to enclose, to enclose, soft language issuing from their lips, their long swishing tails besmeared with stale shite, thrusting upwards their terrible faces . . .
> Help! (138)

"Soft" language is like murmuring, in that softness describes both the volume of speech and the texture of its material presence. The association of language with feces makes explicit the general tendency in these climactic passages to describe language as a soft, substantial element emerging from a semiautonomous bodily orifice. Also, the aural quality of the repeated "hither and thither" suggests that the goat-beings' motion is a kind of indistinct speech in itself.

With these tactile acts of speech, along with the "thrusting upwards" of faces, it seems clear that Joyce has constructed this vision of "lecherous" debasement to parallel the prostitute sequence. While the goat-beings appear to be male, this rhetorical parallel must in some sense suggest a teleological progression from the prostitute to these demonic figures, a progression that would couple debased abjection with the practice of what I call the epiphanic mode of language. However, it is the combined effect of the climactic passages that best demonstrates the power of these shared representational strategies to undermine the thematic demonization of sexuality that these passages might seem to assert if read strictly through Stephen's understanding. Thus the bestial sensuality of the goat vision does not merely correspond to the sin and self-betrayal Stephen associates with the prostitute sequence but also carries forward from that earlier passage the valorization in language of the corporeal and of diffused identity. [3]

Joyce's work toward a pervasive use of such epiphanic language reveals itself at the local level in this chapter in his depiction of Stephen's soul. The removal of references to sin in the *Portrait* goat-vision corresponds to Joyce's general emphasis, in this novel's language, on a tactility that resonates in varied situations rather than on a specific act of "sin." With the explicit moral value of sin thus subordinated to the range of sensations that may or may not seem sinful to Stephen at a given moment, Stephen's soul can be both victim and agent of Stephen's various sins: in short succession (immediately preceding the goat-vision), his soul "pin[es] within him" (137) as he prays not to be sent to Hell, "sighs" as Stephen ascends to his room, and yet is deemed "a living mass of corruption" (137). As Stephen progresses toward confession, the soul acquires a split agency and embodiment that terrifies Stephen:

> But does that part of the body understand or what? The serpent, the most subtle beast of the field . . . Who made it to be like that, a bestial part of the body able to understand bestially and desire bestially? Was that then he or an inhuman thing moved

by a lower soul than his soul? His soul sickened at the thought
of a torpid snaky life feeding itself out of the tender marrow of
his life and fattening upon the slime of lust. O why was that
so? O why? (139-40)

This baffling division of the soul, and its clear identification with
the penis Stephen does not want to acknowledge, is presented with
an ironic appreciation both for Stephen's frantic hypostatization
of his own urges and organs and for the humorous futility of such
an effort. The narration becomes progressively less wry as Stephen
approaches his confession and communion; during this progress,
Stephen's attempt at self-purgation leads him to interpret his soul,
whose above-mentioned ambiguities place it within the epiphanic
mode of language, as debased. His actual confession of "sins of impu-
rity" is portrayed as an utterly foul emission of physicalized language,
from an equally base soul: "His sins trickled from his lips, one by one,
trickled in shameful drops from his soul festering and oozing like a
sore, a squalid stream of vice" (144).

But Joyce makes it clear that such a vomiting-forth cannot rid
one of sexuality, nor can the sin and redemption be reassuringly
embodied outside oneself. In the final sequence between the confession and communion, Joyce portrays the withdrawal from language
and sexuality as a morbidly effacing false purity, invoking the images
of "pale flames of . . . candles" and of leached, overfragrant "masses of
white flowers" (146). The most noticeable rhetorical development in
this sequence is the profound infantilization of Stephen's represented
speech and the repeated ascription of shyness, timidity, and silence to
Stephen and his soul. With such gestures, Joyce frames this ostensible
purification as a regression to Stephen's immediate preadolescence: in
the sequence in section 1 in which Stephen first recognizes his soul
and his desire, Stephen imagines a vaguely sexual union in which he
is utterly impalpable, surrounded by darkness and silence (see 65).
However, Stephen's taking of the communion wafer is not simply an
imposition of a pure silence; it suggests the much more productive
(and quite impure) oral exchanges rendered in similar terms in the
prostitute and the final villanelle passages.

Stephen's vision of the bird-girl at the close of this section illustrates both the continuing power of the regressive force of silence and

impalpability, and the power of the epiphanic mode to undermine this regression. The bird-girl's stylized "sufferance" of Stephen's adoring gaze is a hyperbolic rendering of femininity that, like the swoon of the ephemeral "E. C." figure before the prostitute scene, exceeds Stephen's cognitive and assimilative control. Moreover, her "emerald trail of seaweed" (171) links her with the goat-beings, speckled with stale dung. Such a parallel reinvokes the demonizing portrayal of sexuality and language in the goat-being sequence, but retroactively brings the positive connotations of the present passage into that sequence. A more immediately evident reference to the goat-being sequence is in Joyce's use of "hither and thither" to indicate a murmurous, tactile speech-act:

> [She gently stirred] the water with her foot hither and thither. The first faint noise of gently moving water broke the silence, low and faint and whispering, faint as the bells of sleep; hither and thither, hither and thither: and a faint flame trembled on her cheek.
>
> —Heavenly God! cried Stephen's soul,
> in an outburst of profane joy. (171)

The bird-girl's breaking of silence is portrayed as a necessary reversal of tactile and sensory self-denial, and the reader must in turn reevaluate the nightmarish portrayal of such tactile speech in the goat-beings.

After this valorization of acknowledged speech and sensuality, the fact that the cry of "Heavenly God!" comes from Stephen's soul, and not himself, is somewhat surprising. A profound communication seems to have occurred across, or amidst, this cry, inscribing the bird-girl's murmurous sexuality on Stephen's body in the form of a mimetically inflamed cheek: his body glows, his limbs tremble. But the subsequent narration, at least at the level of staging, explicitly denies the exchange of tactile speech. Stephen is made to turn away from her and stride off, and the "low and faint and whispering" sound of their encounter is repeatedly denied: "Her image had passed into his soul for ever and no word had broken the holy silence of his ecstasy" (172). The dominant rhetorical practice of this sequence, however, undermines this attempt to retroactively separate sexuality and the feminine from spirituality, as Stephen is twice said to run "on and on and on and on" (172), to run recklessly, his blood in a riot.

Ultimately, Stephen appears to move even further from direct interaction with the bird-girl, while nonetheless entering a state of increased tactility and loss of discrete selfhood:

> His soul was swooning into some new world, fantastic, dim, uncertain as under sea, traversed by cloudy shapes and beings. A world, a glimmer, or a flower? Glimmering and trembling, trembling and enfolding, a breaking light, an opening flower, it spread in endless succession to itself, breaking in full crimson and unfolding and paling to palest rose, leaf by leaf and wave of light by wave of light, flooding all the heavens with its soft flushes, every flush deeper than the other (172).

Stephen's swoon has often been taken up by critics within what Carol Shloss refers to as the "second stage of women's critical responsiveness to Joyce": that is, a criticism concerned with "naming the feminine" (628) and challenging the received critical view of women (in Joyce's works and elsewhere) as the archetypal other (628).[4] The limitation of this period in Joyce criticism, as Shloss points out, is a focus on traditional, empirical ideas of character. This assumption of discrete character function allows critics within this second stage, such as Suzette Henke, to regard the swooning passage as Stephen's attempt to impose his "male aesthetic signature [upon] the female body/text" (102) and to view the language of this passage as a transparent vehicle for this exertion. But the materiality that we have seen extending across the language of these climactic moments in *Portrait* at the least complicates their thematic content; and indeed, the representational practice of these moments imposes its own valorization of ambiguity and sexuality upon Stephen far more forcefully than he can "sign" himself as removed from these qualities of self and language. Stephen's swoon in this passage does not retroactively efface his sexual encounter with the prostitute (the other significant swoon in the novel) but rather reinforces the sexual overtones in this passage by connecting with the earlier encounter. Stephen appears to swoon into female genitalia, and perhaps participate in an infinitely self-diffusive female orgasm. Certainly, he is left scarce objective distance from which to demonize this sexual materiality, which even after Stephen awakes remains in the murmurous "low whisper of her [the tide's] waves" (173).

While there are uses of the epiphany manuscripts later in the final chapter of *Portrait*, the sequence early in the chapter in which Stephen composes the villanelle is the culmination of the epiphanic mode of representation that I have discussed in this essay. Joyce here puts Stephen's nascent artistic agency—and artistic practice—at the focus of the continuing tension between Stephen's rigid self-definition in terms of language and sexuality, and Joyce's more interconnected depiction of these aspects of self. From the start of this passage we see Joyce using the same imagery of sensory diffusion of the self as that of the swooning end of chapter 4. Indeed, Stephen is here more intensely immersed, and literally inspired, by the figurative breath of various surrounding and permeating elements: "A spirit filled him, pure as the purest water, sweet as dew, moving as music" (217). That Stephen is said to "inbreathe" this "tremulous morning knowledge" becomes significant after we see the first cycle of represented inspiration, creative thought, poem text, and Stephen's reflections on the process. Stephen first perceives the "form" of inspiration as resolutely indeterminate, and the locus of inspiration is represented in ambiguous and equivocal language:

> The instant of inspiration seemed now to be reflected from all sides at once from a multitude of cloudy circumstance of what had happened or of what might have happened ... An afterglow deepened within his spirit, whence the white flame had passed, deepening to a rose and ardent light (217).

However, in converting this inspiration into poetry Stephen moves immediately to establish concrete, precise associations and imagery: "That rose and ardent light was her strange wilful heart." Over the next few paragraphs, during Stephen's first period of inspired writing (three stanzas' worth), Stephen often uses this declarative tone as if to sum up his operative poetic conceit. But even in the sentences that contain these summary statements, the "roselike glow" and the language associated with it produce a rather nonsummary effect:

> The roselike glow sent forth rays of rhyme; ways, days, blaze, praise, raise. Its rays burned up the world, consumed the hearts

of men and angels: the rays from the rose that was her wilful
heart (217).

The dense pattern of interdependent imagery, sound, and attributed
status in these sentences overspills the forms—of contemplative
thought and of poetic verse—into which Stephen imagines he distills
it. For example, the rhythmic listing, or chanting, of potential line
endings infects Stephen's second repetition of his equation rose-equals-
heart: "the rays from the rose that was her wilful heart." Stephen asks
"And then?" after these first stanzas are produced, as if he had processed
successive units of inspiration.

   This apparent disparity between the represented nature of inspiration, which falls within the epiphanic mode I've described, and the
representation Stephen seeks to create from such inspiration is at
the root of Stephen's conceptual process. Immediately after Stephen
comes up with the first stanza, we read that the "verses passed from
his mind to his lips and, murmuring them over, he felt the rhythmic
movement of a villanelle pass through them" (217–18). Previous critics
of the villanelle sequence have variously regarded this moment as
evidence of the unconscious triumph of Stephen's personality over the
artistic product or as a sign of Stephen's misogynistic dialectic.[5] What
is too easily assumed, in such readings that ascribe textual domination
to Stephen, is that the passage through the lips is necessarily outward.
In the rhetorical and imagistic context of this sequence—particularly
in these nebulous, undulant first paragraphs—Stephen's sensation of
something between his lips must refer both to the prostitute scene
and to the literally "in-spiring" nature of his current creative moment.
The teleology of creation laid out in this sequence clearly points to
Stephen's murmuring as the creative inception, and certainly what
Stephen formulates (and then writes down) begins here. But the
rhetorical and imagistic rendering of this creative process, as seen in
such incantatory passages earlier in the sequence, situates Stephen
within the continuity of the epiphanic mode—which, having been
"inbreathed" (217), exceeds the rigor and unity of his creative formu-
lations. Indeed, being in the act of literary creation emphasizes the
workings of language as performed by decentralized, autonomous
organs of the body, as Stephen's lips are frequently said to murmur
the verses, or, as his inspiration flags, to "stumble through half verses,
stammering and baffled" (218).

As Stephen develops his conception of the poem, his thoughts tend toward a hyperbolic unity and creativity: "The radiant image of the eucharist united again in an instant his bitter and despairing thoughts, their cries arising unbroken in a hymn of thanksgiving" (221). Then follows the fourth stanza, and shortly after, the narration returns him to the confusion of the world: "He knew that all around him life was about to return in common noises, hoarse voices, sleepy prayers." Stephen "shrink[s] from that life," and from the specific implications it contains of his own sexuality in Night-town: "He listened eagerly for any sound," "He heard bursts of hoarse rioting" (99, 100). But his retreat from such conjunctions of sexuality, speech, and physicality is undermined by his own synesthesic, physicalized reaction to (and writing down of) the stanza itself:

> He spoke the verses aloud from the first lines till the music and rhythm suffused his mind, turning it to quiet indulgence; then copied them painfully to feel them the better by seeing them; then lay back on his bolster. (221)

As in the initial, murmuring conception of the poem structure, here Stephen feels the verses acting (tonguelike) directly on his brain and experiences their effect as an overlapping act of writing, feeling, reading, and seeing. With each of Stephen's successive attempts to impose a poetic rigor on himself and his inspiration, Joyce renders his imaginative process in a manner that suggests Stephen is approaching a conscious awareness of the epiphanic mode in his literary work.

This dynamic between Stephen's inspiration and his creative process comes to a climax in the sequence's final passage, which ends with the poem reproduced in its entirety. Stephen's probable masturbation is depicted as a simultaneous penetration and yielding that corresponds to the prostitute scene, as he makes E. C. yield to him as he himself is flooded by "the liquid letters of speech, symbols of the element of mystery" (223).[6] Vicki Mahaffey argues that Stephen's solitary onanism makes his artistic production equally fruitless, in the context of his continued denial of the union of opposites (102). While Stephen's solitary, erotic imagining of E. C. is not directly communicative and unifying, in Mahaffey's sense, the language of this passage does directly identify the epiphanic dynamic of body, speech, and sexuality with the foundation of Stephen's literary process. This language, I believe, is a more subtle and powerful indication of Stephen's direction as an artist than his limited attempts to construct binary, rational forms from his inspiration.

In this final juxtaposition of creative process and artistic product, the evolution of Stephen within the epiphanic mode since *Stephen Hero* is clear. The full text of the poem, as it is positioned directly after Stephen's literary-sexual epiphany, is Stephen's attempt to represent the "liquid letters of speech, [the] symbols of the element of mystery" (223). However, as the "rays of rhyme" passage demonstrates, the poem itself is representative of Stephen's very failure to completely rationalize the murmurous aspects of multiplicity in his life and world. In its isolation, then, the full text of the poem demonstrates a sort of inversion that has taken place in Joyce's representation of sexuality and language since *Stephen Hero*. In that work's conception of the epiphany, as discussed above, the epiphanic exchange itself was isolated graphically within Stephen's evasive theorization of the epiphany in general; in *Portrait*, the isolated poem's text is itself the evasive attempt to summarize, and is now surrounded and outweighed by the epiphanic properties of language that pervade the novel as a whole. I believe this new predominance of nondemonized sexuality in language is a more reliable portent of Joyce's future transformations than are Stephen's final, Icarian pronouncements.

NOTES

1. Beja provides the most extensive study of Joyce's particular uses of epiphanies in the later works.
2. Scholes and Kain give an authoritative account of the enumeration that Joyce devised for the epiphanies.
3. For a similar reading of *A Portrait* as building through a series of correspondences in language and theme, see Ellmann, especially 196.
4. Shloss focuses on Henke's role in editing *Women in Joyce* and on her own article in that collection as representative of this "second stage."
5. See Day and Henke 99.

6. Gose provides an overview of the debate between those who
   believe this sequence depicts masturbation and those who favor
   a more abstract view.

WORKS CITED

Attridge, Derek. "Joyce's Lipspeech: Syntax and the Subject in 'Sirens.'" *James Joyce: The Centennial Symposium*. Ed. Morris Beja et al. Urbana: U of Illinois P, 1986. 55–72.

Beja, Morris. *Epiphany in the Modern Novel*. Seattle: U of Washington P, 1971.

Day, Robert Adams. "The Villanelle Perplex: Reading Joyce." *James Joyce Quarterly* 25 (1987): 69–85.

Ellmann, Maud. "Disremembering Dedalus: 'A Portrait of the Artist as a Young Man.'" *Untying the Text*. Ed. Robert Young. Boston: Routledge, 1981. 192–206.

Gose, Elliot B., Jr. "Destruction and Creation in *A Portrait*." *James Joyce Quarterly* 22 (1985): 259–70.

Henke, Suzette. "Stephen Dedalus and Women: A Portrait of the Artist as a Young Misogynist." *Women in Joyce*. Ed. Suzette Henke and Elaine Unkeless. Urbana: U of Illinois P, 1982. 82–107.

Jones, Ellen Carol. "The Letter Selfpenned to One's Other: Joyce's Writing, Deconstruction, Feminism." *Coping with Joyce: Essays from the Copenhagen Symposium*. Ed. Morris Beja and Shari Benstock. Columbus: Ohio State UP, 1989. 178–95.

Joyce, James. *A Portrait of the Artist as a Young Man: Text, Criticism, and Notes*. Ed. Chester G. Anderson. New York: Viking, 1968.

———. *Stephen Hero*. Ed. John J. Slocum and Herbert Cahoon. New York: New Directions, 1963.

———. *Ulysses: The Corrected Text*. New York: Vintage, 1986.

Mahaffey, Vicki. *Reauthorizing Joyce*. New York: Cambridge UP, 1989.

Scholes, Robert, and Richard M. Kain. *The Workshop of Daedalus: James Joyce and the Raw Materials for* A Portrait of the Artist as a Young Man. Evanston: Northwestern UP, 1965.

Shloss, Carol. "In the Palace of the Magistrates: Joyce/Women/Writing: An Essay Review." *Modern Fiction Studies* 35 (1989): 617–33.

THE RAPE OF THE LOCK
(ALEXANDER POPE)

"*The Rape of the Lock*: A Reification of the Myth of Passive Womanhood"
by Ellen Pollak,
in *The Poetics of Sexual Myth: Gender and Ideology in the Verse of Swift and Pope* (1985)

INTRODUCTION

In her essay on *The Rape of the Lock*, Ellen Pollak explores how Pope's "satire on a culture that objectifies individuals is itself a pretext for his own objectification of the female." By analyzing Pope's symbolism, syntax, and rhetorical strategies, Pollak convincingly demonstrates that *The Rape of the Lock* enshrines passivity and subservience as essential qualities of the "ideal" woman, a woman whose "entire value is tied up with her identity as a piece of property transferable among men."

Where then is man in this . . . picture? Nowhere and everywhere, like the sky, the horizon, an authority which at once determines

Pollak, Ellen. "The Rape of the Lock: A Reification of the Myth of Passive Womanhood." *The Poetics of Sexual Myth: Gender and Ideology in the Verse of Swift and Pope*. Chicago: University of Chicago Press, 1985. 77–107.

and limits a condition.... Man is never inside, femininity is
pure, free, powerful; but man is everywhere around, he presses
on all sides, he makes everything exist; he is in all eternity the
creative absence.... [T]he feminine world ..., a world without
men, but entirely constituted by the gaze of man....

                                            Roland Barthes, *Mythologies*

A satire on the superficial values of fashionable society in the reign
of Queen Anne, Pope's *Rape of the Lock* criticizes the sterility and
social vanity of a world in which appearances have actually become
substitutes for things themselves, where virtue has been reduced to
reputation and men themselves to swordknots (I, 101).[1] The world of
Hampton Court is imaged by Pope as a world of empty forms where
people are dehumanized exteriors while, in the underground Cave of
Spleen (where we might expect to find an inversion of conditions in the
aboveground world), objects are alive: teapots live, goosepies talk. Yet
there are limits to Pope's satire on the irrational materialism of bourgeois values that objectify human beings by giving primacy to surface
over substance. For even as Pope attacks drawing-room society for its
sterile fetishism, he establishes a poetic economy (and specifically an
economy of gender) in which woman is made to function as the sign *not*
of her own subjectivity but of a male desire of which she is the object.
Pope's satire on a culture that objectifies individuals is itself a pretext
for his own objectification of the female. It is, in a sense, a testimony to
the rhetorical genius of Pope that this ideological contradiction at the
center of his text is so fully and so masterfully concealed.

    The enabling contradiction between Pope's satire on commercial
values on the one hand and his objectification of woman on the other
has been obscured, it seems to me, by the overwhelming tendency of
modern criticism to universalize Belinda—to read her not *as woman*
(not in terms of the specificities of her rhetorical construction as a
female) but as a generic representative of a genderless humanity. Thus
the Belle's distinguishing weakness is human vanity, a naive belief in
her own capacity for eternal innocence and immortal beauty, and her
fate is the sobering lesson of all mortal experience—the acquisition
of that difficult but dignifying knowledge that life always involves
some compromise, some loss. Such a reading, to be sure, must have
its place. But by leaving the matrix of assumptions about gender that
underlies Pope's narrative fiction essentially unanalyzed, it obscures

the extent to which this satire on human vanity also functions as a fable of social and sexual initiation in which Belinda is a type not of Everyman, but of Everywoman, and in which the rape is figured as a rite of passage in her "progress" (however dubious a progress it may be) from an intact and strident girlhood to a mutilated but stellarized maturity. When considered in terms of its sexual ideology, in other words, Pope's fictive history of a single virgin's severed hair emerges as nothing less than emblematic of the birth of the female as a social being in eighteenth-century English culture.

As the poem opens Belinda is presented as the very antithesis of a social being. She is, rather, the embodiment of a self-enclosed narcissism. The dominant image of that narcissism is, of course, our vision of the heroine worshiping her own image in the mirror as she performs the Rites of Pride. The epic machinery of the poem further elaborates this idea, the sylphs providing Pope yet another way of representing the autoerotic love of the coquette. As the spirits of dead coquettes—as, in effect, projections of Belinda's own psychic life—they allow the poet to image Belinda's self-involvement as an involvement with beings other than herself, with beings whose sex (like that of Milton's angels) is conveniently, infinitely transformable. In fact, however, sylph embraces (which are the reward Ariel promises Belinda for her rejection of mankind) are self-embraces, and the function of the erotic dream that Ariel conjures over the sleeping Belinda's head is finally to stoke the maiden's sense of self-importance (I, 35). Appealing to her desire for social and economic power, Ariel assures Belinda that the sylphs are an "equipage" in air that bespeaks a far higher distinction than the two pages and a chair that a mortal man could offer her through marriage (I, 45–46).

Thus, early in the poem, Belinda's self-love is identified with her desire for power and, specifically, with her desire for the sort of power she might obtain (retain) by avoiding wedlock and its subjection of the female.[2] Her lock becomes a metaphor for the pleasure she withholds from men in order to secure this type of power. As a product of her art, it is a part of the armor by which she makes herself invulnerable to men.

But as woman's only armor is the art by which she ornaments herself, Belinda's invulnerability as Pope portrays it contains the very seeds of (indeed is an invitation to) its own destruction. And, as we soon discover, Belinda is not invulnerable to men at all. Her power, on

the contrary, is severely limited. Even her guardian sylphs are neither
omniscient nor omnipotent. Although Ariel knows enough to foretell
some dread event in Belinda's ruling star, he cannot actually forestall
the maiden's fate—which is, ultimately, to have her chastity (her sexuality) appropriated by a man. Despite their supernatural protectors,
women *are* finally vulnerable to men; their natural vulnerability is built
into the very supernature, or metaphysics, of Pope's poetic universe.

It is this idea, this message that woman ultimately belongs to
man and that, as such, she is not just a part but also an expression of
him, that Pope's poem repeatedly reaffirms by persistently collapsing
Belinda's subjectivity into her status as an object, and specifically
as an object of male desire and ownership. Manifestly, Belinda is at
the center of Pope's fictional universe, as she is—as the belle of the
ball—at the center of Hampton Court society where all eyes are fixed
on her alone (II, 6). Dramatically speaking, the Baron seems to play a
relatively insignificant role. As a presence in the poem he almost seems
a kind of shadow of Belinda; he doesn't even have a proper name.
Ideologically, however, it is Belinda who is situated on the margins of
this text. For her visibility in the poem not only signals her nonexis-
tence as a subject, but finally points to the latent, and more powerful,
masculine presence of which she has been figured as the sign.
[. . .]

As if expressly to assert the tenet of female uniformity that Pope
would later elaborate more explicitly in "To a Lady," Belinda—despite
her egregious identification as a "coquette"—actually shows herself
to be (like Atossa) "Scarce once herself, by turns all Womankind."
She is, in effect, a type of Everywoman and the battle between the
sylphs and gnomes a psychomachic framework in which the drama of
woman's sexual and social initiation is forever reenacted.[3] Within the
limits of their femaleness, Belinda and Clarissa are represented as fully
differentiated—even antithetical—character-types, but they must also
be understood as constituting behavioral variations on a single set of
exclusively female motivations. If the sylphs and gnomes symbolize
different and inevitably conflicting aspects of Everywoman, coquettes
and prudes are simply individuations of a common female paradigm.

An even more striking affirmation of the notion of female uniformity in the *Rape* is the fact that the machinery of the poem applies
only to women. As Keener observes in his chapter on "Sublunary

Belinda" (a crucial association which links women both to mutability and to fate), while the "sylphs guard women, men are on their own."[4] This circumstance is consistent with the sexual double standard that is generally implicit in Pope's text; most pertinent to the present discussion, it gives imaginative substance to the contrast between the assumed predeterminancy of female existence and the natural autonomy of men. As the ultimately impotent embodiments of the female's need for protection, the sylphs symbolize woman's inherent vulnerability to influences beyond her control.[5] The Baron, in keeping with orthodox doctrine regarding the humors, is susceptible to elemental forces, but as a potentially rational being he also retains the power to resist them. He is incited to action in the *Rape* by the same vapor that precipitates Belinda's downfall, but because as a man he is expected to be more "responsible" for his actions, the effect of capitulation to natural forces is in a curious sense more damaging in his case than in hers.[6] Within the Popeian hierarchy, Belinda may commit a form of hubris in aspiring to a male prerogative, but she operates from a precondition of degradation and defeat while the Baron actively descends into effeminacy. He is not predestined to be a rake at heart; in fact, as we shall see, his vulnerability to Belinda's charms and his consequent assault upon her are paradoxically justified by the poem's definition of female beauty as a form of sexual aggression.[7]

The predetermined character of woman's world, its status as a closed system that exists in a particular relationship to the male world by which it is entirely contained and entirely subsumed, but with which it is not entirely commensurate, is deliberately obscured by Pope's metaphorical contraction of the world to "feminine" proportions. By transforming a velvet card table into a grassy plain, placing whole oceans into coffee cups, all Arabia into a tiny box, or by describing Belinda in terms of military, naval, and Olympian imagery, Pope can temporarily distract attention from Ariel's explicit assertion that "the Fair," though no "less pleasing," are yet "less glorious" than national politics (II, 91–92). But ultimately, like overblown flattery, his lending of epic stature to beings he regards as so intrinsically unheroic only primes them for deflation, and the more stable and comprehensive values of Pope's world are given moot testimony at every turn by Belinda's clearly convoluted sense of them. In her myopic preoccupation with the labors of her toilette, she may remain innocent of the sight of hanging wretches, but Pope's alert reader may not. We are admitted to Belinda's world long enough to come to know its trivial charms, but these are mystic mazes in which we never really lose our way. Pope ornaments the narrowness of the *beau monde* by making it seem to encompass all the world or by crowding it with objects, images, and angel-like spirits; but the sense of paradox that emerges from this opposition between its emptiness and fullness, barrenness and wealth, itself consistently bows to a single sexual ideology in which women are inferior, emptier and narrower than men. Pope's "two-way vision" looks only one way; his paradoxes have a unified intent.[8]

A good example of how Pope's ironies function monologically in the *Rape* comes early in Canto III, in his declaration that sylphs, like women, are "wondrous fond of Place." Belinda is playing *Ombre*:

> *Belinda* now, whom Thirst of Fame invites,
> Burns to encounter two adventrous Knights,
> At *Ombre* singly to decide their Doom;
> And swells her Breast with Conquests yet to come.
> Strait the three Bands prepare in Arms to join,
> Each Band the number of the Sacred Nine.
> Soon as she spreads her Hand, th'Aerial Guard
> Descend, and sit on each important Card:
> First *Ariel* perch'd upon a *Matadore*,
> Then each, according to the Rank they bore;
> For *Sylphs*, yet mindful of their ancient Race,
> Are, as when Women, wondrous fond of Place.
>   (III, 25–36)

The concluding couplet reads at first as a compliment. Sylphs, like women, are wondrously respectful of hierarchy and, "mindful of their ancient Race," of tradition too. But the assertion gives us pause. The ancestors of the sylphs are the coquettes, hardly a "race" known for its happy or compliant subservience. Indeed, Belinda's example just ten lines above shows her thirsting for fame and conquest. Though she extends "Favours to none," the "*diabolick Din*" she makes after the taking of the lock does not, as John Dennis pointed out, reassure us of her modesty.[9] Paradoxically, in their love for order and degree, the sylphs are true to a heritage of self-serving, rivalrous, and insubordinate women who ever seek to be first in "Virtue" by being first in "Face"—whose love for rank is but a love for primacy among women and dominance over men. The "Aerial Guard," after all, perch only on important cards, subserviently abetting Belinda in her powerful compulsion to win.

Like Pope's tribute to the lady who "has her humour most, when she obeys," where—as we shall see—"humour" implies both obliging "femininity" and unruly female whim, this couplet from the *Rape* makes the dual and apparently contradictory assertion that women are at once uniquely power-hungry and wondrously obedient; eager to have their way, they gladly hug their chains. The lines embody both sides of that myth by which women, because of their presupposed lack of rational powers, are by turns grossly sensual and angelically spiritual. Like Clarissa's speech, it accommodates both positive and negative female possibilities by exploiting a false distinction between good and evil women. Both Belinda and the idealized Martha of "To a Lady" are part of that general negativity in Pope which includes, along with fools and knaves, the whole of female kind.

But if women are both naturally willful and naturally obedient, and if both Belinda and Martha are on some level representative of female nature, then clearly a dual concept of what is "natural" must be operating in Pope's view of women. Indeed, one might well ask of Pope's tribute to Martha Blount what Elizabeth Janeway has asked in another context: "Why should anyone be praised for being what she is supposed to be by nature" unless there is some form of "mythic illogic" at work?[10]

I shall argue that the key to this illogic in the "Epistle to a Lady" lies in a functional dichotomy between femaleness and femininity according to which Martha's "true charm" as a woman is represented not as a raw but as a mediated form of femaleness. In *The Rape of the Lock*, this same mediation of femaleness that is a fait accompli in Martha is given dramatic expression in the chronology or "progress" of Belinda's beauty from a state of militant wholeness to one of glorified dismemberment. A woman of sober beauty—like Martha, or like the feminine ideal implicit in Clarissa's speech—is in a sense more "natural" than Belinda, who is promised permanent glory only after she has been "naturalized" or shorn of the emblem and the product of her art. But this process of "naturalization" is also, paradoxically, the process of Belinda's "socialization" as a female—in a word, of her "feminization." And it is not insignificant that the symbolic loss of her much-coveted virginity is realized in the form of a castration or

literal cutting off of that bodily part of her associated most strongly
with those "masculine" attributes of the coquette—her power, skill,
and pride.[11]

The notion of "the natural" in Pope's text is admittedly complex,
since as Clarissa makes clear, Pope's ideal of "femininity" itself involves
a form of "Pow'r" and the skill to use it well (V, 29). But there is a crucial
distinction to be made between Belinda's "artfulness" and that which
either Martha represents or Clarissa recommends, and that distinction
rests squarely on Belinda's resistance to the demands of wedlock—or,
to put the matter in Clarissa's terms, on the coquette's refusal to accept
with good humor the premise that loss is an inherent ("natural")
feature of the female predicament (V, 30). What Clarissa is saying is
that, if one seeks to dominate men by coquettish rejection, one loses
by dying single; and she judges this loss to be worse than the loss of
one's virginity, the gracious and passive yielding of which in marriage
is, in her view, the stuff of woman's "virtue" and the paradoxical basis
of her "gain." It is fitting, then, that the consecrated lock—which bears
Belinda's name—can become a vehicle for the heroine's immortaliza-
tion only *after* it has been (in this case forcibly) given up. On one level
Belinda's ravished hair is a triumphant reminder of her transcendent
artfulness, of her power to purify the blush and repair the smile (I,
141–44); but it can function as a sign of permanence only once it also
becomes the emblem of the sacrifice of that art to a more elevated
cultural ideal. The paradox here, as in Richardson's *Clarissa*, is that the
sign of woman's artfulness and sexual integrity can be transcendently
imaged "only in the fetishistic symbol of male power."[12]

For Belinda, the passage from the simply "female" to the truly
"feminine" must involve not merely a giving up of sexual independence but of all other forms of independence as well; her chastity
is a complex metaphor for these. Her maturation is figured not as a
coming into selfhood but as an abdication of the impulse to autonomy
in every aspect of existence. Pope builds the "naturalness" or inevitability of this circumstance into the very structure of reality in the *Rape*.
As Wasserman has observed, Belinda wants to avoid wedlock and its
concomitant subjugation of the female, but her intention is inexorably
doomed; in the terms of Pope's poetic universe, her chastity is a challenge to the intrusion of reality itself.[13]

Although couched in an allusive context that calls for a "Christian
Greco-Roman" readership,[14] the *Rape* already contains the dominant

features of that bourgeois sexual ideology which Pierre Fauchery identifies as characteristic of the early European novel. Most notably, it mythologizes female destiny in exclusively sexual terms as a natural continuum between virginity and defloration. Writing of *Clarissa*, Fauchery remarks on the binary relationship between virginity and rape so typically exploited in eighteenth-century prose fiction, and his observations shed an interesting retrospective light on Pope's mock-epic synthesis of classical and contemporary sexual themes:

> Rape, in the imaginary society of the century, is presented as the potential destiny of every woman; but it maintains with virginity one of those antithetical relations in which contradiction becomes attraction. Chastity attracts rape as the sacred invites defilement.[15]

One almost immediately senses the relevance of this formulation for a culture where virginity had ambiguous moral status and where singleness was scorned. Both "purity" and its loss are natural and necessary phases of female life as Pope conceives it, and together they embody the truth about woman as she exists in his version of natural and social order; at base, she is impure, and any willful effort to deny or contravene this ontological given can but provoke a violent self-restitution of the axioms of female fate.

POPE'S PARADOX OF FEMALE POWER

John Dennis complained that the a priori nature of Belinda's fate created dramatic absurdities in the *Rape*. Was it not ludicrous, he reasoned, for Umbriel "to take a Journey down to the *central Earth*, for no other Purpose than to give her the *Spleen*, whom he left and found in the Height of it?"[16] But certainly Pope's rather elliptical dramatic mode in this poem is consistent with what we have observed to be the limits within which he imagined the range of female possibility. Defeat is a foregone conclusion for Belinda, and even her resistance to surrender is incorporated and neutralized by Pope's philosophy as a token of unconscious compliance. Indeed, the circularity of the poem's dramatic trajectory and the seemingly superfluous function of its "Machines" are both aspects of a structure of desire which defines Belinda's undoing as fully self-determined.

In the mythic economy of the *Rape* female power is always self-consuming. In the linear progression of the poem, Belinda as an image of strength and wholeness gives way to Belinda as an image of impotent disarray; but in Pope's symbolic system, these two contradictory images are not so much one another's negations as they are complementary and mutually sustaining aspects of Pope's objectification of the female. Through such an objectification, Pope uses his heroine to reflect and reaffirm the passive sexual and economic role of women in mercantile society.

At the root of the myth of female power in Pope is the premise that female sexuality is responsible for the exercise of desire in both men and women. For, indeed, at the dramatic center of the *Rape*, where the Baron performs the action of a desiring subject—

> Th' Adventrous *Baron* the bright Locks admir'd,
> He saw, he wish'd, and to the Prize aspir'd. . ..
>   (II, 29–30)

—Belinda is defined as both the object and the source of that desire:

> This Nymph, to the Destruction of Mankind,
> Nourish'd two Locks, which graceful hung behind
> In equal Curls, and well conspir'd to deck
> With shining Ringlets the smooth Iv'ry Neck.
> Love in these Labyrinths his Slaves detains,
> And mighty Hearts are held in slender Chains.
> . . .
> Fair Tresses Man's Imperial Race insnare,
> And Beauty draws us with a single Hair.
>   (II, 19–28)

In the absence of any concept of female autonomy, Belinda's self-involvement and apparent indifference to the Baron are an automatic challenge to assault, her "ravishing" beauty a passive-aggressive inducement to revenge.[17] Though the agency of the drama is located in the Baron, its motivation is situated in her.
[. . .]

Of all the works regarded by the modern critical establishment as classics of English poetry, Pope's *Rape of the Lock* is perhaps the most liberal in its use of that synecdochic principle by which a part is made to stand for the whole. In it, woman—whom it defines as a mere appendage to man, her world a mere corner of his—represents the whole world in what amounts to a large-scale repetition of that more basic equation by which Belinda's lock, the symbol of her chastity, becomes a proxy for Belinda herself, what Kenneth Burke would call a "fetishistic surrogate" for the whole woman.[18] Now the equation by which Belinda's lock equals her chastity provides a crucial cross-link in this ever-expanding spiral of synecdoche between Pope's criticism of the sterile fetishism of the *beau monde* on the one hand and his positive assertion of a normative ideal of woman on the other. For if, as Pope portrays it, female chastity (i.e., sexuality) is something over which man has a rightful claim, then the lock must, by association, be understood at least transiently as the common property of Belinda and the Baron. Moreover, just as this part of her—which is, symbolically, all of her—is really part of him (and here the notion of the lock as phallus is relevant), so in "wedlock" (the term is never actually used in the poem and yet it seems to function as a silent pun throughout) the good wife is the rightful possession of her husband and a natural extension of him.

In fact, throughout the *Rape*, Pope is engaging in extended play on the notion, already conventional in his day but to which his own work gave new force, that woman's entire value is tied up with her identity as a piece of property transferable among men.

[...]

Thus, although Belinda's victory at cards is a transient fulfillment of her subversively "masculine" power, it also manages to foreshadow the maiden's final defeat and does so in terms which covertly allude to the specifically sexual form that defeat will take. The "livid Paleness" that "spreads o'er all her Look" not only contains a clue to this sexualized interpretation in its use of the familiar key verb, but as Rudat's study of the poem's allusive context would suggest, it intends a silent association between the "approaching Ill" of the lock's removal and the loss of Belinda's "virgin blood" (III, 89–92).[19] Again, like the role of the Amazon Queen of Spades, the progress of the card game is consistent with Pope's treatment of Belinda's aggressive chastity as provocation to assault. "Just in the Jaws of Ruin" comes the virgin's symbolic triumph, prefiguring her later "Screams of Horror" (III, 156) in lines that also suggest exultation at the thrill of jeopardy and the idea of loss.[20]

But the verb "to spread" continues to multiply, appearing again thirty-two lines later in connection with the "fatal" shears that clip the lock. Clarissa has bestowed the "two-edg'd Weapon" on the Baron:

> So Ladies in Romance assist their Knight,
> Present the Spear, and arm him for the Fight.
> He takes the Gift with rev'rence, and extends
> The little Engine on his Fingers' Ends,
> This just behind *Belinda's* Neck he spread,
> As o'er the fragrant Steams she bends her Head . . .
> (III, 129–34)

Given Pope's passing comparison of the scissors to a "Spear" as well as the fact that the Baron wears them on his fingers (where he later wears the phallic lock), it is difficult to resist an association to Fanny Hill's frequent references to the penis as an "engine" or "machine." Still, in Pope's version of the phallic sword, male and female symbolism seems curiously and significantly combined. Indeed, in the very next stanza the Baron's "little Engine" is described as a "glitt'ring *Forfex*" whose wide-spread stance is distinctly suggestive of female anatomy:

> The Peer now spreads the glitt'ring *Forfex* wide,
> T'inclose the Lock; now joins it, to divide.
> (III, 147–48)

The most likely inference to make regarding the intertwining of sexual metaphors in the image of the scissors is that Pope means to symbolize the coming together of man and woman in sexual union. But it seems worthy of special notice that while both male and female anatomies are implicated in this image of consummation at the center of Pope's text, the actual physical working of those doubly gendered shears is *exclusively* under the agency of the Baron; as Pope insinuates by his ambiguous reference to the Baron's "Steel" as "unresisted" (III, 178), Belinda's unconsciousness (or, at best, semi-consciousness) of the Baron's approach condemns her to a form of passive cooperation. Again like Richardson's Clarissa, who is drugged, she is at a physiological disadvantage; she is under the erotic influence of coffee steams.[21]

As activator of the scissors, the Baron is the subject of the verb "to spread," which on the level of the poem's sexual symbolism suggests an appropriation of female sexuality on the part of the male not unlike the male appropriation of female self-display we observed earlier. Indeed, the complex link between display and sexual activity reasserts itself at the moment of the rape in Pope's sudden and arresting allusion to the Baron as "Peer" in a line that strongly hints at male voyeurism.

Pope's division of the functions of motivation and agency between Belinda and the Baron is thus brilliantly carried through his poem down to the very description of the gesture by which the lock is cut. This description embodies two complementary assertions of fact: that spreading and enclosure take place simultaneously in sex and that a closed position is accompanied by the division of sexual partners. But Pope's description of the cutting of the lock has an even broader inclusiveness than this in its yoking of the principles of joining and division. For it not only recalls Belinda's distant, rejecting—in a word, closed—attitude toward men, but it reasserts the motivational connection between that evasiveness and the ultimate consummation of the rape. In one and the same conceit, two joining-separations are contained: the literal severing of the lock, which is consummation itself, and the identification of that consummation with the female aloofness that motivates it. Through the highly sophisticated use of a couplet counterpoint which itself seems to mimic a scissor motion, the evasion and completion of sex are brought into congruence with one another just as the *Rape* as a whole attempts to fashion a congruence between Belinda's far-ranging "influence" and the Baron's assault upon her.

Pope may create a metaphorical framework in which Belinda is an all-pervasive force, a prime mover, and a symbol for the world; but it is the concrete specificity of the Baron's literal deed that we find at the true heart of this poem and the structure and syntax of which determine everything around it. Insofar as "spreading" behavior is engaged in by Belinda for her own sake, it is condemned as an arrogation of masculinity. Insofar as such behavior is contained within the broader context of male display and male spreading, however, it is legitimized. By virtue of anatomical fact, Pope's key verb may be inexorably gender-related, but at the hub of his poem he resolutely establishes a syntax in which woman is not the proper subject of that verb, but its passive object.

NOTES

1. All references to Pope's poems, cited by line number, or by canto or epistle and line number, in my text, are to *The Twickenham Edition of the Poems of Alexander Pope*, gen. ed. John Butt (New Haven: Yale University Press; London: Methuen): vol. 2, *The Rape of the Lock and Other Poems*, ed. Geoffrey Tillotson, 3d ed., (1962); vol. 3, i, *An Essay on Man*, ed. Maynard Mack (1950); vol. 3, ii, *Epistles to Several Persons*, ed. F. W. Bateson, 2d ed. (1961). *The Rape of the Lock* will be abbreviated as *Rape* and *An Essay on Man* as *EM* throughout.

2. Earl Wasserman also reads Belinda's resistance to wedlock as a means of avoiding subjection, in "The Limits of Allusion in *The Rape of the Lock*," *JEGP* 65 (1966): 436.

3. In another connection, Pat Rogers refers to the Cave of Spleen episode as a "miniature psychomachia" in "Faery Lore and *The Rape of the Lock*," *RES*, n.s. 25 (1974): 32.

4. Keener, p. 42.

5. Miller discusses the phenomenon of female vulnerability as it emerges in eighteenth-century prose fiction: "Fictional memoir or epistolary novel, the chronology of the feminine destiny is rooted in sexuality. In a universe ruled by the prerogatives of gender, it is logical and economical to have the movement of the plot triggered by the 'polarizing conjuncture' . . . : the erotic confrontation. The memoir—whose author is most often an orphan—usually opens with an exposition/exposure of the heroine's vulnerability: coded as lack of experience, protection, money. . . . In the epistolary novel where the heroine is often a daughter well-protected by parents determined to guard their offspring's innocence, the challenge to security generally results from the transformation of a masculine figure already in place: from neutral to sexual. . . . A young woman is *vulnerable* (and etymology is relevant here) by nature, by virtue of gender. Absent parents or omnipresent parents simply overload a circuit, overcode a system already set up to transmit only one kind of information" ("The Exquisite Cadavers: Women in Eighteenth-Century Fiction," *Diacritics* 5, no. 4 [Winter 1975]: 39).

6. For discussion of the relation of reason and will to the humors, consult Tillyard, pp. 66–73. Ernst Cassirer is also useful on the

subject of freedom and necessity in Renaissance thought in *The Individual and the Cosmos in Renaissance Philosophy* (Oxford: Clarendon Press, 1963), chap. 3.

7. As Earl Wasserman notes in "The Limits of Allusion," "John Dennis was on the right track without knowing it when he complained that the poet should have asked what strange motive could *induce* or *provoke* 'A well-bred *Lord* t'assault a gentle *Belle*' (I,8). 'The Word *compel*,' Dennis astutely observed, 'supposes the Baron to be a Beast, and not a free agent'" (p. 429).

8. The expression "two-way vision" is William K. Wimsatt's in his introduction to *Alexander Pope: Selected Poetry and Prose* (New York: Holt, Rinehart and Winston, 1951), p. xxi.

9. "Remarks," pp. 334–35.

10. Janeway, p. 52.

11. One thinks, too, of Samson's loss of strength at Delilah's hands. Stanley Edgar Hyman also refers to Belinda's "rape" as a ritual initiation in "The Rape of the Lock," *Hudson Review* 13 (1960): 411.

12. Eagleton, *The Rape of Clarissa*, p. 57.

13. Wasserman, p. 436.

14. Wasserman, p. 427.

15. *La Destinée féminine dans le roman européen du dix-huitième siècle 1713–1807: Essai de gynécomythie romanesque* (Paris: Armand Colin, 1972), p. 317; the translation is Miller's in "Exquisite Cadavers," p. 39.

16. "Remarks," pp. 344–45.

17. For an interesting commentary on the idea of a woman's beauty "ravishing" a man, see Gubar, p. 387. Judith Wilt's discussion of the lexical relationship between "ravishment" and "rape" in "He Could Go No Farther: A Modest Proposal about Lovelace and Clarissa," *PMLA* 92 (1977): 19–20, is also of interest in this connection.

18. *The Philosophy of Literary Form: Studies in Symbolic Action*, 2d ed. (Baton Rouge: Louisiana State University Press, 1967), p. 30. Jeffrey Meyers actually analyzes the Baron as a fetishist in "The Personality of Belinda's Baron: Pope's 'The Rape of the Lock,'" *American Imago* 26 (1969): 71–77.

19. Rudat, p. 53.

20. See Wasserman, who reads the belle's distress at the loss of her lock in terms of an allusive tradition in which the "bride's lamentation is veiled jubilation" (p. 442).

21. On the role of coffee vapors in the *Rape*, see Keener, pp. 43–44. Through an allusion to the *Iliad* in the concluding lines of Canto III of the *Rape*, Pope also effects an important link between Fate and Steel:

> What Wonder then, fair Nymph! thy Hairs shou'd feel
> The conqu'ring Force of unresisted Steel?

[cf. *Iliad*, V. 777: "Urg'd by the Force of unresisted Fate"] Since Pope also establishes a link between the epic sword and the phallus, an implicit association between fate and phallus (i.e., man) emerges. The moral Pope's poem seems intent on repeating is that man is woman's fate.

SONG OF MYSELF
(WALT WHITMAN)

"Whitman's *Song of Myself*:
Homosexual Dream and Vision"
by Robert K. Martin,
in *Partisan Review* (1975)

INTRODUCTION

In this excerpt from his Pushcart Prize-winning essay on
Whitman's "dream-vision poems," Robert K. Martin analyzes
the homosexual imagery and structure of "The Sleepers"
to better understand "the strength" and "inner unity" of
Song of Myself. Characterizing *Song of Myself* as both a
"body/soul dialogue" and a "love poem," Martin traces the
loose structure of the poem from seduction, to fulfillment,
and, finally, "to the vision which follows on sexual experience [. . .and] permits the poet to perceive the unity of all
things." According to Martin, Whitman's "poetry of vision"
springs from "the euphoria of the satisfied lover," where the
speaker imagines that the world is physically embodied in
his partner. Through this sexual encounter with the world,
Whitman's speaker finds peace.

Martin, Robert K. "Whitman's *Song of Myself*: Homosexual Dream and Vision."
Partisan Review, Vol. 42, No.1 (1975); 80–96.

It has become common among critics of Walt Whitman to argue that the protracted debate over the nature of the poet's sexuality, whether he may have been homosexual, heterosexual, or bisexual, is essentially beside the point. This argument has not been based on any reading of the poetry, but rather on the general modern and "liberal" tendency towards acceptance and tolerance. Acceptance and tolerance of homosexuality have not only been disastrous for the development of a homosexual consciousness; they have also led to a critical irresponsibility which seeks to equate all experience and to deny that homosexuals are "really" different from heterosexuals (to test the absurdity, substitute women and men, or blacks and whites).

Homosexuality shares a number of the general functions of all sexuality, but it bears a particular burden, given the social view of homosexuality and the virtual universality of repression of homosexual desires, at least in their most overt or public manifestations. The homosexual artist has a double need to express his sexual drives through his art because he is (or was) far less able than his heterosexual brother to give expression to these drives in his own life. In a society which attaches serious penalties to the open practice of homosexuality, the homosexual will often turn to art as a way of confronting those desires that he cannot acknowledge through action. Through the symbolism of his art he can communicate the facts of his homosexuality to his readers, knowing that those of them who are similarly homosexual will read the signs properly. Thus it was certainly with Whitman. He wrote a large part of his poetry directly out of his own sexual conflicts and fantasies, and he used his poetry to convey the news of his homosexuality to his readers. He knew that they were to be his "cameradoes," his only faithful lovers and only true readers, for all others would (Whitman predicted accurately) fail to see the "message" that would be unmistakable to some:

> This hour I tell things in confidence,
> I might not tell everybody, but I will tell you.
> (Song of Myself, sec. 19)

Whitman's (Mis)readers

Whatever homosexual readers may have thought (and John Addington Symonds was but the first to have recognized Whitman's homosexual meanings; he has been echoed by gay writers from André Gide to Allen Ginsberg to any of a large number of young American poets all of whom take Whitman as a point of reference, exceeded by no other American gay poet with the possible exception of Hart Crane), Whitman's readers in general have made a sorry record of misreading Whitman's poems. If one is charitable, one can suggest that these readers were simply unable to see the homosexual meanings, which were so divorced from their own experiences. But I am not inclined to be charitable. The record of absolute lies and half-truths and distortions is so shameful as to amount to a deliberate attempt to alter reality to suit a particular view of normality. If Whitman is to be a great poet, then he must be straight. If the poetry shows something else, Whitman must be made to alter his own poetry, censor himself. Despite considerable concessions made by Whitman during the course of his career, and the removal of a number of passages, the rabid heterosexualists were not satisfied. Whitman's life must be betrayed, rewritten, and his poems reread in a "safe" manner. Whitman must be saved from himself.

The process of this creation of a new, false Whitman is so well known that I will not spend too much time recounting its details. But it is important to note the extent to which otherwise respectable and reliable critics went in their efforts to "clean" Whitman up. The first stage, the most overt, was directed toward biography, toward proving that Whitman was actively heterosexual in his personal life. In part this stage was provoked by Symonds' famous letter to Whitman and Whitman's equally famous (and comic) reply, in which he boasted of having fathered six illegitimate children. Whitman had played the role of good citizen, especially in his old age, despite the barely concealed friendships with younger men (which are discussed in some detail by Edwin Haviland Miller), and his older friends continued the fiction of his life. But the first critics were not content with such an absence of open homosexuality: they needed proof of heterosexuality. So the New Orleans story was invented, out of nothing but a desire to prove that Whitman was normal. And even otherwise sensitive readers of Whitman, such as Emory Holloway, William Carlos Williams, and Babette Deutsch, continued to believe in the story long after its total fictitiousness had been demonstrated. Doubtless many still do.

The case of Holloway was particularly disappointing since it was he who was responsible, in 1920, for revealing that the poem which seemed to give rise to the New Orleans story, "Once I Pass'd Through a Populous City," had been changed prior to publication by Whitman to alter "I remember only the man who wandered with me there for love of me," to "I remember only a woman I casually met there who detain'd me for love of me." One would have thought that such evidence would have been conclusive. But no, the New Orleans story blooms again whenever someone wants to refuse to believe that Whitman loved other men. Even those critics who must of course admit the textual evidence refuse to accord any significance to it: James E. Miller, Jr., in his important book on *Leaves of Grass*, published in 1957, commented, "Although Holloway's discovery may be biographically revealing, the poem has the 'meaning,' surely of its final version." How convenient when a new-critical principle can be used to buttress what is essentially nothing more than a refusal to admit an unpleasant truth! One wonders what argument would have been used if the homosexual meaning were in fact the published version—as is the case of virtually all the Calamus poems as well as of large numbers of poems scattered throughout the *Leaves of Grass*.

Many critics have at least been honest about this prejudice. Whitman criticism is full of the vocabulary of social opprobrium and the clichés of undigested psychoanalysis. Even homosexuals themselves have used words of scorn—Symonds says "symptoms of emotional abnormality" and Newton Arvin spoke of a "core of abnormality." Others have been more vicious. Mark Van Doren in 1942 was able to write, "Manly love is neither more nor less than an abnormal and deficient love."

Since that time the heterosexual attacks on Whitman have become more subtle, and perhaps ultimately more damaging. They have used sophisticated techniques of literary analysis to demonstrate that sexuality is not an important aspect of Whitman's poetry. The most insistent of these arguments is that advanced by James Miller, in his reading of "Song of Myself," for instance, as an "inverted mystical experience" (he didn't mean the pun on invert there). By seeing patterns of mystic symbolism (which is identical to erotic imagery, except that it does not mean what it purports to mean, but only uses sex to talk about God) at crucial points in the poem, Miller diverts the reader's attention from the poetry's frankly and directly sexual nature. Miller's argument at least had the virtue of making us look again at the "mystical" Whitman and making us return to the visionary poet; in the hands of his less talented followers, the arguments singularly lack charm, as in this recent example from Thomas E. Crawley's *The Structure of Leaves of Grass* (1970): "To associate it (These I Singing in Spring) with any crude, sensuous interpretation of the calamus-symbol is to miss the mystical beauty" or again "the gross interpretation . . . that the root is a symbol of the male sexual organ."

A recent, "liberated" version of Whitman's poetry illustrates the failure of the "liberal" reading. Walter Lowenfels' edition of *The Tenderest Lover: The Erotic Poetry of Walt Whitman* purports to be honest. Lowenfels maintains with pride, "Our text . . . is unexpurgated; erotic lines and passages that Whitman changed or deleted have been restored." But although the text is restored, the editor feels obliged to insist on the interchangeability of the sexes. He writes of the famous "Once I Pass' d Through a Populous City" text, "What is intrinsic to the poem is not the sex of the loved one but the love itself."

Such intellectual softheadedness is characteristic of this reprehensible edition which is only possible because of the critic's need to romanticize (i.e. render abstract) a sexuality which he finds distasteful. One can hardly expect much of anyone who can write such garbage as "Whitman was a prophet of today's sexual revolution . . . In his love poems, youth speaks to youth of all ages, across all centuries and languages." But he goes on to ignore crucial and obvious evidence, and refers to "the unnamed him or her whom Whitman identified only by the number '16' or '164.'" The rankest amateur in cryptography knows that Whitman meant P or PD, Peter Doyle.

The history of Whitman criticism in this connection is shameful. I can think of no parallel example of the willful distortion of meaning and the willful misreading of a poet in order to suit critics' own social or moral prejudices. And it must be added that the very few critics who spoke against this tradition of distortion were generally Europeans, who perhaps did not totally share American Society's total and relentless hostility to the homosexual. It is thanks to the work of Jean Catel, Roger Asselineau, and Frederik Schyberg that Whitman finally can be seen as a poet of sexual love between men. In the last few years there has been the important work done by Edwin Haviland Miller, which has unfortunately not received the attention it deserves (despite his overly normative Freudian bias). One begins to suspect that the history of Whitman misreading is not over.

Whitman's own life was marked by the same pressures toward sexual conformity that now lead to critical distortions. He seems to have felt the need to act out a role, to hide behind the mask of the tough. And he had to learn the strategies of concealment, strategies that, until recently at least, all of us had to learn in order to succeed as homosexuals in a heterosexual world. The changing of texts, the excision of passages, these are but the most obvious of what must have been an enormously painful series of acts performed almost daily in order to conform to someone else's version of normality. And how painful they must have been to the man who was able to give another man a wedding band, who from his youth on wrote with passion only of friendship between men, who cried out in suffering "O unspeakable passionate love" (Song of Myself, sec. 21) for the love, "the secret of my nights and days," which lay hidden "in paths untrodden."

One important consequence of his homosexuality is that Whitman, unlike so many male poets, does not see women as sexual objects even in his ostensibly heterosexual poems. Freed of the need to enslave the opposite sex, the homosexual is free to see women as human beings, and thus we find in Whitman a strong sense of compassion for suffering figures of women—the mother, the prostitute, the spinster. It is not only that he does not see woman as sex object, but that he can thereby see himself as self-enjoying. Whitman's poetry is frequently autoerotic in the sense that he takes his own body as a source of sexual pleasure much as Freud's famous polymorphously perverse child does, and derives pleasure from his own orgasm, rather than from any sense of conquest or aggression.

Whitman makes no distinction between subject and object (a distinction necessary to the position of woman as "other" and as property). All experience becomes a part of himself—"Absorbing all to myself and for this song" (sec. 13)—as the total egotism of the child is restored. The "Song of Myself" is the song of the world, as seer and seen, male and female become one. If Whitman's vision is regressive, it looks back to an earlier ideal of play. We need to see the sensitivity, the *finesse* of Whitman, a sensitivity which has too long been obscured by the image of him as

Walt Whitman, A Kosmos, of Manhattan the son,
Turbulent, fleshy, sensual, eating, drinking and breeding
(Song of Myself, sec. 24)

This was what Whitman wanted to seem to be; but the poetry reveals the happy truth that he was indeed a much deeper, more sensitive person than he dared admit.

WHITMAN'S DREAM-VISION POETRY

The great debate over homosexuality in Whitman's poetry has generally centered on the poems in the Calamus section or those poems which, although not actually placed in that section, seemed to belong there, by similarity of theme or imagery. But this emphasis is somewhat unfortunate for two reasons. First it tends to isolate the "homosexual" poems of Whitman into one neat category which can be labelled and then safely forgotten and put away. Second it tends to assume that Whitman's sexuality is only relevant to his most explicit and frequently didactic poems. On the (hopeful) assumption that most readers are capable of reading Calamus themselves, I have therefore preferred to center my discussion here on another mode of Whitman's poetry, which is perhaps slightly more elusive and yet which seems to me essential to an understanding of the whole body of his work. I refer to what I have called Whitman's dream-vision poems, those poems which are written in a state of the mind somewhere beneath full consciousness and which invoke the experience of the mind in that state.

"The Sleepers" has received a fair amount of attention in recent years, probably due to the general interest in stream of consciousness techniques and also to a new willingness to look more carefully at explicit sexual imagery. I do not wish to give a full reading of the poem here—one may be referred to the helpful comments of Leslie Fiedler and Edwin Haviland Miller in particular, as well as to the reading of James E. Miller—but I do want to look at it sufficiently to suggest that it is similar to "Song of Myself" in its sense of wavering consciousness, in its use of cosmic observation, in its shifts through time and space, and in its sexual imagery.

"The Sleepers" is explicitly about a vision, as the first line informs us, and its action is the movement of the poet within his vision,

> I wander all night in my vision,
> Stepping with light feet, swiftly and noiselessly stepping
>   and stopping,

Bending with open eyes over the shut eyes of sleepers,
Wandering and confused, lost to myself, ill-assorted,
    contradictory,
Pausing, gazing, bending, and stopping.

The first section of the poem is agitated, marked by continual movement. The poet uses the game metaphor to depict the atmosphere of levity which prevails as the covers are lifted and the genitals are revealed.

wild-flapping pennants of joy!

It concludes with a remarkable depiction of orgasm, in which it becomes clear that the naked speaker who has been exposed is using his body as a metaphor for his penis and that the entire exposure motif of the poem operates on these two levels (the exposure of the poet for what he is—the fear of being revealed as a homosexual—and the exposure of the penis which may bring forth castration anxiety in a hostile world). The text is worth quoting in full, especially since Whitman later removed these lines from the 1855 edition and they are therefore not present in most of the editions regularly used.

O hotcheeked and blushing! O foolish hectic!
O for pity's sake, no one must see me now! .... my
    clothes were stolen while I was abed,
Now I am thrust forth, where shall I run?
Pier that I saw dimly last night when I looked from the
windows
Pier out from the main, let me catch myself with you and
    stay. . . . I will not chafe you;
I feel ashamed to go naked about the world,
And am curious to know where my feet stand ... and
    what is this flooding me, childhood or manhood.
    . . . . and the hunger that crosses the bridge between.

The cloth laps a first sweet eating and drinking,
Laps life-swelling yolks. . . . laps ear of rose-corn, milky
    and just ripened:
The white teeth stay, and the boss-tooth advances in darkness,

> And liquor is spilled on lips and bosoms by touching
>   glasses, and the best liquor afterward.

Miller manages to see vaginal imagery here, but I do not see it.
It seems clear to me that what is being depicted is the act known
politely as fellatio—the penis protrudes from the foreskin, the balls
are sucked, the penis is sucked, and finally there is ejaculation in the
mouth. The sexual experience is the starting place for the poem, and
the poet begins his vision with the second section, after the orgasm
when "my sinews are flaccid / Perfume and youth course through
me, and I am their wake." The physical experience leads toward the
spiritual experience which is the dream, and which is also in its turn
physical and sexual.

     The third section brings a fantasy of the destruction of the "beau-
tiful gigantic swimmer," a warning in dream terms of the dangers in
the unconscious world of the sea with its "swift-running eddies." The
swimmer seems to be a sexual object, but is also an ideal presentation
of the self. The dream of the third section is a dream of the destruction
of the self—the clue lies in Whitman's surprising line "will you kill
him in the prime of his middle age?" (Whitman was 35 at the time)
and in the transition to the next section through its first line, "I turn
but do not extricate myself." The poet-dreamer wants to escape from
his dream, but the nightmare is not yet over. In another key passage
that was omitted from later editions Whitman introduces his conflict
with the Satanic through the figure of Lucifer (whom Whitman
seems perhaps to have taken in his literal sense as light-bearer, for it
is the coming of dawn that will destroy the dream and take away the
lover, real or imaginary).

     The theme of slavery is linked to the sexual by the sequence of
the poem, where the poet moves from the mother's vision of the "red
squaw":

> My mother looked in delight and amazement at the stranger,
> She looked at the beauty of her tallborne face and full and
>   pliant limbs,
> The more she looked upon her she loved her

to his own identification with the black slaves. Both evoke guilt
because of their (implicit) double violation of taboo: homosexuality

and miscegenation are the twin crimes so feared in American thought. (And we recall that Whitman's famous letter implied that he had broken the lesser of the two, lest he be found guilty of the greater!)

Starting with section 7 there is a drastic change brought about by the poet's acceptance of the world, an acceptance which is possible through his perception of unity in space and time. The agitation of sexuality, the immediate sensation of guilt following it, and the fantasy of death and loss which accompany its completion give way to a sense of sexual calm and peace. The poet learns to accept the daytime world of disunity ("the rich running day") because it is part of the cycle which always leads back to the night and love and the Great Mother. His love of experience and diversity does not lead him to forget the world of unity and calm, but rather to accept both:

> I love the rich running day, but I do not desert her
>   in whom I lay so long:
> . . .
> I will stop only a time with the night, and rise betimes.
> I will duly pass the day O my mother and duly return to you.

Much as I am indebted to the thoughtful book of Edwin Haviland Miller (*Walt Whitman's Poetry: A Psychological Journey*), I must take issue with his particular emphasis on such a passage as evidence of Whitman's regressive patterns and what he implies to be an unresolved oedipal situation. I do not feel any *personal* maternal qualities in his poem. The mother addressed here seems to me to be a universal mother, goddess of the night, of the dream, of the vision, of all that is excluded from the daylight world of jobs, reason, and fathers. Reading the poem in terms of personal psychology seems to me to miss the essential significance of Whitman's vision, which achieves a return to a state of primal consciousness, which is pre-patriarchal, and cyclical rather than linear. His essentially matriarchal vision leads him to send the poet back to the Night-Mother (forces of darkness, mystery, and the unknown) to be reborn from her. The Mother is the death-sleep which follows upon the male striving of sexuality, but it is also the repose that heals and out of which the fallen penis may rise again:

> Not you will yield forth the dawn again more surely than
> you will yield forth me again,

Not the womb yields the babe in its time more surely than
I shall be yielded from you in my time.

The sexual experience is revealed by this poem to be the gateway
to the visionary—literally because ejaculation leads to sleep and
thus to dream, but metaphorically because it is the realization of
the possibility of transcending the self through sexual ecstasy which
leads to an acceptance of the world. As we fall off to sleep following
orgasm, we are able to see a kind of inner sense in the world, a
world freed from the pressures of the day and in which we have
regained a kind of repose that Freud thought found its only model
in intrauterine existence. Through that vision Whitman could come
to his understanding of the world and greet all men and women
as sleepers, each dreaming his own dream, but each dream like the
others.

"SONG OF MYSELF"

Whitman's most important poem, in terms of length, and in terms
of the themes broached there, is clearly his "Song of Myself." Critics
have attempted to find an adequate way of understanding the poem's
strength and sense of inner unity despite an appearance of disorder,
but no one has fully explained the poem's patterns by looking at
it in the light of "The Sleepers" as a dream-vision based on sexual
experience. I would like to attempt such a reading now with the
clear understanding that I am not denying any epic or mystic or
democratic elements—they are clearly all there but they do not
explain how the poem works, nor do they deal with any of the sexual
structure.

The poem appears, at first glance, to be very unlike "The Sleepers"
in that it seems to be the product of a wholly conscious mind which is
engaged in a number of identifiable traditional poetic functions—e.g.
singing, being an epic poet; debating, being a metaphysical poet. But
a careful look at the poem will reveal that the poem is a monologue
posing as a dialogue, or perhaps a dialogue which turns out to be a
monologue. A dialogue for one speaker might be a nice way of putting
it. The second role is clearly nonspeaking.

The mode of the poem seems to be a body/soul dialogue, such
as those popular in the Renaissance, and known in American

poetry through the example of Anne Bradstreet. But the body does most of the talking, the soul does not seem to respond, and the reader is addressed so often and so insistently as "you" that he indeed becomes a part of the poem. The poem is cast as a love poem; it involves a seduction, a growing desire which leads to final fulfillment and then to the vision which follows on sexual experience and which, as in "The Sleepers", permits the poet to perceive the unity of all things. The poem also ends with a sense of contentment brought on by acceptance but not until the poet has marked the end of the night by bidding farewell to his lover.

The structure of the poem is loose, but nonetheless clear if one follows the basic themes which are developed. I can only outline a few of them here and suggest their similarity to the patterns we have already seen in "The Sleepers." The first section is a very brief introduction, particularly in the 1855 edition, where it consists of only five lines which provide a setting and the argument. In the second section, the process of natural intoxication has begun. The poet concludes this section by asking the you-reader to "stop this day and night with me." It is clear that, in fantasy at least, the request is granted, and the rest of the poem is an account of that day and night. At this very early stage of the poem it is clear that the poet has a sense of acceptance—"I am satisfied" he writes—and that acceptance is based on the metaphor of God as the lover who sleeps with him by night, leaving him "baskets covered with white towels bulging the house with their plenty." In the scarcely concealed sexual symbolism of this section, the genitals are hidden by white towels, not unlike the "cunning covers" of "The Sleepers." It is the coming of God at night which gives the poet a "bulging basket" and permits him to accept the day in the knowledge of a forthcoming night and permits him to ask whether in fact he should

> postpone by acceptation and realization and scream at my
> eyes,
>   That they turn from gazing after and down the road,
>   And forthwith cipher and show me to a cent,
> Exactly the value of one and exactly the value of two,
>   and which is ahead?

In the world of nighttime vision there is no counting, one and two are the same, real and imaginary lovers are equal.

The poet continues his address to you, through the recollection of a previous sexual experience which is the source of his first knowledge of peace:

> I mind how once we lay such a transparent summer morning,
> How you settled your head athwart my hips and gently turn'd
>   upon me,
> And parted the shirt from my bosom-bone, and plunged
>   your tongue to my bare-stript heart,
> And reach'd till you felt my beard, and reach'd till you held my
>   feet.

From this reminder of previous love and the insights it gave, the poet turns to the beginning of a new sexual experience, which begins with undressing of the you; "undrape!" Once undraped the loved one is subject of one of the most interesting passages of this poem, section 8, which depicts the progress of life through sexual metaphor.

> The little one sleeps in its cradle,
> I lift the gauze and look a long time, and silently brush away flies
>   with my hand.
>
> The youngster and the red-faced girl turn aside up the bushy
>   hill,
> I peeringly view them from the top.
>
> The suicide sprawls on the bloody floor of the bedroom,
> I witness the corpse with its dabbled hair, I note where the
>   pistol has fallen.

From childhood to adolescence to death; from birth to reproduction to death; from the "little one . . . in its cradle" to the "bushy hill" to "the bloody floor . . . the pistol has fallen." The sight of nakedness leads in visual terms to a realization of death and suggests the ambivalent attitude toward the male genitals. But it is crucial to see that if one "cannot be shaken away" then one must accept all. He must accept the penis beneath the foreskin, the erect penis, and the penis after coitus. The acceptance of these three stages can lead to an acceptance of the same three stages of life and thereby to an acceptance of life as a whole in all its multiplicity, and so the second half of this leads to the first catalogue, and we begin to understand the meaning in Whitman's work of the catalogue—the expression of ultimate unity of things seen not on their surface but seen *sub specie aeternitatae*, a point of view that for Whitman was best arrived at through a sexual experience.

The following sections of the poem go out, literally, into the world and lead, for instance, to the celebrated section 11, where the abstract vision of section 8 is transformed into a very specific vision of masturbation.

> Twenty-eight young men bathe by the shore,
> Twenty-eight young men and all so friendly;
> Twenty-eight years of womanly life and all so lonesome.
>
> She owns the fine house by the rise of the bank
> She hides handsome and richly drest aft the blinds of the
>   window.
>
> Which of the young men does she like the best?
> Ah the homeliest of them is beautiful to her.
>
> Where are you off to, lady? for I see you,
> You splash in the water there, yet stay stock still in your room
>
> Dancing and laughing along the beach came the twenty-ninth
>   bather,
> The rest did not see her, but she saw them and loved them.
>
> The beards of the young men glisten'd with wet, it ran from
>   their long hair,
> Little streams pass'd all over their bodies.
>
> An unseen hand also pass'd over their bodies,
> It descended tremblingly from their temples and ribs.

The young men float on their backs, their white bellies bulge
   to the sun, they do not ask who seizes fast to them,
They do not know who puffs and declines with pendant and
   bending arch,
They do not think whom they souse with spray.

This poem, or part of the poem, is exquisite in its evocation of
the mood of sexual arousal. As many readers have pointed out,
Whitman achieves the feat here of being both subject and object,
of being the woman voyeur, and also of being the men who are
masturbated. Not only is this one of the loveliest sexual poems I
know, it is also a clear defense of the anonymity of sexual encounter.
In the dream-vision of Whitman there are no persons, but rather
a general feeling of the delight of sexual experience regardless of
the partner. They are totally tactile, since they take place in the
dream-world of closed eyes. The experience could well be repeated
in almost any steam bath of a modern large city. But the important point to see is that not asking, not knowing and not thinking
are integral parts of Whitman's *democratic* vision, and anonymous
sexuality is an important way-station on the path to the destruction of distinctions of age, class, beauty, *and* sex. Whitman loves all
being, and will love, and be loved by, all being. It is perhaps at this
juncture that the implications of Whitman's perspective become
most revolutionary.

The sense of universality of experience leads to the long cata-
logues of the following sections, which introduce the transitional
sections 21 and 22, concerned with the yearning for love. In section
21, Whitman returns to his Body/Soul division to express his desire
to return to the bodily. He concludes the section with the line I have
quoted earlier:

unspeakable passionate love

and then 2 lines omitted in later editions but which make the sexual
male marriage metaphor clear:

Thruster holding me tight and that I hold tight
We hurt each other as the bridegroom and the bride hurt each
   other.

The sense of growing desire and longing culminates in section 24, where playing gives way to direct phallic arousal, and introduction of the calamus theme. The sperm is risen up:

> You my rich blood! Your milky stream pale strippings of my life.

As the poet imagines himself making love, his assertions become bolder. He refuses the stigma that society may attach: "What we do is right and what we affirm is right." The imagery becomes more violent as he asserts his right to homosexual love

> Unscrew the locks from the doors!
> Unscrew the doors themselves from their jambs!

All that is hidden must be exposed; there must be no secrets, in this metaphor strikingly similar to the more modern "Out of the closets into the streets!" As his ire increases, the blood and sperm rise, he introduces his calamus symbol ("Root of washed sweet-flag, timorous pond-snipe, nest of guarded duplicate eggs") as a metaphor for his own genitals, and he is able to sing all of the body, with penis and sperm ("Your milky stream pale strippings of my life"). The extraordinary crescendo of section 24 is based in sexual ecstasy and reaches its culmination in a sexual climax: "Seas of bright juice suffuse heaven."

And yet suddenly the passage comes to an end with the apparent arrival of the dawn, which would destroy the night. The reference is at the same time ambiguous, since the physical dawn would end the nighttime vision, but the day-break of sexual ecstasy would show the poet the possibility of ultimate victory over the day through his sexual powers.

> Dazzling and tremendous how quick the sunrise would kill me,
> If I could not now and always send sunrise out of me.

> We also ascend dazzling and tremendous as the sun
> We found our own my soul in the calm and cool
>   of the daybreak.

Man can make his own sunrise and thereby master the natural world
and escape the necessity of the cyclical pattern—recalling the first
sexual experience, section 5, which also took place in the morning.
Making love in the morning seems to break the tyranny of the day.

The next few sections record the poet and his playful reluctance to
give in, to let himself be brought to orgasm, a coyness which is ended
by rebirth of section 28.

> Is this then a touch? quivering me to a new identity,
> Flames and ether making a rush for my veins,
> Treacherous tip of me reaching and crowding to help them,
> My flesh and blood playing out lightning to strike what is
>   hardly different from myself,
> On all sides prurient provokers stiffening my limbs,
> Straining the udder of my heart for its withheld drip,
> Behaving licentious toward me, taking no denial,
> Depriving me of my best as for a purpose,
> Unbuttoning my clothes, holding me by the bare waist,
> Deluding my confusion with the calm of the sunlight and
>   pasture-fields,
> Immodestly sliding the fellow-senses away,
> They bribed to swap off with touch and go and graze at the
>   edges of me,
> No consideration, no regard for my draining strength or my
>   anger,
> Fetching the rest of the herd around to enjoy them a while,
> Then all uniting to stand on a headland and worry me.
> The sentries desert every other part of me,
> They have left me helpless to a red marauder,
> They all come to the headland to witness and assist against me.
> I am given up by traitors,
> I talk wildly, I have lost my wits, I and nobody else am
>   the greatest traitor,
> I went myself first to the headland, my own hands carried me
>   there.
> You villain touch! what are you doing? my breath is tight in
>   its throat,
> Unclench your floodgates, you are too much for me.

This most extraordinary passage is almost certainly a depiction of anal intercourse, in which Whitman has turned the entire physical experience into mythic proportions and sees himself reborn as he takes into himself the seed of the unnamed lover. The cycle is complete, the sexual anticipation is ended through fulfillment, tension gives way to satisfaction, and the pattern we have now come to recognize is again present: the orgasm is followed by passages of philosophical summary and visionary perception of unity.

Something very similar happens a few sections further on, in section 32, when he turns to the stallion, symbol of the male lover. But the poet who in section 28 was the so-called passive partner in anal intercourse has now become the active partner as Whitman makes vivid the banal sexual metaphor of "riding" someone.

> A gigantic beauty of a stallion, fresh and responsive to my
>   caresses,
> Head high in the forehead, wide between the ears,
> Limbs glossy and supple, tail dusting the ground,
> Eyes full of sparkling wickedness, ears finely cut, flexibly moving.
> Hair nostrils dilate as my heels embrace him.
> His well-built limbs tremble with pleasure as we race around
>   and return

Thus again the sexual leads to the visionary, in this case to the famous section 33, where the poet is "afoot in my vision," recalling the first lines of "The Sleepers."

This vision, like those in "The Sleepers," includes the negative, for the poet is not able to separate sexuality from guilt. Death images are pervasive and culminate in his vision of himself as a crucified victim, in section 38. His racial memory includes all experience, and all suffering. He becomes a sacrificial victim, taking upon himself the sins of the world, and thereby assuring the safety and the sleep of his beloved. Reborn like the resurrected Christ, he can begin his journey across the continent—"Ohio and Massachusetts and Virginia and Wisconsin and New York and New Orleans and Texas and Montreal and San Francisco and Charleston and Savannah and Mexico"—and beyond. He recognizes that his poetic mission will be carried on by his élèves, the poet's disciples, who can learn the meaning of his words only if they have followed out the sexual patterns of the poem and have in fact become the poet's lovers. He is now awake but lets the other sleep:

> Sleep—I and they keep guard all night,
> Not doubt, not decease shall dare to lay finger upon you.

He carries his message of salvation, his Christ-like role to the world and feels certain of the correctness of his mission. Thus assured, he awakens the lover in section 44. "It is time to explain myself—let us stand up." He realizes that he has escaped the trap of reality through the acceptances, including that hardest of all to accept, Death. But once he has accepted it, and acceptance was already implied in section 8, he is already out of time and out of space (to quote Poe, who sometimes seems surprisingly like Whitman). Having achieved that state of ascension, he can now say good-by to the lover, recognizing his transitoriness. The recognition of death means that no earthly love is final; that all lovers will part; and so he parts from his lover, prepared to give himself to the world rather than to any one individual. He cannot take this lover with him, but must ask him to make his own journey.

> Not I, not anyone else can travel that road for you,
> You must travel it for yourself
>
> . . .
> I kiss you a good-by kiss. . .
> Long have you timidly waded holding a plank by the shore,
> Now I will you to be a bold swimmer
> To jump off in the midst of the sea. . .

Having made love, learned about the world, and then bid the world adieu, he is calm again, he has found happiness. Characteristically Whitman's image is physical and sensual:

> Wrench'd and sweaty—calm and cool then my body becomes,
> I sleep—I sleep long.

It is only after the experience of sexual gratification, achieved through the dream, that the visionary experience becomes possible. It is the euphoria of the satisfied lover that gives rise to Whitman's poetry of vision—the poems of realization of unity. Its needs fulfilled, the body expands to encompass the world, through its physical embodiment of the lover, who in his role as "other" is the world. One can accept the death of the world only after transcending unitary death, escaping beyond the fear of the "little death" into a realization that all death brings resurrection, that the penis shall indeed rise again.

* * *

Homosexuals are a constant affront to the society, because they demand to be defined in terms of their sexuality. The homosexual has no existence as a group unless it is through sexual preferences and experiences. He cannot be wished away with the thought that such matters are of no importance, or with the piety that all human experience is basically similar. Whitman's poetry, particularly "Song of Myself," shows how the poet translates his love for the world, his cosmic promiscuity, into a myth of the wandering lover seeking his partners in all places and at all times. The visionary is rooted in the sexual, and Whitman will not let his root be torn out. He remains what he is for those who will read him, despite all that has been done to him. He can be secure in the knowledge he spoke of in "Scented herbage of my breast" and which we have seen to be fundamental to his other poems as well:

> Every year shall you bloom again, out from where you retired
>   you shall emerge again;
> O I do not know whether many passing by will discover you or
>   inhale your faint odor, but I believe a few will;
>
> . . .
>
> Do not fold yourself so in your pink-ringed roots timid leaves!
> Do not remain down there so ashamed, herbage of my breast!
> Come I am determin'd to unbare this broad chest of mine, I
>   have long enough stifled and choked;
> Emblematic and capricious blades I leave you, now you serve
>   me not
> I will say what I have to say by itself,
> I will sound myself and comrades only, I will never again
>   utter a call only their call,

Out of the cycle of the penis is born the cycle of the soul; out of his erections, ejaculations (the pun is crucial), and re-erections comes Whitman's faith in a cycle of the world which will comprehend and conquer death. The real sleep is the sleep of the contented lover who will not die.

SONS AND LOVERS
(D. H. LAWRENCE)

"Sons and Lovers: A Freudian Appreciation"
by Alfred Booth Kuttner,
in The Psychoanalytic Review (1916)

INTRODUCTION

Claiming that D. H. Lawrence's *Sons and Lovers* is "truly creative, in that it is built up internally—as any masterpiece must be—out of the psychic conflicts of the author," Alfred Booth Kuttner analyzes the novel in accordance with the theories of human sexuality propounded by Sigmund Freud. Arguing that the novel is semiautobiographical, with Paul Morel standing in for Lawrence, Kuttner concludes that *Sons and Lovers* corroborates Freud's view of sexual development and yields a great deal of insight into Lawrence's artistic practice.

❦

Poets and novelists often strive for impressiveness in their creations by dealing in strange plots and adventures or in monstrous and unnatural loves. The advantages gained may well be called in question: to be grotesque is hardly ever to be great and the bizarre may survive as a

Kuttner, Alfred Booth. "*Sons and Lovers*: A Freudian Appreciation." *The Psychoanalytic Review* Vol. 3, No. 3 (July 1916): 295–317.

demerit after it is exhausted as a sensation. The great literature of life is after all built around the commonplace. [...] What distinguishes enduring literature is not novelty, but freshness of feeling, and that pointed insight into life which reveals a vivid personality keenly alive. *Sons and Lovers* has the great distinction of being very solidly based upon a veritable commonplace of our emotional life; it deals with a son who loved his mother too dearly, and with a mother who lavished all her affection upon her son.

Neither this distinction nor its undeniable freshness and often amazing style would of itself entitle Mr. D. H. Lawrence's novel to anything beyond an appreciative book review. But it sometimes happens that a piece of literature acquires an added significance by virtue of the support it gives to the scientific study of human motives. Literary records have the advantage of being the fixed and classic expression of human emotions which in the living individual are usually too fluid and elusive for deliberate study. The average man, subjected to what seems to him a kind of psychological vivisection, is apt to grow reticent, and mankind must often be convicted through its literature of impulses which under direct scrutiny it would acknowledge only with the greatest reluctance or else deny altogether. Literature thus becomes an invaluable accessory to the psychologist, who usually does well to regard with suspicion any new generalization from his researches for which the whole range of literary expression yields no corroboration. But if he can succeed in finding support there his position is immensely strengthened. For a new truth about ourselves, which may seem altogether grotesque and impossible when presented to us as an arid theory, often gains unexpected confirmation when presented to us in a powerful work of literature as an authentic piece of life. When at last we recognize ourselves we like the thrill of having made a discovery.

Sons and Lovers possesses this double quality to a high degree. It ranks high, very high as a piece of literature and at the same time it embodies a theory which it illustrates and exemplifies with a completeness that is nothing less than astonishing. [...] *Sons and Lovers* is thus truly creative, in that it is built up internally—as any masterpiece must be—out of the psychic conflicts of the author, and any testimony which it may bear to the truth of the theory involved will therefore be first hand.

The theory to which I have been referring is Professor Sigmund Freud's theory of the psychological evolution of the emotion of love as finally expressed by a man or a woman towards a member of the other sex, and the problem which Mr. Lawrence voices is the struggle of a man to emancipate himself from his maternal allegiance and to transfer his affections to a woman who stands outside of his family circle. What the poet has seen as a personal problem the scientist has formulated as a theory. I shall outline the problem first and then relate it to the theory. If the theory can succeed in generalizing the truth which Mr. Lawrence's novel presents the reader will realize with fresh force that fiction, to be great art, must be based upon human verities.

First we shall see how it happened that the mother in this story came to lavish all her affections upon her son. In the opening chapter Mrs. Morel, the wife of a Derbyshire coal miner, is expecting her third child, the boy Paul, who is to become the central figure of the story. Her life with her husband has already turned out to be a complete fiasco. He is a drunkard and a bully, a man with whom she shares neither intellectual, moral or religious sympathies. What strikes her most about Morel is that he presents a striking contrast to her father, who was to her "*the type of all men.*" For he had been a harsh, puritan type, given to theology and ignoring "all sensuous pleasure," while Morel is the very opposite; warm, sensuous and indulgent, with a "rich ringing laugh" and a "red, moist mouth." It is this sensuous quality in Morel which overwhelms and confounds her; she goes down before the sheer, impersonal male in him. After the sex illusion has worn off somewhat Mrs. Morel makes an attempt to draw nearer to her husband. But the clash of personalities is stronger than the transitory tie of their poetized passion and Morel's habitual drunkenness, his indulgent and shiftless ways, and his temperamental dishonesty are mercilessly flayed by his almost fanatically moral and religious wife. It is very easy for her to loathe him. At the time of the birth of her third child the breach is already irreparable. Mrs. Morel dreads the coming of another child, conceived unwillingly out of a loveless relation, and at the sight of it a sense of guilt steals over her. She will atone: "*With all her force, with all her soul she would make up to it for having brought it into the world unloved. She would love it all the more now it was hers; carry it in her love.*" Towards Paul she feels, as to none of the other children, that she must make up to him for an injury or a sin committed by her and that he must recompense her for all that she has missed in her shattered love for her husband.

All the early formative influences in Paul's life radiate from his mother. Physically he is more delicate than the other children so that his illnesses tend to further her concentration upon him still more. Paul is a "pale, quite child" who seems "*old for his years*" and "*very conscious of what other people felt, particularly his mother. When she fretted he understood, and could have no peace. His soul seemed always attentive to her.*" His mother and for a time his sister Annie, are his only real companions. His brother William is too old to be his playmate and other children play no role in his early childhood. One vicious bond of sympathy unites all the Morel children; their common hate and contempt for their father. This feeling poisons the whole family life. Often, of a windy night in their creaking house, the children lie awake listening in terror for his drunken return, his banging fists and the muffled voice of their mother. The strain is greatest upon Paul. Towards evening he grows restless and stays near his mother, waiting for his father's coming and the usual scene of abuse and violence. Already at an early age these hostile feelings take definite shape. He often prays: "*Lord, let my father die.*" And then, with a kind of guilty conscience: "*Let him not be killed at pit.*" One incident in particular stands out in his memory. Morel has just blackened his wife's eyes and William, then already a tall and muscular youth, threatens to beat him. Paul aches to have him do it; it is his own wish which he cannot carry out. Later, when he is older, he almost does it himself, but for his mother's fainting, and his physical encounters with other men are tinged with a deadly animosity, as if the memory of that earlier hate had lingered on in him. We must remember that Paul had been born into an atmosphere of parental violence; when still a baby his father hurled a drawer at his mother so that the blood had trickled down upon the child's head. Indelible among his earliest impressions must have been that gross and terrifying figure, threatening his life and that of his mother, whose convulsive movements to protect him must have aroused an answering quiver in the child.

The early relations between mother and child are full of a delicate and poetic charm. Paul's admiration for his mother knows no bounds; her presence is always absorbing. Often, at the sight of her, "*his heart contracts with love.*" Everything he does is for her, the flowers he picks as well as the prizes he wins at school. His mother is his intimate and his confidant, he has no other chums. When Morel is confined to the hospital through an accident in the mine, Paul joyfully plays the husband, *"I'm the man in the house now."* He is happiest when alone with her. By this time the interaction between mother and son is complete; she lives in him and he in her. In fact his whole attitude towards her is but the answer which she gradually evokes from him as her whole life finds expression in her son. *"In the end she shared everything with him without knowing. . . . She waited for his coming home in the evening, and then she unburdened herself of all she had pondered, or of all that had occurred to her during the day. He sat and listened with his earnestness. The two shared lives."* The emotional correspondence between them is striking, *"his heart contracted with pain of love of her"* just as from the very beginning she has always *"felt a mixture of anguish in her love for him."* Mother and son are one; the husband is completely effaced and the father exists merely as a rival.

But now Paul is to strike out for himself. He takes up an occupation and finds himself attracted to women. His mother's whole emphasis has always been towards making Paul interested in some other occupation than his father's dirty digging, as a protest against the sordidness of the life that she herself has been compelled to lead with him. She therefore encourages the boy's liking for pretty things, for flowers and sunsets and fancy stuffs, and is delighted when his slender artistic endowment begins to express itself in pencil and paint. Her emotional revolt against her husband here takes an esthetic turn, as people are often driven to beauty by their loathing of the ugly, and it is interesting to note that Mrs. Morel's tendencies to estheticize Paul and to effeminate him go hand in hand, as if the two sprang from a common root. Paul never becomes a real artist. He uses his painting to please his mother and to court his women, but in the crises of his life his art means nothing to him either as a consolation or as a satisfying expression. As his painting is essentially dilettante and unremunerative, his mother apprentices him in a shop for surgical appliances where the process of effeminization goes on through his contact with the girls and women with whom he works. He himself has no ambition. All that he wants is *"quietly to earn his thirty or thirty-five shillings a week somewhere near home, and then, when his father died, have a cottage with his mother, paint and go out as he liked, and live happy ever after."* Not, like any normal boy, to strike out for himself, to adventure, to emulate and surpass his father, but to go on living with his mother forever! That is the real seed of Paul's undoing. We shall now trace the various attempts on his part to emancipate himself from his mother by centering his affections upon some other woman.

The first woman to attract Paul is Miriam Leiver, a shy, exalted and romantic girl who leads a rather lonely life with her parents and brothers on a neighboring farm. Paul's approach is characteristically indirect; he begins by avoiding the girl and cultivating her mother. Meanwhile Miriam, piqued by the neglect of this well-mannered boy, who seems so gentle and superior, has fallen in love with him. Paul is fascinated but uneasy and fights shy of personal intimacy with her. The intensity of her emotions frightens him and impresses him as unwholesome. He finds her growing absorption in him strangely discomfitting: "*Always something in his breast shrank from these close, intimate, dazzled looks of hers.*" His feminine attitude towards her tends to reverse the usual method of courtship; it is Miriam who has to seek him out, to call for him and make sure of his coming again. Paul tries to approach her in two ways; through his art and as her teacher. Both methods are really self-defensive, they are barriers that he erects against Miriam to prevent anything too personal from arising between them, to keep his real self, as it were, inviolate. For as a painter he distracts her attention from himself to his work and as her instructor he wields an authority with which he can keep her emotions in check by overawing her. Something about her is always putting him on edge, he loses his temper at her very easily and feels a dawning impulse of cruelty. "*It made his blood rouse to see her there, as it were, at his mercy.*" Sometimes he feels an actual hatred for her. And immediately he thinks of his mother: "*He was thankful in his heart and soul that he had his mother, so sane and wholesome.*"

Paul resists every intimation that he is falling in love with Miriam. He indignantly repudiates his mother's insinuation that he is courting and hastens to assure Miriam: "*We aren't lovers, we are friends.*" And Miriam, who has already gone so far, tries to fortify herself with a prayer. "*O Lord, let me not love Paul Morel. Keep me from loving him, if I ought not to love him.*" But her love breaks through again and her healthier instincts triumph. Henceforth Paul can do with her as he will. But he can do nothing with her love because he cannot return it. Love seems to him like a "*very terrible thing.*" The honest and more impersonal passion that he feels for her frightens him. "*He was afraid of her. The fact that he might want her as a man wants a woman had in him been suppressed into a shame.*" He cannot even kiss her. And he hates her again because she makes him despise himself. They gradually move to the edge of a quarrel.

And now Mrs. Morel makes her appeal. Almost from the first she has mistrusted Miriam. She fears that Miriam will absorb him and take him away from her. "*She is one of those who will want to suck a man's soul out till he has none of his own left.*" Her jealousy revels in the exaggerated simile of the vampire. "*She exults—she exults as she carries him off from me. . . . She's not like an ordinary woman . . . she wants to absorb him . . . she will suck him up.*" So she throws down the gauntlet to her rival. She makes Paul feel wretched, as only a mother can make a son feel, whenever he has been with Miriam. Her comments grow spiteful and satiric; she no longer takes the trouble to hide her jealousy and plagues him like a cast woman. "*Is there nobody else to talk to? . . . Yes, I know it well—I am old. And therefore I may stand aside; I have nothing more to do with you. You only want me to wait on you—the rest is for Miriam.*" It sounds like a wife's bitter reproach to her husband. Paul writhes under her words and hates Miriam for it. But Mrs. Morel does not stop there. She makes the final, ruthless, cowardly appeal.

"*And I've never—you know, Paul—I've never had a husband—not—really—*"

He stroked his mother's hair, and his mouth was on her throat.

"*Well, I don't love her, mother,*" *he murmured, bowing his head and hiding his eyes on her shoulder in misery. His mother kissed him, a long, fervent kiss.*

"*My boy!*" *she said, in a voice trembling with passionate love.*

Without knowing, he gently stroked her face. Thus she wins him back. He will continue to console her for her husband. There follows the scene where Paul almost thrashes his drunken father and implores his mother not to share the same bed with him. It is a crisis in his life: "*. . . he was at peace because he still loved his mother best. It was the bitter peace of resignation.*"

But there is some resistance in him still. For a time he stands divided between his two loves. "*And he felt dreary and hopeless between the two.*" In church, sitting between them, he feels at peace: "*uniting his two loves under the spell of the place of worship.*" But most of the time he is torn between the two women. He does not understand his feelings. "*And why did he hate Miriam and feel so cruel towards her at the thought of his mother?*" His emotions towards Miriam are constantly changing. Sometimes his passion tries to break through. But it cannot free itself. "*I'm so damned spiritual with* YOU *always!*" He blames her for the humiliating sense of impotence which he feels. It is all her fault. He transfers all his inhibitions to her and consciously echoes his mother's accusations. "*You absorb, absorb, as if you must fill yourself up with love, because you've got a shortage somewhere.*" When her love for him flames out to confound him he takes refuge by talking about his work. There at least some freedom is left for them both. "*All his passion, all his wild blood, went into this intercourse with her, when he talked and conceived his work.*" But at last he tells her that he does not love her, that he cannot love her physically. "*I can only give friend-ship—it's all I'm capable of—it's a flaw in my make-up. . . . Let us have done.*" And finally he writes: "*In all our relations no body enters. I do not talk to you through the senses—rather through the spirit. That is why we cannot love in common sense. Ours is not an everyday affection.*" Thus he tries to spiritualize their relations out of existence. He would persuade himself of his own impotence.

Paul's whole experience with Miriam has thrown him back upon his mother; he gets away from Miriam by returning to her. "*He had come back to his mother. Hers was the strongest tie in life. When he thought round, Miriam shrank away. There was a vague, unreal feeling about her. . . . And in his soul there was a feeling of the satisfaction of self-sacrifice because he was faithful to her*" (his mother). "*She loved him first; he loved her first.*" He is her child again and for a time he feels content. They go off on a charming excursion to Lincoln Cathedral. He behaves like a lover out with his girl, buying her flowers and treating her. Suddenly there surges up in him a childhood memory of the time when his mother was young and fair, before life wrung her dry and withered her. If only he had been her eldest son so that his memory of her could be still more youthful! "*What are you old for!*" he said, mad with his own impotence. "*Why can't you walk, why can't you come with me to places?*" He does not like to have such an old sweetheart.

At the same time his whole outlook upon life also grows childish again. When his sister Annie marries he tries to console his mother. "*But I shan't marry, mother. I shall live with you, and we'll have a servant.*" She doubts him and he proceeds to figure it out. "*I'll give you till seventy-five. There you are, I'm fat and forty-four. Then I'll marry a staid body. See! . . . And we'll have a pretty house, you and me, and a servant, and it'll be just all right.*" His plans for the future have not changed. He thinks at twenty-two as he thought at fourteen, like a child that goes on living a fairy-tale. But it is a false contentment and he pays the penalty for it. In resigning the natural impulse to love he also resigns the impulse to live. Life cannot expand in him, it is turned back upon itself and becomes the impulse to die. Paul makes the great refusal. *"What is happiness!" he cried. "It's nothing to me! How* AM *I to be happy? . . . He had that poignant carelessness about himself, his own suffering, his own life, which is a form of slow suicide."* Mrs. Morel sees the danger and divines the remedy. *"At this rate she knew he would not live. . . . She wished she knew some nice woman—she did not know what she wished, but left it vague."* But now she knows that she can no longer hold her son to her exclusively.

At this point Paul begins to turn to another woman, Clara Dawes, a friend of Miriam. She is married, but lives separated from her husband. Paul has known her for some time before becoming intimate with her. She exerts a frankly sensual attraction upon him without having any of that mystical unattainableness about her which he felt so strongly with Miriam. Her presence has had the effect of gradually seducing him away from Miriam without his knowing it. There would be less difficulty with her. She is a married woman and is unhappy with her husband, like his mother. To love her would not be so momentous a thing, he would be less unfaithful to his mother if he had an affair with a woman who already belonged to someone else. Their relations threaten to become typical of the young man and the woman of thirty. *"She was to him extraordinarily provocative, because of the knowledge she seemed to possess, and gathered fruit of experience."* The question of marriage would hardly enter; he could go on loving his mother. But still he is inhibited. *"Sex had become so complicated in him that he would have denied that he ever could want Clara or Miriam or any woman whom he knew. Sex desire was a sort of detached thing, that did not belong to a woman."* Clara's first service to him is to talk to him like a woman of the world and thus correct his self-delusion about Miriam: *". . . she doesn't want any of your soul communion. That's your own imagination. She wants you."* He objects. *"'You've never tried,' she answered."* Thus she gives him courage to do what he never could have done of his own accord.

The force which drives him back to Miriam is nothing but the sheer, pent-up sexual desire that has alternately been provoked and repressed in him. Now indeed it is a completely detached thing which does not belong to any woman. He has almost entirely succeeded in de-personalizing it. That is why he feels that he can let it run its course. But not in any personal way. "*He did not feel that he wanted marriage with Miriam. He wished he did. He would have given his head to have felt a joyous desire to marry her and have her. Then why couldn't he bring it off? There was some obstacle; and what was the obstacle? It lay in the physical bondage. He shrank from the physical contact. But why? With her he felt bound up inside himself. He could not go out to her. Something struggled in him, but he could not get to her. Why?*" And Miriam does not insist upon marriage, she is willing to try out their feelings for each other. Theirs is a pitiful love-making. He cannot bear the blaze of love in her eyes; it is as if he must first draw a veil over her face and forget her. "*If he were really with her, he had to put aside himself and his desire. If he would have her, he had to put her aside.*" Love brings him only a sense of death: "*He was a youth no longer. But why had he the dull pain in his soul! Why did the thought of death, the after-life, seem so sweet and consoling?*" Love has brought them no satisfaction, only bitterness and disillusion. He turns back to his men friends and to Clara's company and the old quarrel between him and Miriam breaks out afresh. He decides to break off his relations with her. But at last he is to hear the truth about himself from Miriam. "*'Always—it has been so!'*" she cried. *'It has been one long battle between us—you fighting away from me.'*" He tries to tell her that they have had some perfect hours. But she knows that these do not make up the healthy continuity of life. "*Always, from the very beginning—always the same!*" She has called him a child of four. It is the truth, and it goes to the heart of his vanity. She has treated him as a mother treats a perverse child. He cannot stand it. "*He hated her. All these years she had treated him as if he were a hero, and thought of him secretly as an infant, a foolish child. Then why had she left the foolish child to his folly! His heart was hard against her.*"

The full flood of his passion, freed of some of its incubus through his experience with Miriam, now turns to Clara. He tries to wear it out on her in the same impersonal way, and for a time lives in sheer physical ecstasy. With her at least he has had some solace, some relief. His mother has not stood so much between them. But it is only temporary, he cannot give himself to Clara any more than he could give himself to Miriam. Clara loves him or would love him if he could only rise above the mere passion that threw them together. "*'I feel,' she continued slowly, 'as if I hadn't got you, as if all of you weren't there, and as if it weren't* ME *you were taking—'* 'Who then?' 'Something just *for yourself. It has been fine, so that I daren't think of it. But is it me you want, or is it* IT*?'* . . . *'He again felt guilty. Did he leave Clara out of count and take simply woman? But he thought that was splitting a hair.'"* They begin to drift apart. He rehearses his old difficulties with his mother. *"I feel sometimes as if I wronged my women, mother."* But he doesn't know why. *"I even love Clara, and I did Miriam; but to give myself to them in marriage I couldn't. I couldn't belong to* them. They seem to want ME, *and I can't even give it them."*

"You haven't met the right woman."

"And I shall never meet the right woman while you live."

His relations with Clara have brought about a marked change in Paul's attitude towards his mother. It is as if he realized at last that she is destroying his life's happiness. *"Then sometimes he hated her, and pulled at her bondage. His life wanted to free itself of her. It was like a circle where life wanted to turn back upon itself, and got no further. She bore him, loved him, kept him, and his love turned back into her, so that he could not be free to go forward with his own life, really love another woman."* But his realization, as far as it goes, brings no new initiative. He is twenty-four years old now but he still sums up his ambition as before: *"Go somewhere in a pretty house near London with my mother."*

The book now rounds out with the death of Paul's mother. Mrs. Morel gradually wastes away with a slow and changeful illness; it is an incurable tumor, with great pain. Paul takes charge and never leaves his mother until the end. Their intimacy is occasionally disturbed by the clumsy intrusion of Morel, whose presence merely serves to irritate his wife. Paul and she commune with the old tenderness. *"Her blue eyes smiled straight into his, like a girl's—warm, laughing with tender love. It made him pant with terror, agony, and love."* Their reserve drops before the imminence of death, it seems as if they would be frank at last. But there is also the old constraint. *"They were both afraid of the veils that were ripping between them."* He suffers intensely. *"He felt as if his life were being destroyed, piece by piece, within him."* But mingled with his love and his anguish at her suffering there now enters a new feeling: the wish that she should die. Something in him wants her to die; seeing that she cannot live he would free both her and himself by hastening her death. So he gradually cuts down her nourishment and increases the deadliness of her medicine. Here again he approaches close to the source of his trouble; he dimly realizes that he has never lived outside of his mother and therefore has never really lived. The feeling that he cannot live without her and the feeling that he cannot live a life of his own as long as she is alive, here run side by side. But when the death which he himself has hastened overtakes her, he cries with a lover's anguish: " '*My love—my love—oh, my love!' he whispered again and again. 'My love—oh, my love!*'"

But death has not freed Paul from his mother. It has completed his allegiance to her. For death has merely removed the last earthly obstacle to their ideal union; now he can love her as Dante loved his Beatrice. He avows his faithfulness to her by breaking off with the only two other women who have meant anything to him. He is completely resigned, life and death are no longer distinguished in his thinking. Life for him is only where his mother is and she is dead. So why live? He cannot answer, life has become contradictory. "*There seemed no reason why people should go along the street, and houses pile up in the daylight. There seemed no reason why these things should occupy space, instead of leaving it empty. . . . He wanted everything to stand still, so that he could be with her again.*" But life in him is just a hair stronger than death. "*He would not say it. He would not admit that he wanted to die, to have done. He would not own that life had beaten him, or that death had beaten him.*"

The last chapter of the book is called "Derelict." The title emphasizes Mr. Lawrence's already unmistakable meaning. Paul is adrift now; with the death of his mother he has lost his only mooring in life. There is no need to follow him further; when he is through despairing he will hope again and when he has compared one woman to his mother and found her wanting, he will go on to another, in endless repetition. The author's final picture of Paul's state of mind is full of seductive eloquence: "*There was no Time, only Space. Who could say that his mother had lived and did not live? She had been in one place and was in another; that was all. And his soul could not leave her, wherever she was. Now she was gone abroad in the night, and he was with her still. They were together. And yet there was his body, his chest, that leaned against the stile, his hands on the wooden bar. They seemed something. Where was he?—one tiny upright speck of flesh, less than an ear of wheat lost in the field. He could not bear it. On every side the immense dark silence seemed pressing him, so tiny a spark, into extinction, and yet, almost nothing, he could not be extinct. Night, in which everything was lost, went reaching out, beyond stars and sun. Stars and sun, a few bright grains, went spinning round for terror, and holding each other in embrace, there in a darkness that outpassed them all, and left them tiny and daunted. So much, and himself, infinitesimal, at the core of nothingness, and yet not nothing."*

" 'Mother!' he whimpered—'mother!'"

* * *

Such is the condensed account of Paul's love-life. Textual testimony could hardly go further to show that Paul loved his mother too dearly. And shall we now say that it was *because* Mrs. Morel lavished all her affection upon her son? But then, most mothers lavish a good deal of affection upon their sons and it is only natural for sons to love their mothers dearly. Why should an excess of these sacred sentiments produce such devastating results? For it is undoubtedly the intention of the author to show us Paul as a wreck and a ruin, a man damned out of all happiness at the age of twenty-five, who has barely the strength left to will not to die. And why should we accept as a type this man who seems to bear so many ear-marks of degeneracy and abnormal impulse, who is alternately a ruthless egotist and a vicious weakling in his dealings with women, and who in the end stoops to shorten the life of his own mother? Surely the thing is deeper and due to profounder causes. But of these the author gives us no indication. Let us therefore assume for the moment that Paul is by no means a degenerate, but merely an exaggeration of the normal, unhealthily nursed into morbid manifestations by an abnormal environment. If that can be established it may very well be that the story of Paul's love-life simply throws into high relief an intimate and constant relation between parent and child the significance of which has hitherto escaped general observation. Perhaps all men have something of Paul in them. In that case their instinctive recognition of their kinship with the hero of the book would go a great way towards explaining the potency of "Sons and Lovers." We are fond of saying something like that about Hamlet.

The theory which would enable us to assume such a point of view is at once concrete, humanly understandable, and capable of personal verification. For Freud holds that the love instinct, whose sudden efflorescence after the age of puberty is invested with so much poetic charm, is not a belated endowment, but comes as the result of a gradual development which we can trace step by step from our earliest childhood. In fact, according to Freud, the evolution of the mature love instinct begins as soon as the child has sufficiently developed a sense of the otherness of its surroundings to single out its mother as the object of its affections. At first this is entirely instinctive and unconscious and comes as the natural result of the child's dependence upon its mother for food, warmth and comfort. We come preciously close to being born lovers. The mother is the one overwhelming presence of those earliest days, the source from which all good things flow, so that childhood is full of the sense of the mother's omnipotence. From her we first learn how to express affection, and the maternal caresses and the intimate feeling of oneness which we get from her form the easy analogies to love when we feel a conscious passion for another individual of the opposite sex. Our mother is, in a very real sense of the word, our first love.

As soon as the child is capable of making comparisons with other people it proceeds to celebrate the superiorities of its mother. She is the most beautiful, the most accomplished, the most powerful, and no other child's mother can equal her. But meanwhile the influence of the father, that other major constellation of our childhood, is also felt. Though not so gracious, he too is mighty, mightier than the mother, since he dominates her. His presence brings about a striking change in the attitude of the child, according to its sex. The boy, seeing that the mother loves the father, strives to be like him, in order to draw the mother's affection to himself. He takes his father as an ideal and sets about to imitate his masculine qualities. And the girl, becoming aware of the father's love for the mother, tries to attract some of his love to herself by imitating the mother. This is the process of self-identification which is already conditioned by the natural physical similarity where parent and child are of the same sex. Father and son, and mother and daughter, now have a common object of affection. But to the child this means at the same time an active rivalry, for the child is an unbridled egotist, intent upon nothing less than the exclusive possession of the affection of the beloved parent. It therefore manifests unmistakable signs of jealousy, even of frank hostility. So strong is this feeling that a careful examination of the unconscious childhood memories of thousands of individuals, such as is possible with the Freudian method of psycho-analysis, has yet to reveal an infancy in which a death phantasy about the rival parent has not played a part. The childish wish is ruthlessly realized in imagination; the boy suddenly dreams of living in a cottage with his mother after the father, let us say, has been devoured by the lion of last week's circus, while the girl revels in the thought of keeping house for her father after the mother has been conveniently removed. We may feel, then, that we were fellow conspirators with Paul when he prayed to God to have his father slain. For we have had the same wish in common: to eliminate the rival and celebrate a childish marriage with the parent of our choice.

From this naïve attitude the child is normally weaned by the maturing influences of education and by the absolute barriers which its childish wish encounters. It is a slow and gradual process of transference, which continues through childhood and puberty. The child is tenaciously rooted in its parents and does not easily relinquish its hold upon them. Even after it has acquired a dawning sense of the meaning of sex it continues to interweave its immature phantasies of procreation with its former ideal adoration of the parent. Thus the girl, having had a glimmering that the father has something essential to do with her birth, may assign to him a similar function in regard to her dolls, which of course are her children. And the boy, similarly aware that his father has played a mysterious part with regard to the mother when she suddenly introduces another child into the nursery, is likely to usurp the exercise of this function to himself. Both substitutions are merely more sophisticated ways of eliminating the rival parent by making him unnecessary. It must be remembered, of course, that the child can have none of our reservations as to the direction which the erotic impulse may take, and therefore quite innocently directs its crude and imperfect erotic feelings towards its parent, from whom they must then be deflected. This is most favorably accomplished when there are other children in the family. The girl is quick to see the father in her brother and the boy transfers his worship of the mother to his sister. The father's manly qualities are used by the girl to embellish the brother when she sets him up as a love ideal. From him again she slowly extends her love phantasies to other boys of his and her acquaintance. The boy on his part, dowers his sister with the borrowed attributes of his mother and then passes from her to other girls who in turn are selected on the basis of their similarity to the sister and to the mother. In default of brothers or sisters other playmates have to serve the same purpose. The enforced quest of a love object other than the parent thus becomes the great

incentive of our social radiation towards other individuals and to the
world at large.

This process of deflection and transference, which is one of the
main psychic labors of childhood, is facilitated by a parallel process
that constantly represses a part of our thoughts to the unconscious.
The mechanism of repression, as the Freudian psychology describes
it, does not become operative until the age of about four or five, for
at first the child does not repress at all and therefore has no unconscious. But the function of education consists largely in imposing
innumerable taboos upon the child and in teaching it to respect the
thou-shalt-nots. Thoughts and feelings such as the cruder egotistical
impulses and the associations with bodily functions, which seem
quite natural to the child's primitive and necessarily unmoral mind,
gradually fall under the cultural ban proclaimed by parents and
educators, so that the unconscious becomes a receptacle for all the
thoughts that are rendered painful and disagreeable by the slowly
developing sense of shame and of moral and ethical behavior. We
"put away childish things" by putting them into the unconscious.
Our germinating sexual ideas and our naïve erotic attitude towards
our parents become particularly "impermissible" and we therefore
draw an especially heavy veil of forgetfulness over this part of our
childhood. But though we can forget, we cannot obliterate, and the
result of this early fixation upon our parents is to leave in our mind
an indelible imprint, or "imago," of both our mother and our father.
Our parents are always with us in our unconscious. They become our
ultimate criterion by which we judge men and women, and exercise
the most potent influence upon our love choice. The imago of them
that holds us to our unconscious allegiance is a picture, not as we
know them later, old and declining, but as we saw them first, young
and radiant, and dowered, as it seemed to us then, with godlike
gifts. We cannot go on loving them so we do the next best thing;
the boy chooses a woman who resembles his mother as closely as
possible, and the girl mates with the man who reminds her most of
her father.

Such, according to Freud, is the psychological genesis of
the emotion of love. The normal evolution of love from the first
maternal caress is finally accomplished when the individual definitely transfers his allegiance to a self-chosen mate and thereby
steps out of the charmed family circle in which he has been held

from infancy. That this is difficult even under normal circumstance seems already to have been recognized in the Bible, where Christ says with so much solemnity; "For this cause shall a man leave father and mother"; as if only so weighty a reason could induce a child to leave its parents. Freud, in postulating the above development as the norm, proceeds to attach grave and far-reaching consequences to any deviations from this standard. The effect of any disturbance in the balanced and harmonious influence of both parents upon the child, or of any abnormal pressure of circumstances or wilful action that forces the child into a specialized attitude toward either parent, is subtly and unerringly reproduced in the later love-life. The reader himself will probably recall from his own observation, a large number of cases where the love-life has been thwarted, or stunted, or never expressed. He will think of those old bachelors whose warm attachment to their mother has so much superficial charm, as well as of those old maids who so self-effacingly devote themselves to their fathers. He will also recall that almost typical man whose love interest persistently goes where marriage is impossible, preferably to a woman already preempted by another man or to a much older woman, so that his love can never come to rest in its object; he will wonder whether this man too is not preserving his ideal allegiance to his mother by avoiding that final detachment from her which marriage would bring. He will notice a class of men and women who, even though their parents are dead, seem to have resigned marriage and live in a kind of small contentment with a constantly narrowing horizon. Or he may know of actual marriages that are unhappy because the memory of one of the parents has not been sufficiently laid to rest, and the joke about the mother-in-law or the pie that mother used to make, will acquire a new significance for him. And to all these cases thousands must still be added where neurotic and hysteric patients reveal with unmistakable clearness that the ghosts of the parents still walk about in the troubled psyches of these unfortunates, influencing life and happiness with paralyzing effect. These are all manifestations which the reader hitherto has observed only as results, without knowing the causes or trying to ascertain them. With the aid of the Freudian theory such examples may now help him to see, as perhaps he has already begun to see in Paul, the tremendous rôle that the abnormal fixation upon the parent plays in the psychic development of the individual. And in so doing he may perhaps also gain some insight into the part that his own parents have played in his normal psychic growth, just as disease gives us a clearer understanding of health or as Madame Montessori's study of subnormal children has enabled her to formulate general laws of education.

4.

We can now return to *Sons and Lovers* with a new understanding. Why has the attitude of the son to his mother here had such a devastating effect upon his whole life? Why could he not overcome this obstacle like other children and ultimately attain some measure of manhood? Why, in short, was the surrender so complete? In Paul's case the abnormal fixation upon the mother is most obviously conditioned by the father, whose unnatural position in the family is responsible for the distortion of the normal attitude of the child towards its parents. The father ideal simply does not exist for Paul; where there should have been an attractive standard of masculinity to imitate, he can only fear and despise. The child's normal dependence upon the mother is perpetuated because there is no counter-influence to detach it from her. But there is another distortion, equally obvious, which fatally influences the natural development. Paul's early fixation upon his mother is met and enhanced by Mrs. Morel's abnormally concentrated affection for her son. Her unappeased love, which can no longer go out towards her husband, turns to Paul for consolation; she *makes* him love her too well. Her love becomes a veritable Pandora's box of evil. For Paul is now hemmed in on all sides by too much love and too much hate.

If now we compare Paul's boyhood and adolescence with, let us say, the reader's own, we find that the difference is, to a great extent, one of consciousness and unconsciousness. All those psychic processes which are usually unconscious or at least heavily veiled in the normal psycho-sexual development lie close to consciousness in Paul and break through into his waking thoughts at every favorable opportunity. Everything is raw and exposed in him and remains so, kept quick to the touch by the pressure of an abnormal environment which instead of moulding, misshapes him. The normal hostility towards the father which is conditioned in every boy by a natural jealousy of the mother's affection, is nursed in him to a conscious hate through Morel's actual brutality and his mother's undisguised bitterness and contempt. And the normal love for the mother which ordinarily serves as a model for the man's love for other women is in him perverted into abnormal expression almost at his mother's breast, so that he is always conscious of his infatuation with his mother and can never free his love-making from that paralyzing influence. These powerful determinants of the love-life which we acquire from our parents would be too overwhelming in every case were it not for the process of submersion or repression already referred to. This repression usually sets in at an early stage of childhood and acts biologically as a protective mechanism by allowing us to develop a slowly expanding sense of selfhood through which we gradually differentiate ourselves from our parents. In this way the fateful dominance of the parents is broken, though their influence remains in the unconscious as a formative and directing impulse.

In Paul this salutary process never takes place because he cannot free himself from the incubus of his parents long enough to come to some sense of himself. He remains enslaved by his parent complex instead of being moulded and guided by it. One turns back to that astonishing scene at Lincoln Cathedral. Here Paul goes to the roots of his mother's hold upon him. For his passionate reproaches hurled at his mother because she has lost her youth, prove that the mother-imago, in all its pristine magic, has never diminished its sway over him; he has never been able to forget or to subordinate that first helpless infatuation. If only she could be young again so that he could remain her child lover! With that thought and wish so conscious in him nothing else in life can become really desirable, and all-initiative is dried up at the source. Paul cannot expand towards the universe in normal activity and form an independent sex interest because for him his mother has become the universe; she stands between him and life and the other woman. There is a kind of bottomless childishness about him; life in a pretty house with his mother—the iteration sounds like a childish prattle. Miriam feels it when she calls him a child of four which she can no longer nurse. Nor can Clara help him by becoming a wanton substitute for his mother. Only the one impossible ideal holds him, and that means the constant turning in upon himself which is death. Paul goes to pieces because he can never make the mature sexual decision away from his mother, he can never accomplish the physical and emotional transfer.

If now this striking book, taken as it stands, bears such unexpected witness to the truth of Freud's remarkable psycho-sexual theory, it is at least presumable that the author himself and the rest of his work also stand in some very definite relation to this theory. The feeling that *Sons and Lovers* must be autobiographical is considerably strengthened by the somewhat meager personal detail which Mr. Edwin Björkman supplies in an introduction to Mr. Lawrence's first play. Mr. Lawrence was himself the son of a collier in the Derbyshire coal-mining district and his mother seems to have occupied an exceptional position in the family, showing herself to be a woman of great fortitude and initiative, who evidently dominated the household. Mr. Björkman is silent concerning the father, but gives us the interesting information that *Sons and Lovers* was written not long after the mother's death. This information is not sufficient, however, to warrant our inquiry going beyond the author's writings, a step for which, in any case, it would be necessary to have both his permission and his coöperation. We must therefore limit ourselves to the testimony of Mr. Lawrence's work. This consists of two additional novels, a volume of poems, and a play. What is truly astonishing is that all of these, in various disguises and transparent elaborations, hark back to the same problem: the direct and indirect effects of an excessive maternal allegiance and the attempt to become emancipated from it.

Reference has already been made to the poems. This is the way the author ends a love poem:

> "What else—it is perfect enough,
> It is perfectly complete,
> You and I,
> What more—?
> *Strange, how we suffer in spite of this!*"

Why, it may well be asked, should the perfection of love bring suffering? Certainly the love poems of adolescence are not as a rule colored with the feeling of suffering as unmotivated as this. But there is a second poem, entitled End of Another Home-holiday which in the short space of three pages states Paul's whole problem with unmistakable precision. The poet tells how dearly he loves his home and then continues as follows:

> "The light has gone out from under my mother's door.
>   That she should love me so,
>   She, so lonely, greying now,
>   And I leaving her,
>   Bent on my pursuits!"

How curiously that last line comes in, "Bent on my pursuits!" as if he felt that he ought to stay at home. Here we have again the son who cannot leave his mother; the mere thought of doing so fills him with self-reproach. In the next few lines the reproach deepens:

> "Forever, ever by my shoulder pitiful Love will linger,
> Crouching as little houses crouch under the mist when I turn.
> Forever, out of the mist the church lifts up her reproachful
>   finger,
> Pointing my eyes in wretched defiance where love hides her face
>   to mourn."

Even inanimate things point the finger of reproach at him. A little later in the same poem the mother becomes a symbolic figure, following the son through life like a Norn, as she begs for his love.

> "While ever at my side,
>   Frail and sad, with grey bowed head,
>   The beggar-woman, the yearning-eyed
>   Inexorable love goes lagging."
>   *
>   *
>   *
> "But when I draw the scanty cloak of silence over my eyes,
> Piteous Love comes peering under the hood.
> Touches the clasp with trembling fingers, and tries
> To put her ear to the painful sob of my blood,
> While her tears soak through to my breast,
>   Where they bum and cauterize."

The poem ends with the call of the corncrake in the poet's ear, crying monotonously:

> "With a piteous, unalterable plaint, that deadens
>   My confident activity:
> With a hoarse, insistent request that falls
> Unweariedly, unweariedly,
>   Asking something more of me,
>   Yet more of me!"

An interesting, tell-tale clew in these last lines shows how thoroughly this poem is Paul's and to how great an extent Paul and the author are one and the same. For the careful reader will remember that Paul too, coming home over the fields after visiting Miriam is strongly depressed by the call of this same little bird and immediately goes in to his mother to tell her that he still loves her best and that he has broken off with Miriam. Has not his mother too "deadened his confident activity." Her influence could hardly be better described in a single phrase. The whole poem is a protest against the terrible allegiance that the mother exacts, just as Paul, towards the end of the book, reproaches his mother for the failure of his life. It can hardly be doubted that a vital part of the lyricist has gone into Paul.

In reading the two remaining novels and the play our attention is immediately struck by a curious sameness and limitation of motif that underlies them all. In each there is a deadly father or husband hate, a poignant sense of death, and a picture of marriage or love that does not satisfy. Siegmund, the husband in *The Trespasser*, is exposed to a hate so withering that he collapses before it. He is a kind and gentle musician, too effeminate for a man, and entirely devoid of initiative. The hatred of his wife and children is practically unmotivated, we are simply asked to assume it in order to follow him in his affair with Helena. This brings him no solace, he cannot come to rest in her, his love for her simply brings him the sense of death. It is the psychology of Paul transferred to a man of forty, and Helena's struggle to make his love for her real is much like Miriam's. In the play, *The Widowing of Mrs. Holroyd*, the wife seeks to escape from a brutal and drunken husband by eloping with another man. The death of her husband in a mining accident intervenes and brings her a sense of pity and remorse because she never tried to win and hold her husband's love. She had married him without love. Her son hates his father and wishes him dead. Blackmore, the man with whom she wanted to elope, has much of Paul in him; his belief that love can bring happiness is never more than half-hearted. The sense of guilt that the death of the husband brings to both of them, makes the elopement impossible. Death always supervenes upon the impermissible with Mr. Lawrence.

In *The White Peacock* the background is again a ruthless hate for the husband and father. One of the daughters says: "*There is always a sense of death in this house. I believe my mother hated my father before I was born. That was death in her veins for me before I was born. It makes a difference.*" We get a picture of women who marry mean-ingless husbands and men who marry unsatisfying wives. Lettie marries Leslie because George, whom she really loves, lacks the initiative to claim her, and George marries Meg after his abor-tive love for Lettie has made him despair of life. Neither he nor she come to any emotional satisfaction; Lettie consoles herself for her aimlessly empty husband by living in her children, and George ends his "Liebestod" in drink. Lettie's brother, who tells the story, is almost sexless except towards his sister, whom he admires like a lover. One gradually gets a sense of monotony; happiness in love is always impossible in this fictional world of Mr. Lawrence, and hate for the parent or husband is the master passion. The motivation is often indistinct or inadequate in all three stories, and the artistry is inferior. They were evidently only preludes to *Sons and Lovers*.

In the story of Paul the author has reached the final expression of a problem which haunts his every effort. The creative labor of self-realization which makes *Sons and Lovers* such a priceless commen-tary on the love-life of to-day, accomplished itself but slowly in Mr. Lawrence, waiting, no doubt, for his artistic maturity and the final clarity which the death of his mother must have brought. And if, as I have tried to show, he has been able, though unknowingly, to attest the truth of what is perhaps the most far-reaching psychological theory ever propounded, he has also given us an illuminating insight into the mystery of artistic creation. For Mr. Lawrence has escaped the destructive fate that dogs the hapless Paul by the grace of expression: out of the dark struggles of his own soul he has emerged as a triumphant artist. In every epoch the soul of the artist is sick with the problems of his generation. He cures himself by expression in his art. And by producing a catharsis in the spectator through the enjoyment of his art he also heals his fellow beings. His artistic stature is measured by the universality of the problem which his art has transfigured.

TESS OF THE D'URBERVILLES
(THOMAS HARDY)

"Study of Thomas Hardy"
by D. H. Lawrence,
in *Phoenix: The Posthumous Papers*
of D. H. Lawrence (1936)

INTRODUCTION

In his appraisal of Hardy's fiction, D. H. Lawrence discusses the relationships among Tess, Alec, and Angel in *Tess of the d'Ubervilles*, drawing correlations between their sexuality and the sexuality of the characters from Hardy's *Jude the Obscure* and *Return of the Native*. Throughout his analysis, Lawrence expounds upon the dual nature of human beings, claiming that everyone possesses both a masculine and feminine side to their psyche. Ultimately, though "his feeling, his instinct, [and] his sensuous understanding" are "very great and deep," Hardy fails to recognize this dichotomy in his fiction. While tracing this failure through Hardy's novels, Lawrence not only provides insightful ways of reading *Tess* in relation to Hardy's other works, but also delineates a view of human sexuality that will aid readers of Lawrence's own fiction.

Lawrence, D. H. "Study of Thomas Hardy." *Phoenix: The Posthumous Papers of D. H. Lawrence.* Ed. Edward D. McDonald. New York: Viking Press, 1936. pp. 398–516

215

[. . .] Thomas Hardy's metaphysic is something like Tolstoi's. "There is no reconciliation between Love and the Law," says Hardy. "The spirit of Love must always succumb before the blind, stupid, but overwhelming power of the Law."

Already as early as *The Return of the Native* he has come to this theory, in order to explain his own sense of failure. But before that time, from the very start, he has had an overweening theoretic antagonism to the Law. "That which is physical, of the body, is weak, despicable, bad," he said at the very start. He represented his fleshy heroes as villains, but very weak and maundering villains. At its worst, the Law is a weak, craven sensuality: at its best, it is a passive inertia. It is the gap in the armour, it is the hole in the foundation.

Such a metaphysic is almost silly. If it were not that man is much stronger in feeling than in thought, the Wessex novels would be sheer rubbish, as they are already in parts. *The Well-Beloved* is sheer rubbish, fatuity, as is a good deal of *The Dynasts* conception.

But it is not as a metaphysician that one must consider Hardy. He makes a poor show there. For nothing in his work is so pitiable as his clumsy efforts to push events into line with his theory of being, and to make calamity fall on those who represent the principle of Love. He does it exceedingly badly, and owing to this effort his form is execrable in the extreme.

His feeling, his instinct, his sensuous understanding is, however, apart from his metaphysic, very great and deep, deeper than that, perhaps, of any other English novelist. Putting aside his metaphysic, which must always obtrude when he thinks of people, and turning to the earth, to landscape, then he is true to himself.

Always he must start from the earth, from the great source of the Law, and his people move in his landscape almost insignificantly, somewhat like tame animals wandering in the wild. The earth is the manifestation of the Father, of the Creator, Who made us in the Law. God still speaks aloud in His Works, as to Job, so to Hardy, surpassing human conception and the human law. "Dost thou know the balancings of the clouds, the wondrous works of him which is perfect in knowledge? How thy garments are warm, when he quieteth the earth by the south wind? Hast thou with him spread out the sky, which is strong?"

This is the true attitude of Hardy—"With God is terrible majesty." The theory of knowledge, the metaphysic of the man, is much smaller than the man himself. So with Tolstoi.

"Knowest thou the time when the wild goats of the rock bring forth? Or canst thou mark when the hinds do calve? Canst thou number the months that they fulfil? Or knowest thou the time when they bring forth? They bow themselves, they bring forth their young ones, they cast out their sorrows. Their young ones are good in liking, they grow up with corn; they go forth, and return not unto them."

There is a good deal of this in Hardy. But in Hardy there is more than the concept of Job, protesting his integrity. Job says in the end: "Therefore have I uttered that I understood not; things too wonderful for me, which I knew not.

"I have heard of thee by hearing of the ear; but now mine eye seeth thee.

"Wherefore I abhor myself, and repent in dust and ashes."

But Jude ends where Job began, cursing the day and the services of his birth, and in so much cursing the act of the Lord, "Who made him in the womb."

It is the same cry all through Hardy, this curse upon the birth in the flesh, and this unconscious adherence to the flesh. The instincts, the bodily passions are strong and sudden in all Hardy's men. They are too strong and sudden. They fling Jude into the arms of Arabella, years after he has known Sue, and against his own will.

For every man comprises male and female in his being, the male always struggling for predominance. A woman likewise consists in male and female, with female predominant.

And a man who is strongly male tends to deny, to refute the female in him. A real "man" takes no heed for his body, which is the more female part of him. He considers himself only as an instrument, to be used in the service of some idea.

The true female, on the other hand, will eternally hold herself superior to any idea, will hold full life in the body to be the real happiness. The male exists in doing, the female in being. The male lives in the satisfaction of some purpose achieved, the female in the satisfaction of some purpose contained.

[...]

The women approved of are not Female in any real sense. They are passive subjects to the male, the re-echo from the male. As in the Christian religion, the Virgin worship is no real Female worship, but worship of the Female as she is passive and subjected to the male. Hence the sadness of Botticelli's Virgins.

Thus Tess sets out, not as any positive thing, containing all purpose, but as the acquiescent complement to the male. The female in her has become inert. Then Alec d'Urberville comes along, and possesses her. From the man who takes her Tess expects her own consummation, the singling out of herself, the addition of the male complement. She is of an old line, and has the aristocratic quality of respect for the other being. She does not see the other person as an extension of herself, existing in a universe of which she is the centre and pivot. She knows that other people are outside her. Therein she is an aristocrat. And out of this attitude to the other person came her passivity. It is not the same as the passive quality in the other little heroines, such as the girl in *The Woodlanders*, who is passive because she is small.

Tess is passive out of self-acceptance, a true aristocratic quality, amounting almost to self-indifference. She knows she is herself incontrovertibly, and she knows that other people are not herself. This is a very rare quality, even in a woman. And in a civilization so unequal, it is almost a weakness.

Tess never tries to alter or to change anybody, neither to alter nor to change nor to divert. What another person decides, that is his decision. She respects utterly the other's right to be. She is herself always.

But the others do not respect her right to be. Alec d'Urberville sees her as the embodied fulfilment of his own desire: something, that is, belonging to him. She cannot, in his conception, exist apart from him nor have any being apart from his being. For she is the embodiment of his desire.

This is very natural and common in men, this attitude to the world. But in Alec d'Urberville it applies only to the woman of his desire. He cares only for her. Such a man adheres to the female like a parasite.

It is a male quality to resolve a purpose to its fulfilment. It is the male quality, to seek the motive power in the female, and to convey this to a fulfilment; to receive some impulse into his senses, and to transmit it into expression.

Alec d'Urberville does not do this. He is male enough, in his way; but only physically male. He is constitutionally an enemy of the principle of self-subordination, which principle is inherent in every man. It is this principle which makes a man, a true male, see his job through, at no matter what cost. A man is strictly only himself when he is fulfilling some purpose he has conceived: so that the principle is not of self-subordination, but of continuity, of development. Only when insisted on, as in Christianity, does it become self-sacrifice. And this resistance to self-sacrifice on Alec d'Urberville's part does not make him an individualist, an egoist, but rather a non-individual, an incomplete, almost a fragmentary thing.

There seems to be in d'Urberville an inherent antagonism to any progression in himself. Yet he seeks with all his power for the source of stimulus in woman. He takes the deep impulse from the female. In this he is exceptional. No ordinary man could really have betrayed Tess. Even if she had had an illegitimate child to another man, to Angel Clare, for example, it would not have shattered her as did her connexion with Alec d'Urberville. For Alec d'Urberville could reach some of the real sources of the female in a woman, and draw from them. Troy could also do this. And, as a woman instinctively knows, such men are rare. Therefore they have a power over a woman. They draw from the depth of her being.

And what they draw, they betray. With a natural male, what he draws from the source of the female, the impulse he receives from the source he transmits through his own being into utterance, motion, action, expression. But Troy and Alec d'Urberville, what they received they knew only as gratification in the senses; some perverse will prevented them from submitting to it, from becoming instrumental to it.

Which was why Tess was shattered by Alec d'Urberville, and why she murdered him in the end. The murder is badly done, altogether the book is botched, owing to the way of thinking in the author, owing to the weak yet obstinate theory of being. Nevertheless, the murder is true, the whole book is true, in its conception.

Angel Clare has the very opposite qualities to those of Alec d'Urberville. To the latter, the female in himself is the only part of himself he will acknowledge: the body, the senses, that which he shares with the female, which the female shares with him. To Angel Clare, the female in himself is detestable, the body, the senses, that which he will share with a woman, is held degraded. What he wants really is to receive the female impulse other than through the body. But his thinking has made him criticize Christianity, his deeper instinct has forbidden him to deny his body any further, a deadlock in his own being, which denies him any purpose, so that he must take to hand, labour out of sheer impotence to resolve himself, drives him unwill-ingly to woman. But he must see her only as the Female Principle,

he cannot bear to see her as the Woman in the Body. Her he thinks
degraded. To marry her, to have a physical marriage with her, he must
overcome all his ascetic revulsion, he must, in his own mind, put off
his own divinity, his pure maleness, his singleness, his pure completeness, and descend to the heated welter of the flesh. It is objectionable
to him. Yet his body, his life, is too strong for him.

Who is he, that he shall be pure male, and deny the existence of
the female? This is the question the Creator asks of him. Is then the
male the exclusive whole of life?—is he even the higher or supreme
part of life? Angel Clare thinks so: as Christ thought.

Yet it is not so, as even Angel Clare must find out. Life, that is
Two-in-One, Male and Female. Nor is either part greater than the
other.

It is not Angel Clare's fault that he cannot come to Tess when he
finds that she has, in his words, been defiled. It is the result of genera-
tions of ultra-Christian training, which had left in him an inherent
aversion to the female, and to all in himself which pertained to the
female. What he, in his Christian sense, conceived of as Woman, was
only the servant and attendant and administering spirit to the male.
He had no idea that there was such a thing as positive Woman, as the
Female, another great living Principle counterbalancing his own male
principle. He conceived of the world as consisting of the One, the
Male Principle.
[. . .]

Jude is only Tess turned round about. Instead of the heroine
containing the two principles, male and female, at strife within her
one being, it is Jude who contains them both, whilst the two women
with him take the place of the two men to Tess. Arabella is Alec
d'Urberville, Sue is Angel Clare. These represent the same pair of
principles.

But, first, let it be said again that Hardy is a bad artist. Because
he must condemn Alec d'Urberville, according to his own personal
creed, therefore he shows him a vulgar intriguer of coarse lasses, and
as ridiculous convert to evangelism. But Alec d'Urberville, by the
artist's account, is neither of these. It is, in actual life, a rare man who
seeks and seeks among women for one of such character and intrinsic
female being as Tess. The ordinary sensualist avoids such characters.
They implicate him too deeply. An ordinary sensualist would have
been much too common, much too afraid, to turn to Tess. In a way,

d'Urberville was her mate. And his subsequent passion for her is in its way noble enough. But whatever his passion, as a male, he must be a betrayer, even if he had been the most faithful husband on earth. He betrayed the female in a woman, by taking her, and by responding with no male impulse from himself. He roused her, but never satisfied her. He could never satisfy her. It was like a soul-disease in him: he was, in the strict though not the technical sense, impotent. But he must have wanted, later on, not to be so. But he could not help himself. He was spiritually impotent in love.

Arabella was the same. She, like d'Urberville, was converted by an evangelical preacher. It is significant in both of them. They were not just shallow, as Hardy would have made them out.

He is, however, more contemptuous in his personal attitude to the woman than to the man. He insists that she is a pig-killer's daughter; he insists that she drag Jude into pig-killing; he lays stress on her false tail of hair. That is not the point at all. This is only Hardy's bad art. He himself, as an artist, manages in the whole picture of Arabella almost to make insignificant in her these pig-sticking, false-hair crudities. But he must have his personal revenge on her for her coarseness, which offends him, because he is something of an Angel Clare.

The pig-sticking and so forth are not so important in the real picture. As for the false tail of hair, few women dared have been so open and natural about it. Few women, indeed, dared have made Jude marry them. It may have been a case with Arabella of "fools rush in." But she was not such a fool. And her motives are explained in the book. Life is not, in the actual, such a simple affair of getting a fellow and getting married. It is, even for Arabella, an affair on which she places her all. No barmaid marries anybody, the first man she can lay hands on. She cannot. It must be a personal thing to her. And no ordinary woman would want Jude. Moreover, no ordinary woman could have laid her hands on Jude.

It is an absurd fallacy this, that a small man wants a woman bigger and finer than he is himself. A man is as big as his real desires. Let a man, seeing with his eyes a woman of force and being, want her for his own, then that man is intrinsically an equal of that woman. And the same with a woman.

A coarse, shallow woman does not want to marry a sensitive, deep-feeling man. She feels no desire for him, she is not drawn to him, but repelled, knowing he will contemn her. She wants a man to correspond to herself: that is, if she is a young woman looking for a mate, as Arabella was.

What an old, jaded, yet still unsatisfied woman or man wants is another matter. Yet not even one of these will take a young creature of real character, superior in force. Instinct and fear prevent it.

Arabella was, under all her disguise of pig-fat and false hair, and vulgar speech, in character somewhat an aristocrat. She was, like Eustacia, amazingly lawless, even splendidly so. She believed in herself and she was not altered by any outside opinion of herself. Her fault was pride. She thought herself the centre of life, that all which existed belonged to her in so far as she wanted it.

In this she was something like Job. His attitude was "I am strong and rich, and, also, I am a good man." He gave out of his own sense of bounty, and felt no indebtedness. Arabella was almost the same. She felt also strong and abundant, arrogant in her hold on life. She needed a complement; and the nearest thing to her satisfaction was Jude. For as she, intrinsically, was a strong female, by far overpowering her Annies and her friends, so was he a strong male.

The difference between them was not so much a difference of quality, or degree, as a difference of form. Jude, like Tess, wanted full consummation. Arabella, like Alec d'Urberville, had that in her which resisted full consummation, wanted only to enjoy herself in contact with the male. She would have no transmission.

There are two attitudes to love. A man in love with a woman says either: "I, the man, the male, am the supreme, I am the one, and the woman is administered unto me, and this is her highest function, to be administered unto me." This was the conscious attitude of the Greeks. But their unconscious attitude was the reverse: they were in truth afraid of the female principle, their vaunt was empty, they went in deep, inner dread of her. So did the Jews, so do the Italians. But after the Renaissance, there was a change. Then began conscious Woman-reverence, and a lack of instinctive reverence, rather only an instinctive pity. It is according to the balance between the Male and Female principles.

The other attitude of a man in love, besides this of "she is administered unto my maleness," is, "She is the unknown, the undiscovered, into which I plunge to discovery, losing myself."

And what we call real love has always this latter attitude.

The first attitude, which belongs to passion, makes a man feel proud, splendid. It is a powerful stimulant to him, the female administered to him. He feels full of blood, he walks the earth like a Lord. And it is to this state Nietzsche aspires in his *Wille zur Macht*. It is this the passionate nations crave.

And under all this there is, naturally, the sense of fear, transition, and the sadness of mortality. For, the female being herself an independent force, may she not withdraw, and leave a man empty, like ash, as one sees a Jew or an Italian so often?

This first attitude, too, of male pride receiving the female administration may, and often does, contain the corresponding intense fear and reverence of the female, as of the unknown. So that, starting from the male assertion, there came in the old days the full consummation; as often there comes the full consummation now.

But not always. The man may retain all the while the sense of himself, the primary male, receiving gratification. This constant reaction upon himself at length dulls his senses and his sensibility, and makes him mechanical, automatic. He grows gradually incapable of receiving any gratification from the female, and becomes a *roué*, only automatically alive, and frantic with the knowledge thereof.

It is the tendency of the Parisian—or has been—to take this attitude to love, and to intercourse. The woman knows herself all the while as the primary female receiving administration of the male. So she becomes hard and external, and inwardly jaded, tired out. It is the tendency of English women to take this attitude also. And it is this attitude of love, more than anything else, which devitalizes a race, and makes it barren.

It is an attitude natural enough to start with. Every young man must think that it is the highest honour he can do to a woman, to receive from her her female administration to his male being, whilst he meanwhile gives her the gratification of himself. But intimacy usually corrects this, love, or use, or marriage: a married man ceases to think of himself as the primary male: hence often his dullness. Unfortunately, he also fails in many cases to realize the gladness of a man in contact with the unknown in the female, which gives him a sense of richness and oneness with all life, as if, by being part of life, he were infinitely rich. Which is different from the sense of power, of dominating life. The *Wille zur Macht* is a spurious feeling.

For a man who dares to look upon, and to venture within the unknown of the female, losing himself, like a man who gives himself to the sea, or a man who enters a primeval, virgin forest, feels, when he returns, the utmost gladness of singing. This is certainly the gladness of a male bird in his singing, the amazing joy of return from the adventure into the unknown, rich with addition to his soul, rich with the knowledge of the utterly illimitable depth and breadth of the unknown; the ever-yielding extent of the unacquired, the unattained; the inexhaustible riches lain under unknown skies over unknown seas, all the magnificence that is, and yet which is unknown to any of us. And the knowledge of the reality with which it awaits me, the male, the knowledge of the calling and struggling of all the unknown, illimitable Female towards me, unembraced as yet, towards those men who will endlessly follow me, who will endlessly struggle after me, beyond me, further into this calling, unrealized vastness, nearer to the outstretched, eager, advancing unknown in the woman.

[...]

...Jude became exhausted in vitality, bewildered, aimless, lost, pathetically nonproductive.

Again one can see what instinct, what feeling it was which made Arabella's boy bring about the death of the children and of himself. He, sensitive, so bodiless, so selfless as to be a sort of automaton, is very badly suggested, exaggerated, but one can see what is meant. And he feels, as any child will feel, as many children feel today, that they are really anachronisms, accidents, fatal accidents, unreal, false notes in their mothers' lives, that, according to her, they have no being: that, if they have being, then she has not. So he takes away all the children.

And then Sue ceases to be: she strikes the line through her own existence, cancels herself. There exists no more Sue Fawley. She cancels herself. She wishes to cease to exist, as a person, she wishes to be absorbed away, so that she is no longer self-responsible.

For she denied and forsook and broke her own real form, her own independent, cool-lighted mind-life. And now her children are not only dead, but self-slain, those pledges of the physical life for which she abandoned the other.

She has a passion to expiate, to expiate, to expiate. Her children should never have been born: her instinct always knew this. Now their dead bodies drive her mad with a sense of blasphemy. And she blasphemed the Holy Spirit, which told her she is guilty of their birth and their death, of the horrible nothing which they are. She is even guilty of their little, palpitating sufferings and joys of mortal life, now made nothing. She cannot bear it—who could? And she wants to expiate, doubly expiate. Her mind, which she set up in her conceit, and then forswore, she must stamp it out of existence, as one stamps out fire. She would never again think or decide for herself. The world, the past, should have written every decision for her. The last act of her intellect was the utter renunciation of her mind and the embracing of utter orthodoxy, where every belief, every thought, every decision was made ready for her, so that she did not exist self-responsible. And then her loathed body, which had committed the crime of bearing dead children, which had come to life only to spread nihilism like a pestilence, that too should be scourged out of existence. She chose the bitterest penalty in going back to Phillotson.

There was no more Sue. Body, soul, and spirit, she annihilated herself. All that remained of her was the will by which she annihilated herself. That remained fixed, a locked centre of self-hatred, life-hatred so utter that it had no hope of death. It knew that life is life, and there is no death for life.

Jude was too exhausted himself to save her. He says of her she was not worth a man's love. But that was not the point. It was not a question of her worth. It was a question of her being. If he had said she was not capable of receiving a man's love as he wished to bestow it, he might have spoken nearer the truth. But she practically told him this. She made it plain to him what she wanted, what she could take. But he overrode her. She tried hard to abide by her own form. But he forced her. He had no case against her, unless she made the great appeal for him, that he should flow to her, whilst at the same time she could not take him completely, body and spirit both.

She asked for what he could not give—what perhaps no man can give: passionate love without physical desire. She had no blame for him: she had no love for him. Self-love triumphed in her when she first knew him. She almost deliberately asked for more, far more, than she intended to give. Self-hatred triumphed in the end. So it had to be.

As for Jude, he had been dying slowly, but much quicker than she, since the first night she took him. It was best to get it done quickly in the end. And this tragedy is the result of over-development of one principle of human life at the expense of the other; an over-balancing;

a laying of all the stress on the Male, the Love, the Spirit, the Mind, the Consciousness; a denying, a blaspheming against the Female, the Law, the Soul, the Senses, the Feelings. But she is developed to the very extreme, she scarcely lives in the body at all. Being of the feminine gender, she is yet no woman at all, nor male; she is almost neuter. He is nearer the balance, nearer the centre, nearer the wholeness. But the whole human effort, towards pure life in the spirit, towards becoming pure Sue, drags him along; he identifies himself with this effort, destroys himself and her in his adherence to this identification.

But why, in casting off one or another form of religion, has man ceased to be religious altogether? Why will he not recognize Sue and Jude, as Cassandra was recognized long ago, and Achilles, and the Vestals, and the nuns, and the monks? Why must being be denied altogether?

Sue had a being, special and beautiful. Why must not Jude recognize it in all its speciality? Why must man be so utterly irreverent, that he approaches each being as if it were no-being? Why must it be assumed that Sue is an "ordinary" woman—as if such a thing existed? Why must she feel ashamed if she is specialized? And why must Jude, owing to the conception he is brought up in, force her to act as if she were his "ordinary" abstraction, a woman?

She was not a woman. She was Sue Bridehead, something very particular. Why was there no place for her? Cassandra had the Temple of Apollo. Why are we so foul that we have no reverence for that which we are and for that which is amongst us? If we had reverence for our life, our life would take at once religious form. But as it is, in our filthy irreverence, it remains a disgusting slough, where each one of us goes so thoroughly disguised in dirt that we are all alike and indistinguishable.

If we had reverence for what we are, our life would take real form, and Sue would have a place, as Cassandra had a place; she would have a place which does not yet exist, because we are all so vulgar, we have nothing.

"To His Coy Mistress"
(Andrew Marvell)

⁂

"Love and Lust in Andrew Marvell's *'To His Coy Mistress'*"
by Robert C. Evans,
Auburn University at Montgomery

Andrew Marvell's famous seventeenth-century poem "To His Coy Mistress" has often been read as one of the most powerfully urgent and erotic love poems in the English language. In this carefully structured and highly memorable work, the male speaker tries to convince a reluctant woman to have sex with him by arguing that since their time on earth is short, they must make the most of it by not postponing sexual pleasure. They must, in the old Latin phrase, *carpe diem*, or "seize the day"; in other words, they must take advantage of their youthful vigor while they are still young and vigorous. This is an ancient argument, used by plenty of poets long before Marvell (not to mention by many other men who have had no pretensions of being poetic!). Marvell, of course, as a highly talented writer, breathes new life and strong wit into an old plea, but the purpose, tone, and meaning of the poem have been subject to significant debate. Does the poem endorse the speaker's urgent sexual appetites and seductive reasoning, or is the poem in fact an implicit satire not only on this particular lustful speaker but on the whole *carpe diem* tradition and the hedonistic values it represents? Should we take the speaker as seriously as he takes himself and his own sexual desires, or should we see him as the object of the poet's implied mockery or derision?

In a comprehensive survey of criticism dealing with this poem, published in 1977, French Fogle reported that most modern analysts have tended to take the speaker at face value and assume that the poem endorses the speaker's motives and arguments. "Critics of the twentieth century," Fogle states, "seem to have been, by and large, dominated by the idea that (a) the resolution of a *carpe diem* poem is always seduction; (b) the "Coy Mistress" is a *carpe diem* poem; ergo, (c) the resolution of the "Coy Mistress" is necessarily seduction" (125). Again and again Fogle quotes from commentators who not only find the speaker's arguments plausible and persuasive but who also find his character and ingenuity worth admiring. However, it is clear from Fogle's own comments that he himself is deeply skeptical both of the speaker's motives and of his logic. Fogle suggests, for instance, that the poem might be "better seen as an answer to traditional *carpe diem* resolution, as a criticism of traditional flimsy defenses against the tyranny of time" (130). Later, he raises the strong "possibility that in this poem as in others Marvell may be offering a criticism of the very genre he is employing rather than merely effecting a seduction" (132–33).

Fogle was hardly the first critic to express doubts about the character, impulses, and logic of Marvell's speaker, nor has he been the last. Bruce King, for instance, in an article on the poem published in 1969, makes a very strong case for an "ironic" reading of Marvell's lyric; articles by Anthony Low and Paul J. Pival, B.J. Sokol, and Lawrence W. Hyman also support such a reading. Even critics who admire Marvell's speaker and his arguments now often concede that technically those arguments are logically flawed (see, for instance, Hackett), but increasing numbers of analysts find both the arguments and the speaker who makes them not only logically weak but morally dubious. In 1989, for example, Larry Brunner offered a Christian reading of the poem that indicted both the speaker and his suspect, self-serving reasoning, while in 1996 Charles Kay Smith presented one of the most skeptical assessments of the speaker and his rationalizations offered by any analyst thus far. Smith contends that Marvell "has his cavalier speaker develop an exaggeratedly pagan *carpe diem* argument, while employing images that gesture toward biblical concepts of time, without allowing the speaker any awareness that in doing so he also suggests a possible alternative view to his own" (203). He continues: "Elsewhere Marvell's speaker mixes Christian with epicurean images in ways that appear to mock or subvert his seductive message" (203).

Ultimately, Smith concludes, "the many incongruities in phrasing built into 'Coy Mistress', together with its mistaken logic, misuse of literary and philosophic tradition, biblical echoes that subvert the speaker's material interests and call attention to his lack of any spiritual awareness, and echoes of Epicurus, Lucretius and royalists such as Cowley, Davenant and Cartwright, all indicate a satiric strategy" (207). Smith thus takes the speaker far less seriously than the speaker takes himself. More and more critics are coming to see "To His Coy Mistress" as a deeply ironic poem in which the joke is on the self-absorbed, self-confident seducer.

Close examination of the work can provide even more evidence for an ironic interpretation than the previously mentioned critics have already offered. By synthesizing and supplementing the arguments supporting an ironic reading of Marvell's lyric, we can better appreciate the thoroughness with which the poet complicates, qualifies, undercuts, and satirizes the speaker's character, motives, phrasing, and logic. The ironies begin with the very title itself. The woman whom the speaker addresses is "coy" in any number of appropriate senses of that word. She is undemonstrative, "shyly reserved or retiring" and displays a "modest backwardness or shyness (sometimes with an emphasis on the displaying)" so that she does not respond "readily to familiar advances," and her behavior may be interpreted (at least by the poem's speaker) as "distant and disdainful." The very word "coy," then, already implies the speaker's ambivalent attitude toward the woman he courts: her modesty and shyness may make her seem attractively innocent and even alluring, but her reserve and her possible disdain perhaps help to provoke the speaker's frustration and even his latent hostility. Yet the word "coy" is double-edged in other ways as well, for it ultimately derives from the Latin word *quietus* ("at rest, still, quiet" [*OED*]), and so it already implies the serene lack of activity that so exasperates the speaker, who is all too eager to act. Furthermore, the woman is coy in the sense that she never speaks—or is never given a chance to speak—in the poem itself, although apparently it is her previous refusals and her insistence on her honor that have unleashed the speaker's own flood of argumentative talk. The doubly emphasized stress on her coyness, then, is typical of the highly charged diction of this poem, in which even the most seemingly simple words are often brimming with variously meaningful connotations.

Take for instance the titular word "Mistress," which is more complicated than it at first appears. Most obviously it denotes a "woman loved or courted by a man; a female sweetheart," but obviously the speaker is also frustrated that the word has not yet come to mean (at least in his case) a "woman other than his wife with whom a man has a long-lasting sexual relationship" (*OED*). The speaker would obviously like to convert the first-cited meaning into the second, and so, in the process of trying to convince his sweetheart to make this change from one sense of "mistress" to another, the speaker addresses the woman (especially in the first strophe) as if yet another, third, meaning of the word were appropriate: he speaks to her as if she were a "woman, goddess, or thing personified as female, which has control over a person or is regarded as a protecting or guiding influence" (*OED*). In short, he seems, at first, to treat her almost as a superior being or an idol to be worshipped and adored. Yet the phrasing in the first strophe is ironic, since all of this apparent adoration will soon be rejected in favor of language that seems brutally harsh and even crude, making the earlier language of adoration both calculated and self-serving. Two key words of the title—coy and mistress—already hint at the speaker's complex attitudes toward the woman he courts—attitudes that combine ostensible affection with underlying frustration. This frustration is born of the speaker's recognition that the woman whom he addresses is a mistress in yet another sense of the term, since she has "the power to control, use, or dispose of something at will" (*OED*). Indeed, to the extent that the speaker debases himself by the end of the poem by depicting himself as a sort of passionate beast, the woman becomes his mistress in one further sense of the term: she is the "female owner of a pet animal; the woman or girl whom an animal is accustomed to obey" (*OED*). In the present situation, however, the male speaker, who only later explicitly confesses his animalistic lusts, seeks to reverse the terms of control by seeking to make the woman obey *him*. Thus, even before the poem properly begins, its very title is rich with potential complexities.

When the poem proper does in fact commence, its opening line emphasizes, through the use of framing commas, metrical stress, final placement, and subsequent rhyme, the key theme of a supposed lack of "time" (l. 1). The speaker suggests that the only time that matters is earthly or worldly time, whereas Christians of Marvell's day (i.e., the vast majority of the population) held that temporal existence was in many ways the least important aspect of life. The time that really mattered was the time to come, which would be spent eternally either in heaven or in hell. While Christians would have agreed heartily with Marvell's speaker that it was indeed important to make the most of earthly time, their emphasis was not on enjoying fleeting physical pleasures. The good life, for Christians, should be spent seeking the divine grace that would permit them to spend eternity with God (or that would help them to avoid spending it with Satan). Lest these comments seem to take too seriously a poem that should be read as light-hearted and jovial, it should be emphasized that it is the speaker himself who repeatedly introduces religious language and Christian ideas into language that might easily have been phrased in entirely different ways. In other words, the speaker keeps reminding readers of the very standards of morality and spirituality that he seems intent on contravening. Thus, if readers interpret the poem ironically, the speaker has no one but himself to blame for his contradictory logic.

When the poem is read retrospectively—that is, when we read the early lines in light of what comes later—one of the most ironic words in the entire work is the opening suggestion that the lady's coyness is a "crime" (l. 2). In Marvell's day the word could suggest not only wrongdoing but also a moral or ethical sin; furthermore, it could connote a charge, accusation, or matter of accusation (*OED*). From one perspective, the word is merely the opening salvo in a barrage of comic hyperbole, and the exaggerated claim of a possible "crime" seems especially ironic since the woman has just been politely addressed as "lady." From another perspective, however, the word "crime" appears deeply ironic if the speaker's own motives and conduct are interpreted as wrong or sinful. If nothing else, the word suggests the speaker's humorous desperation—his willingness to pull no rhetorical punches to achieve the results he desires. The word, like so much else in this poem, boomerangs on the speaker who employs it: his use of such language makes it hard to take him seriously, and perhaps at this point in the poem he is not even taking himself that way. Perhaps, at this point (and especially in his use of such a loaded word as "crime"), his tongue is still very much in his own cheek.

It is not long, however, before the speaker begins using terms and ideas that clearly demonstrate self-reflexive irony. One of these is the word "rubies" (l. 6), which may have reminded Marvell's Christian readers of virtuous women (as in Proverbs 31:10 [N. Smith

81]). "Who," the Old Testament speaker asks, "can find a virtuous woman? for her price is far above rubies." Marvell's speaker has apparently stumbled across such a woman, although he does not seem to appreciate that fact. Yet, even if a possible allusion to scriptural rubies seems far-fetched, what does seem undeniable—and also undeniably ironic—is the speaker's implied suggestion that his mistress, as a potential seeker of fine gems, is materialistic, vain, shallow, and self-aggrandizing. All these terms would far more appropriately fit the speaker himself than the lady he is courting, about whom we know little more than that she desires to preserve her sexual honor. It is the speaker, not the lady, who demonstrably goes out of his way to try to acquire a material object he considers highly valuable (i.e., her body), and it is the speaker whose values ultimately seem self-serving and superficial. Meanwhile, his implied threat to "complain" if he does not get his way (l. 7) is enacted by this very poem itself, which can be read quite literally as a "complaint" in the technical literary sense of that term ("a plaintive poem, a plaint" [*OED*]). Yet, the verb "complain" also suggests the self-pity that is typical of frustrated would-be lovers, and the word may even suggest an "expression of suffering passing into that of grievance and blame" (*OED*). Such a connotation would reinforce the earlier reference to the lady's "crime," especially since one meaning of complain in Marvell's day could be to "make a formal statement of a grievance" or "to lodge a complaint or bring a charge" (*OED*). Finally, the kind of "complain[ing]" this speaker contemplates also suggests his literal "physical suffering or pain," as well as his "feelings of ill-usage, dissatisfaction, and discontent" (*OED*). It is, after all, primarily her body (and his) with which he is most concerned, and surely one of his motives in courting her is to alleviate his "physical suffering."

As the poem continues, the speaker's references to "the flood" and to "the conversion of the Jews" lend themselves even more obviously to ironic analysis. Clearly, these words remind us of the very sort of religious values the speaker pointedly wants his mistress to ignore, and the reference to "the flood," in particular, unavoidably invokes the divine punishment of sinful crimes. There is no reason for Marvell's speaker to mention these scriptural events unless he intends to be almost blasphemously flippant; in any case, the fact that he does mention them inevitably reminds Marvell's readers of the very values and standards the speaker seeks to transgress. Meanwhile, his joking reference to his "vegetable love" (l. 11) reminds us that the adjective "vegetable," in

Marvell's day, could refer to "an organism endowed with the lowest form of life" (*OED*). The speaker's use of such a term is a kind of oxymoron: "vegetable love" is not truly "love" in the highest or deepest sense at all, and in fact the speaker's ensuing catalogue of the lady's various body parts—including her "eyes" (l. 14), her "forehead" (l. 14), and "each breast" (l. 15)—make it clear that his main interest is not in the qualities of her mind, character, soul, or virtue, but rather her body. Interestingly enough, the forehead in Marvell's day was often associated with such traits of character as shame, decency, or modesty, or alternately assurance, impudence, or audacity (*OED*). Apparently, the mistress, much to the speaker's obvious frustration, has been demonstrating the former of these two sets of qualities, thereby provoking in him the present impudent and audacious response. In any case, it is not the woman's eyes, forehead, or even her breasts in which he is mainly interested, but neither is it by any means her "heart" (l. 18), a word often associated with emotions, intellect, temperament, soul, and spirit in the seventeenth century (*OED*). Rather, it is clear—especially from his almost sacrilegious promise to "adore each breast" (l. 15)—that his chief concern is not the woman's character but her body, and although his blazon (or list of her physical attributes) ends before he has progressed beneath her torso, it is just as apparent that his main focus is both literally and figuratively lower. Ironically, the more the speaker spells out the woman's external physical attributes, the more he reveals about his own inner moral character.

Marvell, if he had wanted to, could easily have made this speaker praise this woman's soul as well as her body; plenty of precedent existed for such poems uniting physical desire and spiritual affection. The fact that Marvell's speaker is so obsessively focused on the mistress's flesh therefore invites us to respond ironically—with suspicion and sarcasm—to his repeated protestations of "love," a word he manages to repeat four times in just the opening strophe (ll. 4, 8, 11, 20). The last of these repetitions seems especially ironic: the speaker proclaims that if he and the mistress possessed unlimited time, he would gladly spend centuries extolling her physical appeal, and he ends by asserting, "For Lady you deserve this state; / Nor would I love at lower rate" (ll. 19–20). Both of these lines arguably collapse under the weight of the irony embedded in them: after all, by so obsessively praising her flesh he has not treated her with much genuine "state" or dignity, and it is hard to imagine a much "lower rate" of affection than the one he has been offering and the one he is about to offer. Indeed, the ironies that undermine the speaker's assertion in the first strophe are as nothing compared to those that follow in the second.

The first of the ironies we find in the second strophe is the speaker's claim that thanks to the passage of time, "yonder all before us lie / Deserts of vast eternity" (ll. 23–24). Although the word "desert" had broader connotations in Marvell's day than it tends to have in our own (it could suggest a wilderness and not simply a dry, barren landscape [OED]), many of Marvell's fellow Christians would have been puzzled by the speaker's claims about eternity. They assumed that eternity would be spent either in heaven or in hell, and although hell might indeed be imagined as a kind of desert, it would not have been in the self-interest of Marvell's speaker to remind his mistress of that fact. Likewise, although the speaker attempts to frighten the lady into giving up her virginity by reminding her of physical death and by raising the prospect that "worms shall try" her "long preserved virginity" (ll. 27–28), both of those sentiments and the grotesque phallic imagery in which they are expressed would be more likely to repulse than to impress most intelligent women. Once again the speaker focuses entirely on the lady's flesh; he pays no attention to the moral or spiritual state her physical virginity symbolizes, and in fact he calls her honor "quaint" (l. 29)—a particularly rich word that in Marvell's era could suggest wisdom, knowledge, skill, cleverness, and ingenuity as well as suggesting cunning, craftiness, scheming, and plotting (OED). From one perspective this woman has indeed been wise and skillful in preserving her virginity, although from the speaker's point of view she has not only been cunning and crafty but also proud and haughty (two more connotations of quaint [OED]). To the speaker, her virginity must also seem quaint in the further senses of being strange, unusual, or unfamiliar (OED); certainly he seems to assume that other women were not as careful about preserving their virginity as she has been. And, of course, as numerous commentators have pointed out previously, in its noun form the word quaint contains a pun on a slang word for vagina. If the speaker is trying to be funny, clever, or ironic in using this meaning of the word, the joke is ultimately on him, since it only reminds us (and her) once more of how little he truly respects the woman he pretends to court. Indeed, in all this imagery of rape-by-worms and in all these supposedly witty (but actually smutty) verbal hi-jinks, one senses an attitude of violent frustration. This speaker might have succeeded in winning the woman's heart (as well as the rest of her) if he actually evinced some genuine love for her. Apparently, she knows his real motives well enough to have resisted him thus far.

It is in line 30, in fact, that he finally abandons all his earlier talk of love and frankly confesses his physical "lust." Although this word did not necessarily refer *only* to physical desire in Marvell's time (it could, for instance, also suggest such other meanings as pleasure, delight, attraction, charm, vigor, appetite, and even friendly inclination [*OED*]), it obviously also carried strong biblical and theological overtones. If Marvell had wanted to avoid reminding us of these, he could easily have had the speaker repeat his earlier tired protestations of "love." Alternatively, the speaker could have chosen any of a number of other terms that would not have carried potentially negative connotations. Instead, he chose a word that necessarily conveys unavoidable overtones of a degrading animal passion (*OED*), and these suggestions are only reinforced by his subsequent suggestion that the couple should behave "like am'rous birds of prey" (l. 38). As various commentators in the "ironic" school have pointed out, this kind of phrasing does not seem designed to communicate a lofty or noble sense of the speaker's desire. The same seems true of much of the other phrasing of the final strophe, especially the imagery of the lovers uniting to form a "ball" in order to engage in "rough strife" (ll. 42–43). Although the "ball" mentioned here has been explicated in various ways (including, quite plausibly, as an allusion to a cannon ball), the most obvious meaning seems to imply the imagery of lovers tightly joined together in sexual intercourse—what Shakespeare's Iago (in his typically cynical way) once called the "beast with two backs." It is a suitably coarse image, coming as it does from this speaker, but it is not the last image of the poem. The final image is an ironic scriptural allusion to the story of Joshua commanding the sun to stand still (N. Smith 85): "Thus, though we cannot make our sun / Stand still, yet we will make him run" (ll. 45–46). Previous commentators have pointed out the way this image once more undercuts the speaker's smug lust, but by now one hopes it is clear that such irony is part and parcel of nearly every line, word, and image in this work. We never hear the lady's response to the speaker's proposals, but there is little in this poem that should make us feel confident that his lust will ever be satisfied.

WORKS CITED

Brunner, Larry. "'Love at Lower Rate': A Christian Reading of 'To His Coy Mistress.'" *Christianity and Literature* 38.3 (1989): 25–44.

Fogel, French. "Marvell's 'Tough Reasonableness' and the Coy Mistress." *Tercentenary Essays in Honor of Andrew Marvell*. Ed. Kenneth Friedenreich. Hamden, CT: Archon, 1977. 121–39.

Hackett, John. "Logic and Rhetoric in Marvell's 'Coy Mistress'." *Tercentenary Essays in Honor of Andrew Marvell*. Ed. Kenneth Friedenreich. Hamden, CT: Archon, 1977. 140–52.

Hyman, Lawrence W. "Marvell's 'Coy Mistress' and Desperate Lover." *Modern Language Notes* 75 (1960): 8–10.

King, Bruce. "Irony in Marvell's 'To His Coy Mistress'." *Southern Review* 5 (1969): 689-703.

Low, Anthony and Paul J. Pival. "Rhetorical Pattern in Marvell's 'To His Coy Mistress'." *Journal of English and Germanic Philology* 68 (1969): 414–21.

Oxford English Dictionary. www.dictionary.oed.com

Pittock, Malcolm. "'Virgins all beware': 'To His Coy Mistress' Revisited." *English* 47 (1998): 215–30.

Smith, Charles Kay. "French Philosophy and English Politics in Interregnum Poetry." *The Stuart Court and Europe: Essays in Politics and Political Culture*. Ed. R. Malcolm Smuts. Cambridge: Cambridge UP, 1996. 177–209.

Smith, Nigel, ed. *The Poems of Andrew Marvell*. Rev. ed. London: Pearson Education, 2007.

Sokol, B.J. "Logic and Illogic in Marvell's 'To His Coy Mistress'." *English Studies: A Journal of English Language and Literature* 71.3 (1990): 244–52.

Acknowledgments

Baudelaire, Charles. "Madame Bovary." *Flaubert: A Collection of Critical Essays. Ed. and trans. by Raymond Giraud*. Englewood Cliffs, NJ: Prentice-Hall, 1964. pp. 88–96. (Originally published in *L'Artiste*, 18 October 1857.) Copyright 1964 by Prentice-Hall, Inc.

Clarke, Charles Cowden. "Much Ado About Nothing." *Shakespeare-Characters; Chiefly Those Subordinate*. London: Smith, Elder, & Co., 1863. pp. 295–316.

Dyer, Gary. "Thieves, Boxers, Sodomites, Poets: Being Flash to Byron's *Don Juan*." *PMLA* Vol. 116, No. 3 (May 2001): 562–78. Copyright 2001 by the Modern Language Association of America.

Emerson, Katherine T. "Two Problems in Donne's 'Farewell to Love.'" *Modern Language Notes* Vol. 72, No. 2 (February 1957): 93–95.

Freud, Sigmund. "The Material and Sources of Dreams." *The Interpretation of Dreams*. Trans. A.A. Brill. New York: MacMillan, 1913. pp. 138–259.

Jacobs, Joshua. "Joyce's Epiphanic Mode: Material Language and the Representation of Sexuality in Stephen Hero and Portrait." *Twentieth Century Literature*, Vol. 46, No. 1 (Spring 2000): 20–33.

Kuttner, Alfred Booth. "*Sons and Lovers*": *A Freudian Appreciation. The Psychoanalytic Review* Vol. 3, No. 3 (July 1916): 295–317.

Lawrence, D. H. "Study of Thomas Hardy." *Phoenix: The Posthumous Papers of D.H. Lawrence*. Ed. Edward D. McDonald. New York: Viking Press, 1936. pp. 398–516. Copyright 1936 by Frieda Lawrence, Renewed 1964 by the Estate of the late Frieda Lawrence Ravagli.

Martin, Robert K. "Whitman's *Song of Myself*: Homosexual Dream and Vision." *Partisan Review*, Vol. 42, No.1 (1975): 80–96.

Pollak, Ellen. "The Rape of the Lock: A Reification of the Myth of Passive Womanhood." *The Poetics of Sexual Myth: Gender and Ideology in the Verse*

of Swift and Pope. Chicago: University of Chicago Press, 1985.
pp. 77–107. Copyright 1985 by Ellen Pollak.

Schorer, Mark. "Introduction." *The Fortunes and Misfortunes of the Famous Moll Flanders &c.* by Daniel Defoe. New York: Random House, 1950.
pp. v–xvii. Copyright 1950 by Random House, Inc.

Index

A

Absolon ("The Miller's Tale"), 101–102

adultery. See *Madame Bovary* (Flaubert)

AIDS epidemic, portrayal in *Angels in America*, 1–2, 6–7

Alisoun ("The Miller's Tale"), 102–103

American Jew, epitaph for, in *Angels in America*, 5

anal intercourse, depiction of, 185–186

ancient Greece, views of sexuality in, 77–78

Angels in America (Kushner), 1–7

Annabel (*Lolita*), 56

Aphrodite (*Lyrics*), 67–69

Arabella (*Jude the Obscure*), 220–222

Aristophanes
    Lysistrata, 78–82
    portrayal in *Symposium*, 82–86

Athenian men, sexual activity of, 80–81

Athenian women, social position of, 80

B

Baldwin, James: *Giovanni's Room*, 43–51

Baudelaire, Charles, 87–94

Beatrice (*Much Ado About Nothing*), 118–119, 120–124

Being-Love, in *A Doll's House*, 13–14

Belinda (*The Rape of the Lock*), 154–156, 159, 160, 162–163

Benedick (*Much Ado About Nothing*), 119–120, 123–126

bird-girl (*Portrait of the Artist as a Young Man*), 144–146

blackmail, sodomy and, 27–28

boxing, 21, 22–23, 32n6

Brunnemer, Kristen, 9–17

Byron, Lord: *Don Juan*, 19–33

C

cant, meanings of, 30

Canterbury Tales (Chaucer), 95–104

carpe diem poems, 227–228

Chaucer, Geoffrey: "The Miller's Tale," 95–104

Clare, Angel (*Tess of the d'Urbervilles*), 219–220

Clarissa (*The Rape of the Lock*), 159–160, 164

Clarke, Charles Cowden, 117–128

Claudio (*Much Ado About Nothing*), 127

closet, Giovanni's Room as, 46–47

Cornelius, Michael G., 95–104

crime, flash language and, 21, 28

239